Conversations at the Edges of Things

Conversations at the Edges of Things

Reflections for the Church in Honor of John Goldingay

Edited by
FRANCIS BRIDGER *and* JAMES T. BUTLER

◆PICKWICK *Publications* • Eugene, Oregon

CONVERSATIONS AT THE EDGES OF THINGS
Reflections for the Church in Honor of John Goldingay

Copyright © 2012 Wipf and Stock Publishers. All rights reserved. Except for brief quotations in critical publications or reviews, no part of this book may be reproduced in any manner without prior written permission from the publisher. Write: Permissions, Wipf and Stock Publishers, 199 W. 8th Ave., Suite 3, Eugene, OR 97401.

Pickwick Publications
An Imprint of Wipf and Stock Publishers
199 W. 8th Ave., Suite 3
Eugene, OR 97401

www.wipfandstock.com

ISBN 13: 978-1-61097-951-1

Cataloguing-in-Publication data:

Conversations at the edges of things : reflections for the church in honor of John Goldingay / edited by Francis Bridger and James T. Butler.

xiv + 186 pp. ; 23 cm. Includes bibliographical references.

ISBN 13: 978-1-61097-951-1

1. Bible. O.T. Criticism, interpretation, etc. 2. Bible. N.T. Criticism, interpretation, etc. 3. Theology. 4. Pastoral counseling. I. Bridger, Francis. II. Butler, James T. III. Goldingay, John. IV. Title.

BS540 C5 2012

Manufactured in the U.S.A.

Contents

List of Contributors / vii

Foreword / ix

Introduction / xiii

1 1 Corinthians 14 and Tongues Revisited—*Colin Buchanan* / 1

2 Ruth in Two Canons—*James T. Butler* / 14

3 Old Testament Narratives and Ethics: A Journey in Understanding—*Athena E. Gorospe* / 27

4 What Holds the Bible Together? —*Marianne Meye Thompson* / 39

5 Models of Commitment in Paul: A Fine Balance? —*Stephen Travis* / 49

6 In Praise of Mystery—*Graham Buxton* / 58

7 Evangelical Mary—*Christopher Cocksworth* / 67

8 Why Psychology Needs Theology (and John Goldingay) —*Nancey Murphy* / 76

9 Theology with Passion—*Gordon Oliver* / 86

Contents

10   Growing Old in Gethsemane—*Tom Smail* / 96

11   Biblical Principles of Calling and Training for Mission
     —*Roger Bowen* / 105

12   The Gift of Community: Social Theology for the Twenty-First
     Century—*Francis Bridger* / 116

13   To the Man in the Pink Shirt—*Anne Long* / 126

14   When Choristers Grow Up—*Vivienne Faull* / 134

15   Encountering Abraham in Africa: Reflections of an
     Ethnomusicologist on the Road—*Roberta R. King* / 142

16   Filming the Bible: Crossing the Red Sea—*Philip Jenson* / 154

17   Pausing for Thought—*Sarah Goldingay* / 162

18   A Paradigm for the Interpretation of Sacred Space
     —*Kathleen Scott Goldingay* / 169

     Bibliography / 181

Contributors

REVD CANON ROGER BOWEN, formerly General Director of Crosslinks Missionary Society, UK

REVD DR FRANCIS BRIDGER, Ecclesiastical Professor of Anglican Studies and Executive Director of the Center for Anglican Communion Studies at Fuller Theological Seminary, Pasadena, USA

RT REVD COLIN BUCHANAN, formerly Bishop of Woolwich, UK

PROF JAMES T. BUTLER, Associate Professor of Old Testament at Fuller Theological Seminary, Pasadena, USA

REVD DR GRAHAM BUXTON, Director of Postgraduate Studies in Ministry and Theology at Tabor College, Adelaide, Australia

LORD CAREY OF CLIFTON, 103rd Archbishop of Canterbury 1991–2002, UK

RT REVD CHRISTOPHER COCKSWORTH, Bishop of Coventry, UK

VERY REVD VIVIENNE FAULL, Dean of Leicester Cathedral, UK

KATHLEEN SCOTT GOLDINGAY, retired architect; MA in Theology, Fuller Theological Seminary, Pasadena, USA

DR. SARAH GOLDINGAY, Lecturer in Drama at the University of Exeter, UK

DR. ATHENA GOROSPE, Associate Professor of Old Testament at Asian Theological Seminary, Manila, Philippines

REVD DR. PHILIP JENSON, Lecturer in Old Testament at Ridley Hall, Cambridge, UK

Contributors

Dr. Roberta R. King, Associate Professor of Communication and Ethnomusicology at Fuller Theological Seminary, Pasadena, USA

Revd Canon Anne Long, formerly Director of the Christian Listening Project at the Acorn Trust, UK

Dr. Nancey Murphy, Professor of Christian Philosophy at Fuller Theological Seminary, Pasadena, USA

Revd Canon Gordon Oliver, Rector of Meopham in the Diocese of Rochester, UK

Canon Tom Smail, formerly Rector of Sanderstead in the Diocese of Southwark, UK

Dr. Marianne Meye Thompson, George Eldon Ladd Professor of New Testament at Fuller Theological Seminary, Pasadena, USA

Dr. Stephen Travis, formerly Vice-Principal at St. John's College, Nottingham, UK

Foreword

LORD CAREY OF CLIFTON

Conversations at the Edges of Things is an appropriate title for a book honoring Professor John Goldingay because one of John's great gifts is his ability to address issues on the fringe of church life and his willingness to explore matters that some Christians would prefer to avoid.

My links with John go back forty-five years to the time we were both young theological teachers at Oak Hill Theological College in Southgate, London. John was serving a curacy as an assistant priest in the nearby town of Finchley and had been roped in to do some part-time teaching. I was thirty one and John a mere twenty five year old. As Oak Hill was traditionally a college for older students, we were younger than many of those we taught. We threw ourselves into college life with enthusiasm, although the demands of his curacy made it more difficult for John. Even so, he stood out by his knowledge and love of his chosen subject and his interest in his students. The principal of Oak Hill, Maurice Wood (later Bishop of Norwich), looked upon us with benign indulgence and was genuinely sad when John and I decided quite independently of each other to join the faculty of St. John's College Nottingham in 1970 under the leadership of Michael Green. At our farewell I enjoyed misusing in my speech the text from Genesis 22:5 where Abraham says to his servants, "You stay here with the donkey whilst I and the lad (John) go yonder." Fortunately, Maurice took it all in good part.

St. John's College Nottingham gave both of us more opportunity to develop as teachers and scholars. The college had recently relocated from its home in Northwood: a clear act of faith. But John and I were excited to be invited to work with Michael Green, Colin Buchanan, Julian Charley,

Foreword

Anne Long, Charles Napier and other gifted people with the aim of creating an Evangelical College, rooted in the faith of the Church but open to new ideas. John was an excellent teacher and showed early promise of great potential to become an outstanding scholar.

Our two families loved the open and generous community life of St. John's. The Goldingay home was an open house for single students, and John and Ann together were at the heart of serious learning and great community-building. In 1975 I returned to parish ministry and John remained at St. John's College for twenty seven years, the last nine of which he served as principal.

What were some of his achievements during his long ministry in England? The first was undoubtedly the way John pioneered and transformed the teaching of the Old Testament in English theological colleges. It was usual for such colleges to employ as teachers those (principally male at that time) who were predominantly teachers rather than academics. Scholarship was largely left to university faculties. John was among the first to break this mould, contributing to Old Testament studies and gaining respect among those in university departments. The second contribution was no less significant. In the nineteen sixties and seventies, through to the eighties, there was a tendency for Evangelical colleges to regard the tools of biblical scholarship with suspicion, and the fruits of such scholarship with fear. John and others broke decisively with this tradition, believing that if Christians could not engage in rigorous research, examining the texts of scripture with open minds, then there was something false and unhealthy about their own fundamental assumptions. The confidence that exists today in our theological colleges owes much to the fresh and open stance to scholarship of scholars such as John. Not for him a patchwork of beliefs, but a theological identity with a solid foundation in Scripture and a clear profile.

It was once said of Dr. Thomas Arnold, the renowned nineteenth century Head of Rugby School, that "he started the day with every question being an open question." I don't think John Goldingay was far behind. He, too, engaged with every question—the only difference was that his thought was grounded in a firm Evangelical faith and a commitment to the Old Testament as part of that heritage of faith. This was demonstrated throughout John's long tenure at St. John's that culminated in his distinguished period as principal. During this time innovative styles of learning continued as he presided over the growth of St. John's Extension Studies and pioneered the development of creative programs for mixed mode ordination training and for urban ministry.

In 1997, John was invited by Fuller Theological Seminary to become the David Allan Hubbard Professor of Old Testament. Before his departure to take up the post, I invited John to accept a Lambeth Doctorate in Divinity for his services to the Church of England and to the Anglican Communion as a teacher, theologian, and Old Testament scholar. Lambeth degrees possess a number of unusual features. The first relates to their history. Prior to the Reformation there were three principal routes by which scholarly learning was taught. To the usual routes of Oxford and Cambridge there was a more rare route where the Archbishop of Canterbury, acting for the Pope, possessed authority to bestow degrees on those who had already distinguished themselves in Church and society. At the Reformation the right to grant degrees in this way passed from the Pope to the Archbishop of Canterbury and to this day this third 'university' has conferred hundreds of degrees in law, music, theology, art, and other disciplines.

The second feature is significant because Lambeth degrees are not honorary degrees. They are real degrees and can only be given to people whose scholarship is evident in their writings and teachings. Thus, on July 11, 1997, in the chapel at Lambeth Palace in London I conferred a DD on Professor John Goldingay for his remarkable career and ministry as a theologian in Old Testament studies and for being a Christian on the frontier between the world and the Church.

Sadly, Ann, who started the journey with him, died from the effects of multiple sclerosis in 2009; but, unquestionably, she made a significant contribution to their joint ministry over the years. John's testimony to her life, *Remembering Ann*, is a moving tribute to all that she gave for nearly half a century. Her patience in suffering and her cheerfulness in coping with the inevitable decline in abilities are as much a tribute to her love for John and her commitment to their shared ministry, as to the grace of God in her life.

The move to Pasadena gave John space to write and deepen his reputation as an international scholar. His writings from 1997 onwards show the depth of his scholarship and his ability to relate theology to life, as well as illustrating the breadth of his scope. Who else among Old Testament scholars could muse on such diverse subjects as *The Church and the Gifts of the Spirit*, *The Bible and Sexuality*, *Humour in the Book of Acts*, *Men Behaving Badly*, and *Theological College Training in the Context of a Lifetime's*

Foreword

Journey? It was also at Fuller Seminary that John latterly met Kathleen, whose contribution to John's life has led to much happiness and fulfilment.

Though John Goldingay has a huge sense of fun and has always been relaxed in the company of others, I have no doubt that he is a demanding teacher, anxious to give the best to his students and to get the best from them in return. We live at a time when Western culture tempts Christians to assume that even their faith can be enjoyed and possessed with the minimum of effort. But great teachers are those whose career illustrates that the Christian life is more of a mountain climb than a stroll through a pleasant valley. This *Festschrift* is a celebration of a long punishing ascent of seventy years, with some dangers and sadness on the way, but always with a glimpse of an eternal summit ahead.

Keep climbing, John.
George Carey

George Carey was the 103rd Archbishop of Canterbury (1991–2002). In 2002 he was made a Life Peer in the House of Lords as the Rt Hon and Rt Rev. The Lord Carey of Clifton.

Introduction

FRANCIS BRIDGER *and* JAMES BUTLER

BOTH OF US HAVE been friends and colleagues of John Goldingay for some considerable time: Francis since 1982 and Jim since 1997. So it seemed to us only right that we should find some way of marking John's seventieth birthday year with a tribute to his lifelong ministry of writing, teaching and service to the church and academy. But how to celebrate such a prolific writer and teacher? The traditional answer to this question would be to invite fellow academics to contribute learned essays in honor of their learned colleague and then to gather them together in a collection known as a *Festschrift*. But, true to the Goldingay style, we wanted to do it differently. And so we chose to produce a volume that reflected his characteristic willingness to explore unusual topics or to discuss theology in a way that pushes readers and hearers to the edges of their thinking. Thus were this book and its title born.

What follows is a *Festschrift* with a difference. Instead of inviting FOJs (Friends of John) to write around a single theme, we simply asked them to choose any topic that excited them, or that touched their hearts, and offer it to John as an act of celebration: to bring a gift to the party of their very own making that he—and others—would enjoy.

We deliberately asked for essays that would be of general interest to a wide range of readers and would cover a wide range of topics. This was not to be a book for academic readers only. As a glance at the contents page will reveal, we got exactly what we asked for: a kaleidoscope of subjects lovingly crafted by a group of people drawn from all stages of John's ministry on both sides of the Atlantic. We also encouraged writers to adopt literary and creative styles appropriate to themselves rather than conform to a predetermined template. The result is a potpourri of gifts in which lectures

Introduction

sit alongside letters, and essays alongside expositions. There is, we believe, something here for everyone. What binds the pieces together is their authors' deep and abiding affection for the one whom they seek to honor.

Finally, a word about structure. The collection begins with a foreword from the former Archbishop of Canterbury, Lord Carey of Clifton, who in his early years served with John on the faculty of two UK Anglican theological institutions, Oak Hill College, London, and St. John's College, Nottingham. It was George Carey, also, who as Archbishop in 1997 awarded John a Lambeth doctorate in recognition of John's outstanding contribution "to the Church of England and to the Anglican Communion as a teacher, theologian and Old Testament scholar." The warmth of Lord Carey's tribute sets the tone for the rest of the book and we are grateful to him for it.

The chapters that follow are organized into areas of theology that have occupied John's writings throughout his career, beginning (of course) with Scripture, moving through philosophy and systematic theology, and then into practical theology. No methodological agenda is implied here. We simply wanted to start with the area closest to John's heart. The last section—practical theology—includes reflections on worship, ethics, mission and popular culture, all of which John has written about in numerous places, at numerous times, with the blend of learning and accessibility that marks out his Old Testament works. The book concludes with two moving chapters written by John's daughter in law, Dr. Sarah Goldingay, who teaches at the University of Exeter in England, and his wife Kathleen who, as Lord Carey observes, has brought John renewed happiness in recent years following the death of Ann.

In between the first and final chapters, readers will find (we hope) a stimulating set of essays contributed by colleagues from the UK, Australia, the Philippines, and the USA. Space does not permit us here to elaborate on each but we would wish to draw attention to just one, namely that of John's former colleague, Canon Tom Smail. Tom's chapter is especially poignant since, unknown to him when he submitted it, this was to be the last essay that he would ever publish: for in February 2012, much to the sadness of those who knew him, Tom died after a short illness. We are honored, therefore, to offer his final piece of writing in a volume dedicated to his friend and colleague over many years, John E. Goldingay.

John, with Tom and all who have contributed to this volume, we salute you!

Pentecost 2012

1

1 Corinthians and Tongues Revisited

COLIN BUCHANAN

I ONCE OWNED A backstreet, one-horse publishing house called Grove Books. It functioned from the premises of St John's College, Nottingham, and developed a series of 10,000-word "Grove Booklets on Ministry and Worship." In the series' first year, 1971–72, there appeared a booklet by a certain John Goldingay, entitled *The Church and the Gifts of the Spirit: A Practical Exposition of 1 Corinthians* 12–14. It brought together a number of Bible expositions he had delivered in the College chapel. His exposition stayed within what I shall call the conventional understanding; but his concern was above all pastoral, that believers should be accepting of one another's gifts and should live together in love. The series has run to the present day. But, despite all other Charismatic and contemporary pressures, it has never returned to 1 Corinthians 12. Yet life in the Christian assembly, the subject matter of 1 Corinthians 14, must be of continuing interest—and my investigation here arises from my growing suspicion that the conventional understanding, and particularly the understanding of "tongues," has proceeded on a wholly mistaken presupposition.[1]

---

1. I have been encouraged to make this "revisit" by another erstwhile St. John's College colleague of John Goldingay, Dr. Stephen Travis, New Testament lecturer (and finally vice-principal) at the college from 1969 to 2005. His encouragement took the form "There is a case to answer."

Conversations at the Edges of Things

To address 1 Corinthians 14 we need first to examine "gifts" (Greek, *charismata*). This Greek word *does not occur in* 1 Corinthians 14, though all the English versions insert it in 14:1, many in 14:14, and some also in page, chapter or section headings—all of them gratuitously! *Charisma* does occur in 1 Corinthians 12, but its meaning is more elusive than my Charismatic friends seem to think. It is relatively rare elsewhere in the New Testament, but a full view includes Romans 12, where the listed "gifts" are not only prophesying and teaching, but also hospitality, sharing, and showing pity. These "gifts" of ordinary discipleship start to indicate that *charisma* is *not* a technical theological term for a defined special role as "given" by God. The use in 1 Pet 4:10–11 confirms this; for Peter mentions *charisma*, but quite artlessly; as in Rom 12, a different word (say of "abilities" or "calling") would have done instead. He simply commends a wide open use of speaking and serving, and *all* such activities by disciples he calls *charismata*.

Putting Romans 12 alongside 1 Corinthians 12 reveals that Paul is arguing in opposite directions in the two chapters. In Rom 12 he argues *from* the given unity of the body *to* discovering (and exercising) the individual functions (unreflectively called "gifts") within the body; whereas in 1 Corinthians 12 he argues *from* a listed set of functions apparently named and prized in differing individual ways in Corinth *to* insisting that the Corinthians really grasp the unity of the body and exercise their functions harmoniously to promote it (sealed, says ch. 13, by loving each other). Only "healings" are here called "gifts"—other activities are simply named, warranting my neutral term "functions."

Paul's purpose means that he is *not* objectively listing important functions (let alone listing them in priority), but is writing *ad homines*, naming a range of functions which come to mind *because they have been reported to him as claimed and prized by individual Corinthians*. Thus he begins by mentioning 'the spiritual things' (1 Cor 12:1), quite probably a cover term the Corinthians used for their different activities, each acclaimed as from (or "in") the Spirit with a distinctive profile in the congregation. Paul plays down the individual activities, and puts *charismata* into their place. Thus *charismata* occur in 12:4 where he cites a variety of them, but in 12:5 there is also a variety of *diakoniai*, and in 12:6 a variety of *energēmata*. A parallel English use would cite a variety of, say, "abilities, roles, and ways of working." Such broad abstract nouns do not suggest, whether separately or cumulatively, a defined and institutionalized listing of specific identified functions. So it is here: there are varying functions, and because these come from God (12:7–11), they may sometimes (and sometimes not) be called "gifts."[2] But the actual lists are compiled *ad homines*; they illustrate variety rather than canonize particular activities; and they neither expound the character of this or that activity, nor engage in any deliberate order of priorities.[3]

We thus approach 1 Corinthians 14 not as a charter for discovering particular "gifts" with an expectation of then exercising them, but rather as a particular divisive case of people (or their supporters) promoting differing favored activities. Paul will want the various functions of the body to contribute to harmony—which may mean restraint as much as use. He will now have to expound different functions in order to evaluate them comparatively. But his aim is still the harmony and "building up" of the body of Christ. He allows (14:1) the quest for "spiritual activities" (in effect using speech marks himself, quoting the Corinthians back to themselves), but now, in addressing an actual conflict, he specifically names prophecy as the preferred *pneumatikon*, and gives the Corinthians his reasons.

So we ask how to render *glōssai* and *diermēneuō* in English. The great tradition, beginning with Tyndale, canonized in the King James Version, and followed by all main English versions since, has been to adopt the terms "tongues" and "interpret." Other English words exist—"languages" and "translate"—but, at first sight, the tradition is valid. English does sometimes use "tongues" for "languages" and "interpret" for "translate"; they can be interchanged. But in 1 Corinthians 12–14 the interchangeability has been forfeited: for "tongues" and "interpret," while innocent English equivalents for the Greek, have acquired a special religious sense *from the KJV use in this chapter*. And it is that use we must revisit.

The translators of the KJV New Testament knew the words "language" and "translate," but *always* translated *glōssa* as "tongue," and *hermēneuō* or *diermēneuō* as "interpret."[4] "Tongue" was their normal word for "language,"

---

2. "The point is that *any* word or deed which embodies grace or makes it present to others is properly speaking a charism." Dunn, *1 Corinthians*, 82.

3. The "first . . . second . . . third . . . etc" in 12:28, while it may have a semi-chronological background (i.e. "apostles" were first in point of time), is wholly compatible with Paul striking off (e.g. as we might one by one on the fingers of a hand) a loose list of functions and/or of the persons who exercise them, in order to ensure he has picked up all those reported to him as being assertive or as having raised profiles in Corinth. The *ad homines* character of the list (except possibly those "apostles") is confirmed by his rhetorical questions in 12:29–30.

4. "Language" occurs once only in the KJV New Testament; in Acts 2:6 it translates

not, as for us, a slightly poetic or esoteric alternative to it.⁵ They admittedly confused the picture slightly with the italicized "*unknown*" prefixed to "tongues" as a conjectural gloss (it is no more), but the question is whether they rightly saw in *glōssa* itself, without qualification, a language unknown on earth—i.e., that which is today most usefully termed "glossolalia."⁶

I offer an interesting contemporary check. John Calvin worked from the Greek text, though with the Vulgate open as he wrote in Latin. To him *glōssai* always refers to *known* languages. He knows of many languages; he commends learning them; he condemns his opponents for stopping people learning them; he believes that in Paul's day some may have had miraculous knowledge of languages not learned by normal processes; but he never concedes that Paul would have approved truly unknown languages:

> For it is incredible (at least we do not read of any instance) that there were any people who spoke by the influence of the Spirit, in a language they did not themselves know. For the gift of tongues was not bestowed merely for the purpose of making a noise, but rather for the purpose of communication, of course. For how laughable it would have been had the tongue of a Roman been directed by the Spirit of God to utter Greek words, when he himself had no knowledge of Greek whatever. He would have been like the parrots, magpies and crows which men train to make human sounds!⁷

---

dialektos. (In the Old Testament it occurs roughly as often as "tongues" in this meaning). *Dialektos* itself is rendered "tongues" in Acts 2:8, as also elsewhere in Acts; and "translate" in the KJV never refers to languages (save in the sub-title to the finished Bible "translated out of the original tongues . . ."!); translation is what God did to Enoch "that he should not see death" (Heb 11:5). In the Gospels and Acts *methermēneuō*, another compound of *hermēneuō*, also means "translate." And, everywhere else in the New Testament, modern versions employ "languages" and "translate," whereas in 1 Corinthians 12–14 they have stuck with the KJV "tongues" and "interpret" almost certainly because these English terms have acquired special religious significance, which, I submit, was not there in Paul's original Greek.

5. Thus in Rev 5:9; 7:9; 11:9; 13:7 the KJV has "tongue" but modern versions have generally moved to the more comfortable "language." Shakespeare's contemporaneous use of "tongue" in *Henry V* (Act V, Scene II) in the flirtatious interchange between Henry and the French princess is comparable, though there "tongue" is conveniently ambiguous. Curiously Acts 2 also has a play on "tongues"—cf. the uses in 2:3 and 2:4.

6. Because the meaning of "tongue" is the very matter in question, I cannot use "tongue" to denote "a language unknown on earth" (however much others do). So I resort to "glossolalia" which is almost invariably used univocally in theological discussion.

7. Calvin, *First Corinthians*, 291. Was Calvin, unembarrassed by any English dilemma of having two different words to render *glōssa*, in fact expounding it in the most natural and likely meaning of the normal use in Greek?

With English-speaking Christians it has happened differently. "Languages" in time overtook "tongues" in street-level usage, but the hauntingly suggestive "tongues" persisted in the KJV, and so greatly guided biblical exegesis that commentators never queried that Paul was discussing glossolalia. The general Protestant belief until the twentieth century was that this (along with "interpretation") was one of the special powers by which the Holy Spirit sustained the apostolic church until the New Testament could be written and exert its authority.[8] This view has been dubbed "cessationist." As it could not be road-tested, it often grew imaginatively colourful. Take this, for example: "... *to speak with tongues*; this, as it appears from 1 Cor. xiv.7 sqq., is the gift of men who, rapt in an ecstasy and no longer quite masters of their own reason and consciousness, pour forth their glowing spiritual emotions in strange utterances, rugged, dark, disconnected, quite unfitted to instruct or to influence the mind of others . . ."[9]

So, as Pentecostalism was born in glossolalia in the first years of the twentieth century, the recipients unsurprisingly concluded that "this" was the "that" of which Paul had written.[10] The KJV insertion, "*unknown*," confirmed it. "Interpretation" arose alongside it. The promise of Pentecost was being fulfilled. The "gifts" had *not* ceased—they were *here*, vibrant evidence of the power of the Holy Spirit. And, whether viewed as long-ceased or presently active, the gift of "tongues" was deeply institutionalized in the Church's corporate mind. Modern versions of the Scriptures have persisted with "tongues" here (while readily using "languages" elsewhere), and many have expanded the point in chapter-headings or notes.[11] "Tongues" has be-

---

8. Matthew Henry in the eighteenth century and Charles Hodge in the nineteenth typically believe that Paul is describing glossolalia, while silent on any such contemporary practice.

9. Grimm-Thayer, *Greek-English Lexicon* on *glossa*.

10. The question of "this" being "that" derives from Peter's words in Acts 2:16 in the KJV, and was taken as a chapter heading about Charismatic phenomena in the Church of England Doctrine Commission's Report, *We Believe in the Holy Spirit*.

11. I cite the RV (1881), Weymouth (1902), Moffatt (1913), Phillips (1947), the RSV (1952), the NEB (1961, 1970), *The Living Bible* (1971), the NIV (1973), the GNB (1976), the *New Jerusalem Bible* (1985), the *Revised English Bible* (1989), the NRSV (1989), and *The Message* (2003). Without exception they know that *glōssai* are "tongues"; and some have the further information, in text or notes, that the tongues were "ecstatic" (a speculation comparable to "*unknown*"!). All of them, I contend, derive their choice of English wording *from the KJV tradition*, not from the Greek. My NIV alone has a small footnote that says "or *languages*." Commentators read as though approaching the text already debating whether the "gifts" have ceased or not, and whether glossolalia was ecstatic or not, and then addressing these issues with vigour, without recognizing they had evaded a more fundamental question.

come a focused theological term, denoting a particular religious phenomenon; the Bible translators have set it in concrete, and the commentators have expounded it; but perhaps in the Greek it is not so.

So we come to the received convention: that some people have the "gift of tongues" and when they utter unknown sounds others will "interpret" (though no verification is possible).[12] Some think "tongues" is not simply one gift among several, but is *the* privileged key to the presence of the Holy Spirit. Others identify congregations where "the gifts are exercised," usually denoting tongues, interpretation, prophecy and perhaps healing. That scenario is what the phrase "the gifts" implies, and they provide a "masonic" recognition-symbol giving reassuring evidence of the presence of the Spirit. But does 1 Corinthians 14 really describe such a mountain top of spiritual experience, vital to all believers, but airbrushed from the rest of the New Testament?

Instead, I try the effect of translating *glōssai* as "languages," as surely any translator with a mental *tabula rasa* would want to do.[13] Can it be done such that Paul then speaks consistently through the three chapters? And what does the translation do to our understanding of church life in

---

12. There seems no difference here between those who exercise these "gifts" today and the cessationists—both sets, translators and commentators alike, *know* what was happening in Corinth, the only difference being that the non-practitioners are somewhat more likely to slip in words like "ecstatic."

13. I should acknowledge that I was first put onto this line of thought through a certain Hudson Mackenzie writing in New Zealand in the early nineteen seventies. I found later support from an offprint of an article by a pseudonymous "Medicus simplex" reprinted from *In the Service of Medicine* (a journal of the Christian Medical Fellowship) in 1973, entitled "Ecstatic Speech in the Bible." I assimilated this approach slowly in the nineteen seventies, and *just* safeguarded my developing thought in my Grove Booklet, *Encountering Charismatic Worship*, with the statement ". . . in the New Testament there are *no* 'tongues'—only the ordinary, uninstitutionalized, term for 'languages.' But 'speaking in languages' does not have the 'special event' feel to it which 'speaking in tongues' does . . ." (p. 14 n. 4). When I drafted the report, *The Charismatic Movement in the Church of England* (1981), I was less able to express that reservation; but in the chapter "Is This That?" in the Doctrine Commission report, *We Believe in the Holy Spirit* (1991) I was able to include the words "With regard to tongues, are we dealing with unknown sounds which require interpretation, or with unknown sounds which require expression in intelligible speech, or are we dealing with foreign languages known to the speaker and with their translation into a language known to the hearer?" (p. 50). In this I was encouraged by Anthony Thiselton whose conclusion (see note 19 below) shaped the second of the three choices listed. Finally, in my own, *Is the Church of England Biblical?* (1998), I aired the whole subject (and resolved the questions!) in an appendix, including my own translation of 1 Corinthians 14. The book sold out, but in 13 years the appendix has brought not one response, letter, e-mail or remark! So this can hardly do worse.

Corinth, and any implications for to-day? I begin by asking what was going on in 1 Corinthians 14 and offer some preliminary points:

1. Paul is responding to a report about things going askew in Corinth. It is, like idol meats, an issue that he has to address because it is divisive. But the matter itself is secondary in his thinking, one which might have run its course without further attention, had there not been division. There is a hint of contrast, even relief, in leaving a secondary issue behind, when he can start chapter fifteen by saying "I delivered to you *as of first importance* that Christ . . . etc."

2. This "secondary" issue is that while some insist on using their own *glōssai*, others use prophecy, which is "in clear" and concerns the things of God.[14] The two sets of practitioners, or their supporters, compete with each other. Any idea that Paul, having once beamed on "gifts" in ch. 12, goes on here by deliberate choice to discuss the relationship of two outstanding ones, and, in effect, to promote their use, is to misunderstand both ch. 12 and the role of the discussion here. Even if "tongues," "interpretation" and "prophecy" were to be classified as special "gifts" (from which I demur), they could not possibly be "*the* gifts." Chapter 14 brackets them together not as tiptop accomplishments which people should long to exercise, but as contingent features of church life which have led to some unnecessary polarizing. And not only are these functions *not* called "gifts" in ch. 14, but, as we have seen, they are not so identified in chs. 12 and 13 either. What Paul is after in all three chapters is not a highlighting or commending of particular functions, but the turning of each function to build up the harmonious working of the whole body.

3. In ch. 14, Paul resolves the presenting issue by appealing to a higher principle than either party has allowed. The vital requirement is that those who speak in the assembly should actually *communicate* to others (the acknowledged fact that God himself can understand anything in any language is strictly irrelevant).[15] The point about communication is made early in the chapter where *glōssai* need translation, but also later on where prophets must not all speak at once, but

---

14. The thrust of my argument is not affected by the differing understandings of "prophecy" which may be around, so I refrain from weighing them up.

15. Some commentators derive from 14:2 that the *grammar* of a "tongue" is addressed to God, i.e., it is praise, not exhortation. But it is far more likely that Paul is saying that, whatever the grammatical form, it is only God who will be able to "hear" it.

rather one at a time! Both cautions are designed to ensure that clear communication occurs. The dynamics which Paul seeks for the assembly are a wholesale participation through *clear interactive verbal communication*.

4. Communication is needed to "build each other up" ("edify"). Presumably this implies teaching and exhortation (perhaps the sphere of prophecy), but can obviously include testimony, questioning, quoting scripture, discussion, praying, singing and giving thanks (these last three intriguingly mentioned in 14:15–17).

I add four further hints to help us determine the situation the apostle seeks to address:

a. Paul expects anyone speaking "in a *glōssa*" to "interpret" it (14:5, 13).[16]

b. Paul has more ability than his readers in *glōssai*, but does not use that ability in the assembly (14:18).

c. Prophecy is found elsewhere in the churches to which Paul writes (cf. Rom 12:6; 1 Thess 5:20; 1 Tim 4:14; Eph 2:20). It appears elsewhere as an unobtrusive norm, not as controversial; so it is *glōssai* which are the unique local feature rocking the Corinthian boat.

d. There is no suggestion that whoever "speaks in a *glōssa*" does not personally understand that *glōssa*.[17]

5. Of these hints, (a) and (d) clearly challenge the conventional understanding of "tongues" and "interpretation" and (c) also fits ill with it.

6. So we ask: what is implied in (2) above in 'use their own *glōssai*'? And a linked question is: what do 'pray with the mind' and 'pray with the spirit' mean?

I submit that we should translate *glōssai* as "languages" and, in the first instance, understand them as "languages natural to the speaker" (which may not be the *lingua franca* of the assembly). So they are "*other* languages," not "*unknown* tongues." To pray, sing or speak "with the

---

16. The versions often invent an unwarranted third person (e.g., "someone") in 14:5, but generally recognize that the speaker has the task in 14:13.

17. In 14:2 Paul says "mysteries" are spoken, but this does not imply they are "mystifying" the speaker. Quite the reverse, the very enunciating of them is apparently building up the speaker.

spirit" is to use the form of speech which is natural to the speaker; for the speaker's "spirit" voices his or her instinctive speech, whereas to pray, sing or speak "with the mind" is cerebrally to translate into a language to communicate to the assembly, i.e., using the *lingua franca*.[18] The upshot therefore of what was going on differs from the conventional Pentecostalist/Charismatic account, since now glossolalia are simply not mentioned. Instead we are to visualize a *lingua franca* (Greek); but there are migrant believers present who insist on speaking in their own languages as being the way to express themselves (and possibly also to assert themselves as important or as having a stake in church life). To integrate them into the life of the congregation Paul allows them to speak freely in their first language, and then to translate it into Greek (14:5, 13), or, alternatively, to check before speaking that someone else present can translate the language for them (14:27–28). But if neither way of translation is available, any would-be speaker should keep silent. The notion of *other* languages best fits the sense.[19]

18. All commentators acknowledge that *pneuma* must sometimes refer to the person's own spirit (as in 14:14–16)—the question is what that implies. I suggest that my hypothesis provides consistency.

19. This is the point to follow the Thiselton trail (see note 13 above). He published a learned article on this topic in 1979 (Thiselton, "The 'Interpretation' of Tongues"), and continued his exposition in his magisterial commentary of 2000 (*First Epistle to the Corinthians*). He begins not with *glōssa*, but *hermēneia*, and from Philo and Josephus derives a variant meaning "to put into words." That leads him to posit that "tongues" means "a kind of non-conceptual outlet for a powerful welling up of emotions." He is specifically *not* calling this a divine language, but postulating a human confusion, a mental congestion, affecting the not-so-literate convert. I attempted a full answer in my appendix to *Is the Church of England Biblical?* which I summarize thus: The Thiselton case needs to be cross-examined as follows:

1. Is it methodologically secure to argue from an attractive possible meaning for "interpret" to a highly speculative meaning for "tongues"?

2. As many of Philo's and Josephus's uses of *hermēneuō* and its compounds are normal instances of "translate" or "interpret," how significant are the cases where it *must* mean "put into words"? He reckons it has two (perhaps more) separable meanings and jumps from one to another in different uses. But this disjunction may be overly sharp—if we use "render" in English, it derives its exact meaning from its context, but could hardly itself determine the meaning of the context.

3. Would this meaning of *glōssai* amount to anything differing from glossolalia in practice? But, also, do even semi-literate converts in fact work that way psychologically: to be overwhelmed into uttering an unreflective jumble of sound, but to know what it means in such a way that they can then "put it into words"? Furthermore, can we understand *glōssa* in such a way that the one thing it *cannot* be is a language? (known or unknown) And, lastly, while it makes fair sense for someone who has

If we check this against 1 Corinthians 12–13, then in 12:10 *genē glōssōn* will be "kinds of languages" (i.e., various people with different languages), and *hermēneia glōssōn* will be "translation of languages" (i.e., people able to deliver a translation). The same understandings fit perfectly well in 12:28, 30. A question remains regarding ch. 13, for devotees of glossolalia in ch. 14 invoke "languages of angels" (13:1) as confirmation that something more-than-terrestrial is current. But the passage generally deals with over the top remote hypotheses (as, for example, in Paul's statement "giving my body to be burned"). These illustrate how much *more* weighty is love than even impossibly remote attainments. So there is no need for it to refer to actually experienced current practice; it quite naturally does not.[20]

The issue of different languages may hardly have been a problem in most parts of the Mediterranean (where Christians regularly used Greek). But equally it is not impossible to imagine it as a real issue in Corinth, the crossroads of the Mediterranean world. Acts 2 suggests that from Pentecost onwards, there were groups of believers with different first languages around the Eastern Mediterranean and Black Sea regions—and if they ever migrated as individuals, families or groups to Corinth (as Priscilla and Aquila once did from Rome), then an insistence on speaking their own languages could well have threatened the peace of the assembly.

I dare not claim that this code-breaking resolution solves all the problems of chapter fourteen. It leaves unexplored the exact nature of New Testament prophecy, the curious quotation from Isaiah about foreign languages, and also those apparently not very PC instructions about women ministering in the assembly. But, I submit, it does give a key to the main sweep: that is, to Paul's handling of a divisive, but actually quite secondary, wholly understandable, local issue.

That said, such a case as I have outlined, if once established, has far-reaching implications. I do not stay here on the contemporary outworkings in the assembly.[21] But what of contemporary glossolalia? For the thrust of

---

uttered the *glōssa* to "put it into words" (as in 14.5,13), how is *someone else* (in 14:26–27) to gather the jumbled sound and "put it into words" for the congregation?

20. However, the "languages of mortals" (NRSV) fits this understanding rather better—he has been referring to *genē glōssōn*, and now he sweeps those *genēe* into one comprehensive condition "though I do the whole round of earthly languages, or even if I could speak the language of angels, that would profit me nothing . . ."

21. The "liturgical" implications involve a mutual ministering of the word (i.e., a true liturgical "formation"), by direct "prophetic" exhortation, by prayer and thanksgiving which draw the church into "Amen," and by song. It perhaps questions those kinds of

my revisiting is to remove any scriptural charter from glossolalia. However, I must quickly add, that does *not* invalidate them—it puts them instead with, for example, the "Toronto Blessing," as experiences which appear to come from God, but are not promised in Scripture, and therefore cannot be sought for others as part of God's universal dispensation. However, this exposition makes "interpretation" more questionable, as diminishing the rationale that glossolalia is to convey a message to an assembly. So, where glossolalia occurs in private prayer, let the persons concerned be glad. Where it occurs in public, let them at least be cautious. And let no-one be encouraged to seek "the gift of tongues" as evidence of the coming of the Holy Spirit.

AUTHOR'S TRANSLATION OF 1 CORINTHIANS 14[22]

Pursue love; and do also be zealous about the things of the spirit,[23] though go rather for prophesying. Whoever speaks in another language is not communicating with the people around, but with God; no-one around can pick it up; the speaker is uttering mysteries 'in the spirit'. But whoever prophesies is communicating to the people around upbuilding and encouragement and empathy. So whoever speaks in another language builds himself up; but whoever prophesies builds the church up. It is not that I object to you all using other languages, but I would prefer you to prophesy; for prophesying is a better activity than speaking other languages—unless of course the speaker translates the message in order that the church may be built up. Similarly with lifeless things that give sound, whether flute or harp: if they do not give clarity to their sounds, how will the content be known of what the flute or harp is playing? And if the trumpet gives an unclear note, who will prepare for battle? And thus if you, by using another language, give an unclear message, how shall the content be known of what you are saying? For you will be talking into the air.

---

prayer meeting where all pray aloud at once. It may also imply that a congregation with more than one language should not divide into separate language groups, but work at being bilingual or multi-lingual.

22. I have ignored the constraints of inclusive language and translate singular masculines, where "common," as masculine singular.

23. I.e., "the leading of your individual spirits" (where those lead to using other languages).

Now there are many kinds of sounds around in the world, and none of them is without meaning; but if I do not know the force of what is being said, then I shall be a gibbering stranger to whoever is speaking, and the speaker will be a gibbering stranger to me. Similarly, you too, even while you are keen on "spirits," should seek to excel in what builds up the church.[24]

Therefore, whoever speaks in another language, should pray that he may translate it aright. For if I pray in another language, my spirit is praying indeed, but my mind is not communicating to those around. What then? Well, I will pray with my spirit, but I will pray also with my mind; I will sing with my spirit, but I will sing also with my mind. For if you bless God with your spirit, how shall the ordinary individual say "amen" to your thanksgiving, since he does not know what you have said? Oh yes, you are giving thanks well enough, but the other person is not being built up.

Now for what it is worth, I thank my God that I do speak other languages more than all of you, but in church I prefer to speak five words where my mind communicates, in order to instruct others, rather than ten thousand words in another language. Brothers, do not be young children as far as your minds are concerned (but do be children as far as evil is concerned); no, in use of your minds be mature. For it is written in the law, "through men of other languages and alien lips, I will speak to this people; and even then they will not hear me" says the Lord."

Other languages, then, are for a sign not to believers, but to unbelievers, and prophecy is not for unbelievers, but for believers. So if the whole church has gathered together, and all are speaking other languages, and ordinary individuals or unbelievers come in, will they not say "You are mad"? But if all are prophesying, and some unbeliever or ordinary individual comes in, he will be convicted by all, he will be judged by all, and thus the secrets of his heart will become plain, and he will fall on his face and worship God, and exclaim "Surely God is among you."

So what is the situation, brothers? When you come together, each of you has a contribution, this one a psalm, this one a teaching, this one another language, this one a revelation, this one ability to translate; let all things be done for building up the church. If anyone does speak in another language, let two or at most three do so, one at a time, and then let one person translate them. But if there is no translator present, then let the would-be speaker keep quiet in church, and simply speak to himself and to God.

---

24. The plural "spirits" is difficult to translate, but I suspect it is a condensed form of "indulging the instincts of your own spirits."

And so with the prophets, let two or three speak and the others discern what is being said; but if a revelation comes to another seated person, then let the first speaker keep quiet. You can all prophesy, doing it one by one, in order that all may learn, and all may be encouraged. And the spirits of the prophets are subject to the prophets; for God is not a God of disorder, but of peace, as it is in all the churches of his holy people.

Let your women [wives?] keep quiet in the churches; for it is not fitting for them to speak, but to be under authority, as the law also says. But if they wish to learn anything, let them ask their husbands at home; for it is wrong for women [wives?] to speak in church. Or did the word of God only come out from you? Or has it reached only you? If anyone sees fit to prophesy or speak from his spirit, let him recognize that what I am writing to you is the commandment of the Lord. If anyone disregards this, let him himself be disregarded.

So, my brothers, have a zeal for prophecy, without forbidding speaking in other languages. But let all things be done decently and in order.

2

Ruth in Two Canons

JAMES T. BUTLER

CANONS AND THE ORDER OF BOOKS

CANONS OF SCRIPTURE ARE both the historical products and the continuing stimulus of "conversations at the edges of things." In their origins, Jewish and Christian canons[1] emerged as communities defined and then defended their boundaries, so that the broad and gradual recognition of authoritative writings was followed by more acute discussions about authoritative lists. Evidence about the earliest stages of these developments is sparse and open to varied interpretations, but the disputes eventually involved not only what books were included in the different collections but in some cases the forms of the books and the order in which they would be listed.

In recent decades "canon" has become a topic of new and productive discussion among biblical scholars. Partly out of theological interests

---

1. We will distinguish between "Christian" and "Jewish" canons, calling these respectively "Old Testament" and "Tanak," without considering the varieties of content within various Christian canons or the varieties of order that can be found in manuscripts and printings of the Jewish canon. We will return later to a brief example of the possible significance of variant orders of the Jewish canon.

and partly out of a turn from genetic to "end-form" questions, authors of commentaries and surveys have moved the topic from a brief paragraph at the end of a section called "text and canon" to lengthier discussions of "purpose" and "reception history."

In a wide-ranging lecture on some of the ramifications of these developments, John Goldingay has suggested that there are at least three ways in which the form of the canon may be of theological significance: one may pay attention to the canonical shape of individual books, or to the ordering of the books in the canon, or (most importantly, he thinks) to what he calls "the rhetorical form" of the canon.[2] The present essay is an attempt to think a little further about the second of these aspects of canonical "formfulness." What significance should we ascribe to the order of the books of a particular canon? And what may we learn from observing the different orders of books in different canons?[3] Using the book of Ruth as a case study, I will argue that placing books in a canonical order is an investment of a faith community in fostering promising intertextual conversations.

RUTH IN CHRISTIAN CANONS: THE ANCESTRESS OF DAVID

Thematically, Ruth fits very well in the long narrative sequence with which the Old Testament begins: the opening temporal clause ("In the days of the 'judging' of the judges . . .") links it with the preceding book of Judges, and the closing genealogy ends with the name of David, who will be the hero of the following books of Samuel. These links are not simply clues by which later traditionists have located the book within a plausible chronological sequence. Instead, they are constructions that function to draw the reader into deeper and more programmatic forms of intertextual conversation about this crucial transition from charismatic to hereditary office.

---

2. John Goldingay, "Old Testament Theology and Canon," 2–4.

3. In connection with book order, Goldingay notes parenthetically "I do not think we have to choose between the Hebrew-Aramaic and Greek ordering of the books; while the former was adopted by the synagogue and the latter by the church, both may be of Jewish origin" ("Old Testament Theology and Canon," 3–4). I take this to mean that, though different canonical orders may entail differences of significance, Jewish and Christian readers may find themselves edified rather than offended by these differences. But, as Goldingay himself notes, this is not always true, and Jewish readers generally find the closing of the Christian canons with prophecy to be especially problematic.

Conversations at the Edges of Things

Ruth as Sequel to Judges

The concluding chapters of Judges offer two stories (chs. 17–18, 19–21) that together form an appendix to the book united by the significant refrain "in those days there was no king in the land" (17:6; 18:1; 19:1; 21:25). Both stories concern "sojourning" Levites (17:7; 19:1; Heb. *gur*), a social phenomenon uniquely anticipated in the book of Deuteronomy (Deut 18:6). Both stories also give prominence to Bethlehem. The Levite of chs. 17–18 leaves Bethlehem and ends up being established as the head of a priestly house in the new tribal sanctuary at Dan, while the second Levite featured in chs. 19–21 first finds excellent hospitality in Bethlehem before going on to a very violent reception in the Benjaminite town of Gibeah.

Both stories have wider significance. The first Levite becomes a discredit to the lineage of Moses (18:30) and an anticipation of the besetting sin of the northern kingdom, Jeroboam's rival sanctuaries at Dan and Bethel (1 Kings 12).[4] In the second story, Judges 19 mirrors Genesis 19, as the warm hospitality of Bethlehem reminds us of Abraham's reception of angelic guests at Hebron and the "outrage at Gibeah" recapitulates the sin of Sodom.[5] Both Levites would have done well to stay in Bethlehem, the hometown of David: the first will be disgraced forever as the founder of the idolatrous priesthood of Dan, and the travels of the latter nearly lead to the decimation of an entire tribe. Gibeah of Benjamin, the hometown of Saul, is effectively contrasted with Bethlehem of Judah, the hometown of David.

The book of Ruth does not just come after these stories, but it both continues and reverses their themes. It begins with a family who leaves Bethlehem to "sojourn" (1:1 *gur*), but the ensuing catastrophe is overcome when Naomi and Ruth return, and virtuous, socially restorative behavior leads to the preparation of David's lineage in his birthplace. Sojourning, Bethlehem, and Davidic anticipations are revisited in Ruth, but with positive characterization and outcome.

---

4. The reference in Judg 18:30 to the duration of Jonathan's priesthood at Dan until "the captivity of the land" seems to explain why Jeroboam, when establishing his alternate cults at Dan and Bethel, needs to supply only Bethel with priests (1 Kgs 12:29, 32).

5. The intertextuality of Genesis 19 and Judges 19 has been explored from many vantage points: Niditch, "The 'Sodomite' Theme in Judges 19–20"; Lasine, "Guest and Host in Judges 19"; Penchansky, "Staying the Night: Intertextuality in Genesis and Judges."

Ruth as Prequel of Samuel

It was the standard opinion of an earlier day that the book of Ruth had been adapted for its canonical position before Samuel by the addition of the concluding genealogy linking its protagonists to David. In his classic *Introduction*, Eissfeldt devoted the largest part of his brief treatment of Ruth to a demonstration that 4:17b–22 are secondary to the book, concluding that "the Ruth narrative had originally nothing at all to do with David, but has only secondarily been made into a narrative concerning David's ancestors."[6]

Eissfeldt may be right about the concluding genealogy being a later addition to the story. The phrase in 4:18, "these are the generations" (*'eleh toledoth*), is particularly striking since it is the primary structural device of the final form of Genesis.[7] The expression occurs just twice outside of Genesis, in Num 3:1 to mark "the descendents of Aaron and Moses" and in Ruth to introduce "the descendents of Perez."[8] With this device, the canonical form of the book of Ruth completes the genealogical grounding of the second of the two hereditary offices of Israel's later history—in the larger biblical narrative, the *toledoth* first reach from creation to the offspring of Jacob/Israel, then to the establishment of the priesthood in the Mosaic period, and finally to the appearance of a royal house in the midst of the nations.

But Eissfeldt does not explain why Ruth would be chosen as a vehicle for this Davidic genealogy in the first place, nor does he appreciate the rich intertextuality with which it is associated. Is it possible, as some have argued, that David actually had Moabite ancestry? The silence regarding his mother's name, along with the allusion to his putting his parents into the protection of the king of Moab as he fled the deranged Saul (1 Sam 22:3–4), could suggest that the early tradition was reticent about David's lineage because of potential criticism. And would a later association with Moab be likely unless it was an actual biographical detail seeking a winsome explanation?

---

6. Eissfeldt, *Introduction*, 480.

7. There are ten occurrences in Genesis, five in the Primeval History (Gen 2:4; 5:1; 6:9; 10:1; 11:10) and five in the Ancestral Narratives (11:27; 25:12; 25:19; 36:1=9; 37:2), reaching from creation to the family of Jacob/Israel.

8. Num 3:1 has also often been regarded as secondary, since it is redundant to 3:2ff. and no genealogy is given for Moses. See, in addition to the commentaries, Johnson, *Purpose of the Biblical Genealogies*, 14–27.

Finally, in the present form of the text the concluding genealogy links up with the setting in Bethlehem and the allusion in 4:12 to "the house of Perez, whom Tamar bore to Judah." Surely the story of Judah and Tamar in Genesis 38 offers an unconventional background for a blessing here, unless it is intended to evoke comparisons with the unconventional act of a foreign woman, who as a widow had consented to redeem the line of her husband's family through levirate marriage, but finally could achieve her virtuous intent only through a dangerous and sexually provocative approach in a liminal setting. Judah's commendation of Tamar's faithfulness (Gen 38:26: "more righteous than I") reminds us of Boaz' praise of Ruth on the threshing floor (3:10: "this last instance of your loyalty is better than the first"), both men paying tribute to foreign women for family loyalty expressed in necessarily unconventional ways.

And there may be one last irony in this canonical pedigree for David. Various interpreters have noted that Genesis develops intertextual comparisons between the Tamar account in Genesis 38 and the earlier story about Lot's daughters in Genesis 19. Could it be that we are to think of the firstborn daughter of Lot, the mother of Moab, who is thus a progenitor of Ruth's family (Gen 19:37); of Tamar, the mother of Perez who preserved the line of Judah; and Ruth the Moabitess, the mother of Obed, as three "ancestresses of David"? This sequence of family preservation by assertive females moves from greater moral liability to greater moral approbation. In the end, though, what could have been an ethnic slur about the incestuous origins of Moab is redeemed by a Moabite woman whose virtues are celebrated. In a treatment of the "canonical contexts of Genesis 38," Esther Menn writes:

> No doubt the theme of foreign blood common to all of these birth narratives is an appropriate symbol for David's expansion of Israel to include a number of foreign territories and peoples. In this way, the royal ancestresses correspond to David and his son Solomon's foreign wives, as concrete expressions of this expansionist drive. But the shrewdness and resourcefulness of David's ancestresses, their opportunism and daring, their effective control of history through unorthodox means, also correspond more generally to the character of David's reign. A usurper and empire builder, David, like his royal ancestresses placed at a safe narrative distance, succeeds magnificently through the unconventional.[9]

---

9. Menn, *Judah and Tamar in Ancient Jewish Exegesis*, 102–3.

RUTH IN THE JEWISH CANON: RUTH AS CONVERT AND AS "WOMAN OF MERIT"

A. The Book of Ruth as the Festival Scroll for Shabuʻoth: Ruth as Convert and Model of Covenant Faithfulness

In virtually all extant Hebrew texts of the Tanak, both manuscript and print, Ruth is found not at the juncture of Judges and Samuel, but in the last section of the canon, the Writings, among the five festival scrolls or Megilloth.[10] Particularly in German manuscripts and in the early printed editions deriving from them, we find the book order that is common in Western synagogue use today: Psalms, Proverbs, Job (in the Talmud called the "greater" or "former" Writings), the Megilloth (in the order of their use in the calendar: Song of Songs, Ruth, Lamentations, Ecclesiastes, Esther), and finally Daniel, Ezra-Nehemiah, and 1–2 Chronicles (the "lesser" or "latter" Writings). In the liturgical tradition, Ruth is read at the festival of Shabuʻoth (Weeks/Pentecost), which was associated biblically with the wheat harvest and in post-biblical times with the covenant following the giving of the Torah at Sinai. If Ruth's association with harvest time is the likely reason that the book was first associated with Shabuʻoth, her adoption of Naomi's people and God, acknowledged by Boaz as her taking refuge under the wings of Yahweh, becomes the model of a convert's introduction into the covenant of Sinai.[11] In this way, the Jewish canon has appropriated Ruth as part of a textual commentary on the liturgical calendar.

---

10. It cannot be decided with certainty whether Ruth's earliest canonical setting was associated with Judges or whether it was originally a part of the Writings. Scholars who assign a late date to the work as a commentary on the foreign marriage crisis of Ezra-Nehemiah often have assumed the latter. The Talmud places Ruth before Psalms at the beginning of the Writings, obviously with the intent of providing the family background of David. Whether or not it was originally included among the Prophets or the Writings, its inclusion among the liturgical collection of the Megilloth is post-Talmudic, perhaps eleventh century CE. Wolfenson, "Implications of the Place of Ruth," 167–78, concludes that the question of Ruth's original location is not only impossible to decide, but probably meaningless since the Jewish canon was long a normative list without a normative order.

11. For good measure, Ruth's genealogical connection with David is celebrated with the tradition that David both was born and died on Shabuʻoth.

The Book of Ruth as a Sequel to Proverbs: Ruth as a "Foreign Woman" who is acclaimed as a "Woman of Merit"

Since 1937, scholarship in both Jewish and Christian circles has availed itself of an older manuscript tradition which displays a different order for the Writings.[12] Here Ruth is at the beginning of the Megilloth (Ruth, Song of Songs, Ecclesiastes, Lamentations, Esther), apparently following a supposed chronological order of authors rather than the calendar order of the associated festivals. What is less often noted about this earlier order, however, is the sequence of the first three books of the Writings, which runs Psalms-Job-Proverbs instead of the later Psalms-Proverbs-Job. Hence, the earliest book order of the Hebrew canon for which we have manuscript evidence juxtaposes the books of Proverbs and Ruth. What consequences does this canonical ordering have for readers of Ruth?

Ruth as a "Woman of Merit" ('esheth ḥayil)

Not a few scholars reading their *Biblia Hebraica* texts have noticed a striking parallel between the last unit of Proverbs (Prov 31:10–31), an alphabetic acrostic poem about the "woman of merit" (*'esheth ḥayil*),[13] and Boaz' commendation of Ruth with the same phrase (Ruth 3:11) about four pages later.[14] The expression is rare in the Hebrew Bible, occurring elsewhere only in Prov 12:4. Commentators have detailed the correspondences between the description of Proverbs and the things recounted of Ruth. Sakenfeld notes that as a childless widow Ruth is not being praised for her family or wealth, but "the overall theme of the woman who takes the initiative inside and outside the household area to provide for her family is remarkably

---

12. The third edition of *Biblia Hebraica* abandoned the traditional Rabbinic Bible of ben Chayyim for the oldest complete Ben Asher manuscript known, Codex Leningradensis, dating from the early eleventh century CE. More recently the Ben Asher text of the slightly earlier, damaged Aleppo Codex has become the basis of another important scholarly edition. For our purposes, it is enough to note that both of these early manuscripts, as well as other Masoretic and later Sephardic manuscripts, follow the specific book order that we will discuss, including the juxtaposition of Proverbs with Ruth. Wolfenson's article predates these developments but collates useful information ("Implications of the Place of Ruth," 152–67).

13. For a recent study that gives an overview of research on this passage, and which attempts to correct idealistic theological readings with a careful socio-economic analysis of the female roles in Proverbs 1–9 and 31, see Yoder, *Wisdom as a Woman of Substance*.

14. Cf., already in 1975, Campbell, *Ruth*, 34.

appropriate": "She does good, not harm (see Prov. 31:12); she 'works with willing hands' (31:13) and 'provides food for her household' (31:15); 'strength and dignity are her clothing' (31:25); 'the teaching of kindness (*ḥesed*) is on her tongue' (31:26); 'she does not eat the bread of idleness' (31:27); 'she fears the Lord' (31:30)."[15] Two items in the description of Proverbs 31 seem to receive special emphasis as they are associated with Boaz' threshing floor commendation of Ruth as a "woman of merit" (Ruth 3:10–11). Boaz begins by commending the totality of Ruth's behavior, first in caring for Naomi and now in seeking to redeem her husband's lineage, by characterizing it as her "loyalty" (*ḥesed*). Then he declares that "all the *gate* of my people know that you are a *woman of merit*": this sentence brings together the opening and the closing lines of the poem in Proverbs, which begins with "a woman of merit" (31:10) and closes with her deeds being praised "in the gates" (31:31).

Ruth as a "Foreign Woman" (nokriyah) Who Is Acclaimed a "Woman of Merit"

But the significance of Ruth as a canonical sequel to Proverbs is not exhausted with the parallel of Prov 31:10 and Ruth 3:11. Another term that has high significance in Proverbs is *nokriyah*, which is variously translated as "foreign woman," "adulteress," "seductress," and synonyms, depending on how the context is understood (2:16; 5:20; 6:24; 7:5; 23:27). Scholarly literature on the identity of the *nokriyah* in Proverbs has become enormous and can scarcely be summarized here. One pole of interpretation contends that the phrase simply designates an adulteress—a woman who is "other" or "foreign" because she is married to someone else.[16] Another view relates the phrase to its use in the crises over marriages in Ezra-Nehemiah and Malachi, understanding the danger to be women of a different national group serving other gods (e.g., Neh 13:23–27: "women of Ashdod, Ammon, and Moab" are likened to the "foreign women" who made Solomon to sin).[17] Finally, more complex views have been put forward to locate the "foreign woman" in the complex social definitions of tiny Persian Yehud, with its

---

15. Sakenfeld, *Ruth*, 62.

16. Cf. Fox, *Proverbs 1–9*, 134–41.

17. Tan, *'Foreignness' of the Foreign Woman*, emphasizes that the "foreignness" is just that, albeit developed into a literary trope indebted to the ideology of the Deuteronomistic literature.

authorized golah community and "others" seeking assimilation through marriage.[18] What is clear is that the series of warnings about the "foreign woman" in Proverbs 1–9 is paralleled with descriptions of the appeal of personified Wisdom, until they culminate in the parallel figures of Woman Wisdom and Woman Folly (9:1–6 and 9:13–18). Redactionally, Woman Wisdom of Proverbs 1–9 seems to be embodied by the "woman of merit" in Proverbs 31, bringing a frame to the book as a whole.[19]

Ruth, following Proverbs immediately in this early canonical ordering, seems both to follow and radically to revise Proverbs' antithesis between the "foreign woman" who becomes the type of Woman Folly and the "woman of merit" who embodies Woman Wisdom. In Ruth, by contrast, it is the "foreign woman" who is declared the "woman of merit."

The literary structure of the book of Ruth dramatizes her two identities, as both a "foreign woman" (2:10, *nokriyah*) and a "woman of merit" (3:11, *'esheth ḥayil*), exposing them separately but also bringing them into juxtaposition by a variety of devices. At the center of the book's chiastic or "envelope" structure,[20] the inner symmetry of chapters 2 and 3 provides the dramatic action that resolves the tension of the outer symmetry between chapters 1 and 4: through two dialogue-filled encounters of the protagonists, Ruth and Boaz, first in the fields (2) and then on the threshing floor (3), a Judean family that had been devastated by crisis and death (1) is given new life and royal progeny (4).

THE DIALOGUE OF CHAPTER 2: RUTH AS A "FOREIGN WOMAN"

At the heart of the dynamic inner units of this symmetry are the dialogues between Ruth and Boaz. In the first of these (2:8–13), Ruth identifies herself as a "foreign woman" (*nokriyah*). This is the only time this term is used in the book, but it brings into sharp focus the status entailed for Ruth as a "Moabitess."

---

18. Blenkinsopp, "Social Context of the 'Outside Woman'"; Smith-Christopher, "Exclusion, Transformation, and Inclusion of the 'Foreigner'"; Washington, "Strange Woman"; Yee, "Other Woman."

19. The significance of this bracketing and its resultant "literary recontextualization" of Proverbs was first argued in the thesis of Claudia Camp, *Wisdom and the Feminine.*

20. Of the various outlines, that of Stephen Bertman is clearest in showing the essential features of this structure ("Symmetrical Design," 165–68).

Ruth's name appears twelve times in the book, and in half of these occurrences she is further identified as a "Moabitess" (1:4, 22; 2:2, 21; 4:5, 10). She is initially identified, with Orpah, as one of the Moabite women that Naomi's sons married in their painful and finally catastrophic exile from Judah (1:4). In two references she is redundantly signaled as "the Moabitess . . . from the land of Moab" (1:22; 2:6), and the gleaning episode in which Ruth acknowledges her status as a foreigner is further bracketed by two allusions to her as "Ruth the Moabitess" (2:2, 21). Finally, in the language of legal transactions in ch. 4, "Ruth the Moabitess" is a deal breaker for one kinsman (4:5) and the emphatic acquisition of the other (4:10). As Bush suggests, this was probably simply Ruth's full name in Bethlehem, where as a resident alien the patronymic of her family would have been replaced by the gentilic of her nationality (cf. "Uriah the Hittite").[21] Still, the degree of repetition suggests emphasis, and associations with Moabite women are consistently negative elsewhere in Israel's traditions (cf. Num 25:1; 1 Kgs 11:1, 7–8; Neh 13:23–27). Outside of Ruth, the only association of the terms "Moabitess" and "foreign woman" (*nokriyah*) comes in the description of Solomon's "foreign wives" (1 Kgs 11:1; Neh 13:26–27). When Ruth says that she is a "foreigner," the reader recognizes that her specific nationality is particularly problematic in Israel.

The introduction of Ruth as a foreign woman among the gleaners also carries signals of her social status. Boaz first asks "To whom does this young woman belong?" Then he gives her instructions: "Keep close to my young women . . . I have ordered the young men not to bother you" (2:5, 8–9). The setting is reminiscent of the opening instructions of Proverbs, which offer stern reminders that "foreign women" can be a sexual provocation to young men, since they do not "belong" to a father or a husband. But, contrary to Proverbs' vantage point of protective parental counsel of young men, Boaz is acknowledging the dangers of the situation for the "foreign woman."

Finally, Ruth's acknowledgement (2:10) of her status as a "foreign woman" (*nokriyah*) is further underlined by the wordplay with the verb translated "take notice of" in the same verse (root *nkr*): "Why have I found favor in your sight, that you should *take notice of* me, when I am a *foreign woman*?" The play not only draws attention to the words, but may have the force of ironically bringing together normally contrasting homonyms: "to have regard for" does not typically find its object in a "foreigner."[22] Ruth

21. Bush, *Ruth/Esther*, 138.
22. Ibid., 123.

acknowledges this incongruity by speaking of it as "favor" (*hen*),[23] but Boaz quickly praises her "deeds" on behalf of Naomi, for which he wishes her Yahweh's full "reward" or "wages"[24] (2:11–12). The effect of the play, then, is to raise first the oddity of Boaz' "regard" for a "foreigner," and then to disclaim that this foreigner has received any special regard or favor at all, but only the reward of her faithfulness.

THE DIALOGUE OF CHAPTER 3: RUTH AS A "WOMAN OF MERIT"

In the dialogue of chapter 3, Boaz's commendation of Ruth in the busy gleaning fields is surprisingly elevated in the potentially compromising context of the midnight encounter on the threshing floor. Ruth appeals to Boaz to spread his "cloak" (*kanaph*) over her as kinsman-redeemer (*go'el*).[25] To the importunate widow who has uncovered him, Boaz declares, "I will do for you all that you ask, for all the gate of my people know that you are a 'woman of merit' (*'esheth hayil*)." Boaz himself was first introduced to the reader as a "powerful man of merit" (2:1; NRSV: "prominent rich man") in a phrase that links together the two common ways of predicating "merit, valor, wealth" (*hayil*) of a male (*'ish gibbor hayil*). His "*hayil*" could be assumed as that of a wealthy landowner when he is introduced, but it is quickly disambiguated by his actions in the story; his "merit" reciprocates that which he finds demonstrated in the young Moabitess. His reference to Ruth's "latest loyalty" surpassing her first (3:10)[26] is another element tying the two dialogues of chs. 2 and 3 together, and it demonstrates

---

23. Naomi later expresses the same surprise that someone has "taken notice" of Ruth, and invokes blessing on him (2:19).

24. The term translated "reward" derives from the root "to hire," and elsewhere is used only in the context of Jacob's service with Laban ("my wages," Gen 31:7,41).

25. Here in 3:9 Ruth takes up the terms of Boaz's invocation of Yahweh's care in 2:12 and frames it as a strategic appeal: from the "wings" (*kanaphaim*) of Yahweh's care to the "cloak" (*kanaph*) of the kinsman's acceptance of levirate marriage. Some Masoretic witnesses enhance this parallel by making "cloak" plural.

26 Boaz' commendation, "you have not gone after young men, whether poor or rich," is ambiguous. Does it mean that she has "acted neither from passion nor greed" (Hubbard, *Ruth*, 215)? Or does it acknowledge the substantial risk that Ruth has taken, without knowing Boaz's response? The later comparison between Ruth and Tamar (4:12) may suggest that the measure of Ruth's commitments has been taken from the hazards of her actions.

the surprising heightening of his regard: this "foreigner" is now not only worthy of blessing, but she is exemplary as a "woman of merit," fully his counterpart. "Conversations at the edges of things," indeed!

The surprising juxtaposition of "foreign woman" and "woman of merit" in Ruth 2–3 both echoes the usage of Proverbs and radically expands it. Jennifer Koosed catches something of this:

> Proverbs presents a bifurcated picture of women—Woman Wisdom is countered by Dame Folly; the strange woman is countered by the virtuous wife. Ruth may be identified with the virtuous wife by Boaz's words, but a more careful examination of women in Proverbs and Ruth's character indicate that the compliment is more complex. The strange woman who is contrasted with the 'esheth hayil in Proverbs is a woman who uses her sexuality to drag men into Sheol. The adjective strange may also be an indication that the woman is not just an adulteress but also a foreigner. Ruth may embody all of the virtues explicated in Proverbs 31 and attributed to the perfect wife. But she is also the foreign woman who seduces the righteous Israelite man. The foreign woman is the 'esheth hayil; the seductress is the virtuous wife. Ruth parodies Proverbs.[27]

Does Ruth destabilize what we know about "foreign women," and perhaps even the relative value of social proprieties in maintaining family order? The book clearly cites Tamar as an exemplar—one who, if less clearly than Ruth a "foreigner," was much more clearly than Ruth a seductress. If we are surprised by the ancient story that has the patriarch Judah declare Tamar "more righteous than I," should we not be surprised when Ruth is declared, by a man whom she has uncovered at midnight, a "valorous woman"? This may not revoke the counsel given in Proverbs 1–9 about the dangers that young men should avoid, but it complicates such counsel by reminding us of how societies create the very social categories that they deplore. And how the tribe of Judah was sustained crucially, at least twice, by women who appear to have transgressed the rules, fixed in the Torah and commended in the torah of parental teaching, about appropriate social boundaries.

John Goldingay has written some words about "the canon's fuzzy edges," referring to the inscrutable decisions made about "everything in the canon and everything outside it." I would also appropriate his counsel for the "fuzzy edges" that we have been exploring inside the canon, where different configurations of books can confirm or revise or reconfigure

---

27. Koosed, *Gleaning Ruth*, 92.

a community's treasured readings. Can such "fuzzy edges" be "a sign of grace and a hidden hint of the gospel," reminding us that God "works through human processes, with their oddities, and declines to bypass them supernaturally"?[28]

John, I will look forward to crossing the ten paces between our office doors sometime to have further conversation about the edges of the canon and their contribution to the hermeneutical courage and vitality of the church.

---

28. Goldingay, *Models for Scripture*, 182.

3

Old Testament Narratives and Ethics
A Journey in Understanding

ATHENA E. GOROSPE

ETHICAL REFLECTION ON THE Old Testament has long been centered on the prescriptive genres of law, prophecy, and wisdom, but in recent years scholars have begun to recognize the importance of narrative for their work in this area.[1] This turn to narratives to address ethical questions is not isolated from developments in other fields of study. Ethical criticism—the study of literature for its ethical/moral value and in relation to the life questions of its readers[2]—is enjoying a significant resurgence through the incisive writing of a new breed of moral philosophers who are beginning to engage classical literary works with ethical issues in mind.[3]

---

1. See for example Barton, *Ethics and the Old Testament*; Birch, *Let Justice Roll Down*; Janzen, *Old Testament Ethics*.

2. Ethical criticism, according to Booth (*The Company We Keep*, 11), is "any effort to show how the virtues of narratives relate to the virtues of selves and societies, or how the ethos of any story affects or is affected by the ethos—the collection of virtues—of any given reader."

3. Parker, "The Turn to Ethics in the 1990's," 1–17. This group of moral philosophers, according to Haines ("Deepening the Self," 21–38), is reacting against the Enlightenment's view of a divided moral language (between a "specificatory, descriptive, scientific,

Conversations at the Edges of Things

As we seek to understand and appropriate biblical texts for ethical issues, these developments in the study of narrative texts, and of the characteristics of narrative as a mode of discourse, promise to open up new ways of reading that could both form and challenge us ethically. In this essay, I survey the various ways by which Old Testament narratives have been appropriated ethically by tracing my own journey through successive stages of understanding, offering in effect a personal narrative regarding the discovery of the potentials of narrative.

SUNDAY SCHOOL AND THE ETHICAL MODEL APPROACH

It was at children's Sunday School that I had my first encounter with Old Testament stories. I remember the teacher telling the story of how God called Samuel, and somehow I felt I was there with Samuel, hearing this mysterious voice in the middle of the night. Then there were the stories of David and Goliath, of Noah and the Ark, and the runaway Jonah. I enjoyed those stories and they fired up my young imagination. I often felt that I was there in the scene with the biblical characters, cheering them along, laughing with gentle humor at their foibles, or being horrified at their grave mistakes.

I must confess that I did not enjoy the moral lessons drawn by the teacher, which always came at the end of the stories, as much as I did the stories themselves. In the moral lessons, the biblical characters were always presented as models of ethical behavior. Thus, Abraham was an example of faith, David of courage, and Moses of dedicated leadership. Then there were the "bad" examples: Cain the murderer, Esau the greedy man, and Saul the disobedient.[4] The characters were presented as either good or bad, to be emulated or avoided. I remember the teacher turning to me, after the story was told and the moral lesson was given, saying: "Now, how about you? Will you be like David (or Moses, or Joseph, or Daniel)?" I often squirmed when this time came, for there was no way I could be as good as these

---

fact-oriented component and a recommendatory, prescriptive, emotional, action-oriented component") and a divided self (the reasoning self and the emotive self). They advocate a way of doing ethics which integrates these divides, and they see literature as a locus of ethical reflection that makes such integration possible.

4. Janzen (*Old Testament Ethics*, 7) mentions this first encounter of Christians with Old Testament stories. Much of popular devotional literature uses this approach to Old Testament stories.

biblical characters were. Moreover, the stories were also mostly about men, although a few stories about women were thrown in occasionally.

I was disappointed later on when I realized that the good characters were not all that good, and the bad characters were not all that bad, and that there were characters who seemed to be ethically ambiguous. Jacob, for example, was hard to place (how could the Lord bless him when he was so deceptive?), and Saul seemed to me to have been unfairly punished for such a small mistake, while David got off scot free.

So I became increasingly dissatisfied with this way of reading narratives. In the first place, the biblical characters' actions were not always consistent with the virtue or exemplary attitude attributed to them. At the same time, there were disagreements on exactly how to read a character's actions or attitudes. There were many narratives where explicit evaluation was not given by the teller of the tale. Without this clear evaluation, it became confusing whom to identify with and to follow.[5] And then there were the practices that we would surely regard as morally objectionable which were often completely glossed over in the discussion of the virtues of the characters.[6]

PULPIT SERMONS AND THE PRINCIPLE BEHIND THE STORY

In an evangelical seminary where I took my MDiv degree, the devotional ethical model approach was still the prevalent mode of dealing with biblical narratives. But this time the moral of the story was replaced by the "lesson" of the passage, or the "principle" behind the story, which distilled the attitude or virtue being advocated into one essential statement or phrase. To be sure, attention was given to the ethical-forming function of scripture for personal life, and this I appreciated, but I often felt a sense of loss over the parts of the story which were glossed over because they did not contribute to, or sometimes were opposed to, the ideal portrait which was being presented. At that time, having gone through a particularly difficult period in my life, I was reading scripture voraciously, searching for what

---

5. As Goldingay (*Approaches*, 40) asks, "Who and what in the story has the narrative's own approval?"

6. Birch, *Let Justice Roll Down* (42–43), mentions polygamy, holy war, subordination of women, and excessive nationalism. One can also add to the list slavery, violence, lying, favoritism, elitism, and racism.

was life-giving, caught up in the stories with my own world suspended, as I heard the "sound of a different drummer." So the reduction of the story to a one-line maxim somehow made me feel that something compellingly alluring and potentially transforming was lost.

The sermons based on ethical principles were sometimes inspiring, but often they were based on extended generalizations not supported by a close reading of the text or an idealization of a small detail which got blown out of proportion to the rest of the story.[7]

Thus, I came to see that asking such questions—"What is the moral of the story? How do these characters provide a good or bad example? What lesson or principle can we derive from the story?—is an inadequate approach. Surely there must be other, less reductive ways of reading biblical narratives ethically.

WHAT THE STORY MEANT: USING HISTORICAL-CRITICAL EXEGESIS

Entering a ThM program offered me a context to discover another way of looking at narratives. Now the questions completely shifted from the moral/ethical realm and became purely historical: What did the original author/redactor intend to communicate to the original audience? What were the earlier stages of composition behind the present text? Thus, moralizing turned to reconstruction.

Reconstructing the historical context appealed to my ordering instinct and my sense of history, but it took me away from the world *in* the text to focus exclusively on the world *behind* the text.[8] After the reconstruction was done, I discovered that there was little energy left to spend on understanding what the story meant, let alone working out its ethical implications.

---

7. Janzen (*Old Testament Ethics*, 29) talks about the loss involved in reducing the ethical yield of stories to principles that can then be transferred to other situations. He illustrates how this reduction to abstract principles makes the story unnecessary: "Thus, a Sunday school class studying the story of Ruth and Boaz (Ruth 2) has not finished its task until the story has led to an abstract maxim, such as 'Help the needy!' At that point, no great loss is felt if the pupils forget the story on their way home, as long as they hold on tightly to the principle 'Help the needy.'"

8. Brueggemann aptly comments: "Such treatment of the text does not at all attend to the statements of the text itself, but is in effect a sustained raid on the text, looking for clues that support historical reconstruction. It is odd that an enterprise as preoccupied with the text as Scripture study is, should in the end have so little genuine interest in the text and its rhetorical, artistic character" (*Theology*, 54).

As Goldingay comments, "biblical interpretation often seems to spend vast amounts of effort discussing or establishing when a given story was written and then runs out of steam before going on to interpret it."[9]

Thus, when historical work is prioritized, theological and ethical reflection often comes home limping, so that the end result is not at all commensurate to the amount of work invested in the whole process. I had amassed a wealth of historical information and intriguing theories, but the fragmented and mangled story lay before me, empty of meaning, with no power to change or shape me morally.

Moreover, reconstructing the sources behind the text can lead one to cut up the narrative altogether.[10] As an Asian embedded in a culture which emphasizes interconnectedness and holism, I felt confused as I jumped from one section of the text to another in order to take up the flow of the narrative, since the critical dissection went against a view of life which strives for wholeness.[11]

I remember going to the program director, frustrated and dissatisfied, seeking answers on how to make the results of the whole process more relevant. I was told that we do the historical-critical work first; only after this can we tackle the religious-ethical issues and the question of relevance. But either we never got to talk about religious-ethical issues for lack of time, or we were not able to bridge the gap between the historical/compositional issues and the religious-ethical questions. It is difficult (and for some, impossible) to make the quantum leap from questions of history, which make up the starting point of the enterprise, to questions of theology and morality, the desired ending for readers who regard the text as scripture. Thus, our appropriation of the text appeared forced or strained. The starting questions did not yield the answers demanded by the ending questions.[12]

---

9. Goldingay, *Models for Interpretation*, 34.

10. A forceful example of this problem can be seen in the famous Genesis commentary of von Rad, who arranges his exposition in such a way as to clearly delineate the sources. Thus, Gen 1:1—2:4a, which belongs to P, is immediately followed by ch. 5, another P account. He then returns to 2:4b and takes up the J account until he reaches the end of ch. 4, then jumping to ch. 6. The Flood story, which is considered a composite account, is divided by von Rad as he assigns verses and fragments to their respective sources. Thus one no longer reads the narrative as a continuous text.

11. Sugirtharajah (*Asian Biblical Hermeneutics*, 12) mentions how the Anglicist historical-critical approach replaced the Indian narrative approach, which views text as "authorless narrative wholes."

12. The practitioners of historical approaches, according to Goldingay (*Models for Interpretation*, 19), are "asking questions whose answers the text by definition conceals."

In summary, the "critical reconstruction of the reported events" which "constituted the subject matter of narrative texts" in historical criticism[13] was useful for me in understanding certain aspects of the narrative, but not in ethically informing and shaping me and others who journeyed with me.

WRITING A ThM THESIS: NARRATIVES AS LITERATURE

It was partly in reaction to the dry and unimaginative treatment of narratives in historical criticism that I decided to try a different tack when I was writing my ThM thesis. In the early 90s, scholars in the Philippines were only beginning to feel the impact of the new literary methods in biblical studies. Feeling intuitively that such approaches had much to offer in working with narratives, I decided to explore them in addressing the Samson stories.[14] This study introduced me to the work of literary theorists like Robert Alter, Meir Sternberg, and Adele Berlin.[15] Their reading of narratives provided me with food for thought, fresh and insightful reading, and sensitivity to the different nuances of the text, while using a methodology that was familiar to readers who had taken literature courses.

I had begun teaching at a seminary at that time, and as I read the narratives using this approach, my Asian students responded in amazing ways. It was not as foreign to them as working on the sources, and they felt at home analyzing plot, rhetorical patterns, character, structure, point of view. It was very empowering—people read together, became deeply involved with the story, worked hard to think things through, shared, discussed, and felt that they were not entirely left in the hands of biblical scholars to understand and appropriate the text which they believe can give them life. In all of these readings, there was no explicit intention to apply the text after the analysis of the narrative was over—there was no moral lesson, so to speak. The students just retold the story, putting emphasis in the retelling on themes that the narrative style opened up. We laughed at the humor behind the story of Ehud and Eglon the king; cried at the loss of one so young as Jephthah's daughter; mourned with

---

13. Frei, *Eclipse of Biblical Narrative*, 9.

14. Gorospe, "Comedy and Humor in Samson" (ThM thesis, Asia Graduate School of Theology, Manila, 1995), using Exum and Whedbee, "Isaac, Samson, and Saul," 5–40, as a starting point.

15. Alter, *Art of Biblical Narrative*; Sternberg, *Poetics of Biblical Narrative*; Berlin, *Poetics and Interpretation*.

bitter pain the strife between David and his son Absalom; wondered at the nature of political power as we observed the change in Solomon at the latter part of his reign; and were challenged by the change in Esther from a passive woman to an empowered one.

At Sunday School, where I later became the teacher rather than the learner, many found the new narrative approach interesting, participative, and insightful. Minor characters came alive, seemingly insignificant details became pregnant with meaning, the past and the future formed a connection as a result of recognizing common experiences of people who lived in a different and unfamiliar world. As people reading together shared in the emotions of grief, joy, shame, horror, amusement, disapproval, and loss, they also felt that they were growing in insight. I could never describe what the precise effects were, for the ending was always open, suggestive, leading forward, without any completion or the sense that we had finally got it all down. I wondered afterwards whether the challenge to their moral life had something to do with the unexpected jolt of a reading that was different from what they used to see in the narrative. Or having been drawn unwittingly into the world of the story, were they disarmed and thus caught off-guard?[16]

Such dynamics, however, were not present in many of the studies being done using formalist and structuralist approaches.[17] These studies were interesting; the analysis of structure, characterization, plot, style, etc., produced unexpected readings, or sometimes supported previous readings more strongly. But they often failed to address the moral or ethical questions, remaining instead as descriptive as the historical-critical ones.[18] The reason for this is that the text is seen as a closed aesthetic system, with great artistry but no relation to the world of the reader. Thus, these literary studies can become purely descriptive, and the Bible, while treated as a classic, is considered to be devoid of any authority or theological relevance.[19]

---

16. This is rather similar to the effect on David when Nathan the prophet confronted him with a story (2 Sam 12:11–15), or the effect on Isaiah's hearers when he chanted the Song of the Vineyard (Isa 5:1–7).

17. Goldingay discusses formalist and structural approaches in *Models for Interpretation*, 21–27.

18. The reason for this, according to Goldingay, is that such purely literary approaches allow us to distance ourselves from the text, so that we do not yet permit the text to "press its questions on us, only to overhear it talking to itself" (*Models for Interpretation*, 39).

19. Cf. Childs, *Biblical Theology*, 20.

GEMS FROM MARTHA NUSSBAUM: NARRATIVES AND ETHICAL PERCEPTION

When I began my PhD program, I was able to bring further resources to this question of how the Old Testament narratives may form us ethically. At the suggestion of my mentor John Goldingay and drawing upon the works of John Barton,[20] I explored the writings of Martha Nussbaum,[21] a moral philosopher at the University of Chicago. In contrast to other moral philosophers, Nussbaum has used Greek tragedies and English novels as her material for ethical and moral reflection because she believes that narrative addresses certain questions in life that cannot be addressed by other forms.[22]

Nussbaum claims that narratives offer certain unique features for ethical perception. First, they pay attention to particularity, with specific situations, characters and relationships.[23] Thus, in reading and responding to a narrative, one is led to respond to the specific features of one's situation rather than to apply a general principle that fits all situations. This results in greater flexibility, in responses that are contextual and resourceful, and in sensitivity to the non-repeatable elements of a given situation. By being attentive to particularity, one's ethical perception is thus developed.

Second, stories evoke emotions. Often emotions have been seen as hindering rather than aiding ethical perception, so that narrative is undervalued as merely illustrative while "objective" scientific inquiry is preferred. According to Nussbaum, however, emotions are an essential part not only of cognition but also of moral perception.[24] Emotions guide the reader to be able to perceive clearly the situation and to make an appropriate response.[25] In one of my classes, for example, a student strongly reacted against the Levite's conduct in Judges 19. This reaction, I think, is entirely appropriate since it came from the perception that a grave wrong was done. As I told my students afterwards, it is more worrying if we do not react at all, since our indifference may indicate a lack of sensitivity to injustice.

---

20. Barton, *Ethics and the Old Testament*, 19–36; Barton, "Reading for Life," 66–76.
21. Nussbaum, *Love's Knowledge*; Nussbaum, *The Fragility of Goodness*.
22. Nussbaum, *Love's Knowledge*, 4–5.
23. Ibid., 37–38.
24. Ibid., 40–41, 79.
25. Ibid., 79.

Third, narrative makes room for the surprise and the unexpected. The openness of stories and their multivalent character lead to the acknowledgment of uncertainty and unpredictability, of ambiguity and paradox in life. Storied portrayals of life's contingencies are important for ethical understanding because they force us to acknowledge that "human aspirations to live well can be checked by uncontrolled events."[26]

As I considered Old Testament narratives, I recognized that the qualities that Nussbaum cites are also evident in these texts. Unlike law, prophetic oracles, wisdom sayings, and the psalms, narratives are less open to generalization and schematization. Although it is possible, for example, to generalize that Joseph and Daniel and Solomon are full of wisdom (the text describes them as such; cf. Gen 41:39; 1 Kgs 3:28; Dan 1:17–20), the quality of "wisdom" itself receives its meaning from the particularities of each story. To answer the question why these men are wise is actually to tell their stories all over again.

And even though Old Testament narratives rarely contain any extensive descriptions of emotional display, they do evoke these emotions. Indeed, the sparseness of emotional description is actually an advantage, making it possible for us as readers to imagine in different ways what the feelings of the characters or the sentiments of the narrator might be. This reticence allows, and even compels, readers to speculate, "to fill gaps, to give voice about the silences of character, even when they are unaware of doing so."[27]

Finally, biblical narratives create ambiguity and surprise for us both in their depiction of human characters, who often do not conform to stereotypes, and in their characterization of God, who acts sometimes in paradoxical, puzzling, and even contradictory ways.[28] This freedom of narrative captures a view of life where not everything is known, predicted, or controlled.

---

26. Ibid., 43.

27. Gunn and Fewell, *Narrative in the Hebrew Bible*, 51.

28. Patrick (*Rendering of God*, 82), for instance, while arguing for the consistency in the character of Yahweh, struggles with "out of character" depictions, like Yahweh's attack on Moses after the latter's commission (Exod 4:24–26), or "Yahweh's encounter with Jacob in a nocturnal wrestling match" (Gen 32:22–32). In the depiction of God as a literary character, Miles (*God: A Biography*) shows a God who has disparate elements in his personality. Penchansky's (*What Rough Beast?*) negative portrayal of God is drawn exclusively from narratives.

My interaction with Nussbaum helped me to understand how narrative achieves its ethical effects. It was at the next point of my journey, however, that I was able to see how ethics plays into the actual interpretation of texts.

PAUL RICOEUR AND THE ETHICAL POSSIBILITIES OF A STORY

When I eventually came to do a PhD dissertation on Old Testament narrative ethics, I turned to Paul Ricoeur for a philosophical hermeneutical framework for my work. Ricoeur, whose three-volume *Time and Narrative*[29] is a classic in narrative theory, introduced me to the concept of narrative identity and how it relates to ethical identity.

Ricoeur thinks that our narrative identity—that is, the identity we acquire through the mediation of a narrative—is formed as we interact with the narrative identity of the characters in a story.[30] In turn, the narrative identity of the characters is shaped by the dynamic interplay of concordance and discordance in the plot.[31] Even though there are multiple events, diverse elements, and different levels of time in a story, the plot mediates all of these to produce a "synthesis of the heterogeneous."[32] Thus, even as the plot moves towards its logical conclusion, it is also thwarted in surprising and unexpected ways. This action of concordance-discordance is reflected in the narrative identity of the characters themselves who oscillate between an identity that exhibits permanence through time (sameness or consistency) and that which changes through time (selfhood or constancy).[33]

Through the narrative identity of the characters in the story, as expressed in the dialectic of sameness and selfhood, it becomes possible for us imaginatively to conduct mental experiments with various possibilities for action and life, and thus to shape our own narrative identity. Because the narrative opens up a plurality of roles and plots, we can explore various

---

29. Ricoeur, *Time and Narrative*.
30. Ricoeur, "Narrative Identity," 188.
31. Ibid., 195.
32. Ricoeur, "Life in Quest of a Narrative," 21; Ricoeur, *Time and Narrative*, 1:65–67.
33. Ricoeur, *Oneself as Another*, 149; Ricoeur, "Narrative Identity," 195–96. See also the discussion of Ricoeur's notion of narrative identity in Gorospe, *Narrative and Identity*, 36–45.

ethical possibilities as we try on different models by an act of imagination.[34] However, since narrative imagination is open-ended, narrative identity is also an unstable and seamless identity, continually configured and refigured by the narratives that we appropriate. "Just as it is possible to compose several plots on the subject of the same incidents . . . so it is always possible to weave different, even opposed, plots about our lives."[35] And so we are in continuous search for a narrative that would make intelligible the scattered fragments and discordances of our own existence.[36]

Ethics, however, calls for a decision of the will, and "this decision cannot be provided by narrative."[37] Narrative can only provide possibilities for action. It exercises the imagination more than the will.[38] As Ricoeur emphasizes, "you may try different configurations, different ways of plotting character, but when you come to ethics we have to take a stand." [39]

What then translates narrative identity into ethical identity? According to Ricoeur, it is the "call of the other."[40] "[T]o the question 'Where are you?' asked by another who needs me," the response is "'Here I am!'" "Because someone is counting on me, I am *accountable for* my actions before another."[41] This response of "Here I am!" to the call of the other "marks a halt in the wandering that may well result from the self's confrontation with a multitude of models for action and life, some of which go so far as to paralyze the capacity for firm action."[42] It converts the narrative's imaginative variations, which are already imbued with ethical elements, into a definite ethical stance. The act of commitment transforms the "I can try anything" of imagination into the "Here is where I stand!" of ethics.[43]

---

34. Ricoeur, *Oneself as Another*, 159.
35. Ricoeur, *Time and Narrative*, 3:248.
36. Ricoeur, "Life in Quest of a Narrative," 31–32.
37. Hettema, *Reading for Good*, 117.
38. Ricoeur, *Time and Narrative*, 3:249.
39. Ricoeur et al., "Conversation," in *Whole and Divided Self*, 223.
40. Sweeney, "Ricoeur on Ethics and Narrative," 201.
41. Ricoeur, *Oneself as Another*, 165.
42. Ibid., 167.
43. Ibid., 167–68.

AND THE JOURNEY GOES ON . . .

My journey in understanding the ethics of Old Testament narratives has not ended. One question that I think about is how my earlier understanding of Old Testament narratives as providing ethical models and principles relates to my later understanding of narratives as presenting ethical possibilities.[44] Since every part of one's life journey has value, I cannot just dismiss the earlier stages as totally useless, in the same way that one cannot just discard the earlier history of interpretation of a text as having no contribution at all to its meaning for a contemporary audience.

Back in my seminary in Manila, Philippines, I continually have seen the value of a communal reading of narratives. Because of narrative's imaginative variations and because biblical narratives in particular do not often prescribe the response of the reader, it becomes important to read the text with others. Here the ethical evaluation shifts to the hearers and readers of the story. The sharing of varying responses can lead to the questioning of the community's deepest values, and to a searching of what genuinely to hold as good. It also paves the way by which people can discern when to take the decisive step and say, "Here I stand!"

---

44. This was a question posed to me by Michael Graves.

4

What Holds the Bible Together?

MARIANNE MEYE THOMPSON

IN 1971, GEORGE LADD published an article titled "The Search for Perspective" in a special anniversary edition of the journal *Interpretation*.[1] He had been asked by the editors of the journal to address the question, "Where are we in New Testament theology?," and to do so from his own personal perspective. In answering that question, Ladd indirectly addressed the question of the Bible's unity, locating it in salvation history or *Heilsgeschichte*—a word we all took great delight in uttering as seminarians. Ladd argued that there was a single perspective on the theology of history that ran through the Bible. Ladd also acknowledged that not all agreed: some argued that the Bible contained many theologies of history, so that to speak of the unity of the Bible in terms of a single salvation history made little sense.

In the generation since that article and George Ladd's tenure at Fuller Seminary, the emphasis on the lack of a unified voice in Scripture has become more insistent, and from various angles. On the one hand, Jon Levenson, for example, contends that he cannot find, and does not feel compelled to find, the kind of narrative unity that the New Testament finds in the Old or that some scholars find in the Bible as a whole.[2] And, indeed, neither can

---

1. Ladd, "Search for Perspective."
2. Levenson, *Hebrew Bible*; see especially ch. 2: "Why Jews are Not Interested in Biblical Theology."

many other biblical scholars. Levenson would not be alone in reckoning that abandoning the quest or need for such unity would be a gain rather than a loss.

At the same time, but in a somewhat different vein, we have been reminded that postmodernism can be characterized as an "incredulity towards metanarratives,"[3] where by metanarrative we mean something like a comprehensive account that seeks to explain the way things are. When translated to biblical studies, such incredulity is directed against efforts not only to find unity, but even *coherence*, in the biblical canon, because any such readings could only be ideologically determined constructs imposed upon the diverse materials of the Bible. What is at stake in either of these positions?

IS THE UNITY OF THE BIBLE IMPORTANT?

A recent article in *Theology Today* has this provocative title, "The Urgency of Reading the Bible as One Story." In this article, Michael Goheen argues that "it is only in reading the Bible as one story that we can understand the Bible's authority, that we can understand our identity as God's people as missional, and that we can counter other meta-stories that compete for our allegiance."[4] For Goheen, issues of Christian identity and mission are closely tied together with the question of the coherence of the biblical story. More than Christian identity is at stake, however. The biblical story is the story of the whole world, not just of the religious adherents of Judaism or Christianity. Unless the Bible is read as one story, and as the story not just of people of a certain faith, but as the story of the world, there is little hope of countering those stories that compete with and contradict the Gospel, be these the stories of Islam, capitalism, or whatever other competing narratives would compel human commitment. Is Goheen unduly alarmist?

As I was pondering Goheen's essay, I had two encounters with students. One student told me that while he felt quite confident in exegeting any specific passage, he simply did not know how to read Scripture as a whole, especially when it came to making judgments regarding such matters as war and non-violence, where the canon seemed to offer different witnesses. If Scripture speaks with many voices, how do we hear it shaping

---

3. Cf. the oft-cited line of Jean-François Lyotard: "Simplifying to the extreme, I define postmodern as incredulity toward metanarratives" (*Postmodern Condition*, xxiv).

4. Goheen, "Urgency," 469.

our life of discipleship? Another student told me that he simply did not know how the Christian story held together. He now found the convictions he brought to seminary too simplistic, but he was unable at the moment to articulate the coherence of his faith, or of the Christian story more generally. Consequently, he wondered whether such coherence even existed.

At first these appear to be two different questions: one student asks how the Bible holds together; another asks how the Christian story holds together. But while phrased differently, these questions are inseparably related. Indeed, it has been the conviction of the church from its beginning that the coherence of the biblical story and the coherence of the Christian story are necessary correlates of one another. Those who tell the Christian story differently do so because they read a different Bible—and vice versa. Take as an example Marcion, the second century Christian revisionist, better known to us as a heretic. In reading the two testaments, Marcion concluded that they spoke of two different gods, one "judicial, harsh, mighty in war; the other mild, placid, and simply good and excellent."[5] Identifying the former god as the god who had created the world and the evil within it, he discarded the OT and excised large parts of the Gospels from his canon to attain the "purer" Pauline gospel.

In response to Marcion, the early church Father Tertullian argued extensively for the unity and integrity of the one God. The God who created the world was also the God and Father of our Lord Jesus Christ; the God who made the world is also the God who remakes and saves the world. Tertullian further assumed that the Scriptures contain a coherent account of God's activity from the creation of the world to its final redemption, with its decisive turning point in the coming of Jesus Christ. Because there is movement and change in Scripture's implied narrative—for example, with regard to the law—the coherence of the Bible depends not on the uniformity of its theological assertions, but on the identity and integrity of the one God, creator and redeemer. That one God is the subject of the account of that creative and redeeming activity, which has a beginning, middle and end. We may agree with Tertullian that the unity of God and of the Bible belong inseparably together, that the *unity and integrity of God* hold the Bible together. If God is divided, then so is the Bible, and that is of course exactly what Marcion argued.

Nor is that all. Tertullian goes on mockingly to ask Marcion, "As for that idle god"—meaning the "mild" God who sent Jesus—"who has neither

---

5. Tertullian, *The Five Books against Marcion* 1.6 (ANF 3:275).

any work nor any prophecy, nor accordingly any time, to show for himself, what has he ever done to bring about the fulness of time, or to wait patiently its completion?"[6] The one God of the Bible is no idle god; this God works and waits. To put it somewhat differently, the one God of the Bible, the God of Israel who is the God and Father of our Lord Jesus Christ, is the subject of sentences with active verbs: God creates, sends, calls, loves, promises, redeems, fulfills, works, waits, and completes.[7]

If, then, the unity of the Bible depends on the unity of God, then the activity of this one God, what this one God does, comprises its *one story*. To be sure, the one story of which I speak, and to which the Fathers implicitly referred, is not articulated as such in the Bible. Nowhere is there a summary of it in so many words, nor is the Bible obviously a single story, consisting as it does of a variety of forms of literature, including poetry, proverbs, epistles, apocalypses, prophetic oracles, narrative accounts and more. There were and are different ways of construing the biblical account and its constituent parts. But this was also recognized by the Fathers, who knew that any heretics worth their salt would have appealed to the Bible to ground their beliefs. The charge against the heretics was not merely faulty biblical interpretation, but advocacy of a divisive ecclesiology: the heretics read the Bible wrongly in part because they read it apart from a commitment to the unity of God as grounded in the apostolic witness and the apostolic community.

These active verbs—creates, sends, calls, loves, promises, redeems, fulfills, works, waits, and completes—require objects. God creates a world; in this world he places a people whom he calls, loves, sends, instructs, and redeems; and God works and waits to complete his purposes and fulfill his promises to them and to all creation. So the story of this one God is the one story of *one people*. To be sure, they are not the only objects of God's activity—God makes it rain on all peoples, not just God's covenant people (Matt 5:45)—but the biblical witness is that at the beginning, middle, and

---

6. Tertullian, *The Five Books against Marcion* 5.4 (*ANF* 3:436).

7. In the first volume of his *Old Testament Theology*, John Goldingay links the crucial narrative quality of the Old Testament with the priority of its testimony about what God has done: "The fact that the Old Testament narrative opens with narrative and is dominated by narrative makes narrative form the appropriate starting point for Old Testament theology. As a whole, this narrative tells how God began, God started over, God promised, God delivered, God sealed, God gave, God accommodated, God wrestled, God preserved." These nine verbs predicating divine action become the chapter headings for his 788 page exposition of "Israel's Gospel," followed by "God sent" as a characterization of the New Testament continuation of this narrative (*Israel's Gospel*, 36).

end of that story stands the creation, call, commissioning, and redemption of a people who will honor and worship God and fulfill his purposes for them in the world that God has made.

This account of the Bible's unity depends on and is grounded in the conviction that God's revelation in Jesus Christ is at the center of God's work of creation and redemption, at the center of the biblical story, and at the center of the calling and identity of the people of God. Oddly enough, Marcion read the biblical account in such a way that the manifestation of God in Christ demanded the *rejection* of the unity of God, of the unity of the Bible, and of the unity of the one people of God. But, for many reasons, the church has not and cannot read the Bible that way. Not least among these reasons is that Jesus did not think of the people whom he was calling as a people distinct from God's people, Israel, or that the one he called "Abba" was any other than the God of Israel, or that what we call the Old Testament was a witness to an alien God. Still, in practice many Christians do read the mission of Jesus much as Marcion did—namely, as a casting off of the God of Israel, the people of Israel, and the Scriptures of Israel. No wonder that to reject these required that Marcion also reject the Gospels, except for an edited version of Luke. If we take seriously the historical particularity of Jesus' mission as the Gospels portray it, we will not find the introduction of a new God, a new story, or a new people, but we will find God's purposes for his people coming to fruition: and this is the heart of the one story of the Bible. I would like, then, to look briefly at Jesus' mission in the Gospels, and how that mission embodies and furthers the biblical story of God's purpose to create one people for himself.

THE MISSION OF JESUS

It has been said that first century Judaism was characterized by debates about the question, what does it mean to be the people of God? When will God act to restore his people to wholeness, and what shape will that deliverance take? Who will be counted among God's people, among the elect? According to the gospel accounts, Jesus saw his mission as a mission to gather the people of Israel together. His announcement of God's kingdom was an announcement that the time for God's universal rule and restoration of his people to wholeness had drawn near. In light of that coming kingdom, Jesus' mission was to find the lost sheep of the house of Israel; to seek out the one sheep who had gotten lost and bring it back to the fold with the other ninety-nine; to sweep until that missing coin had been found; to welcome home the younger brother, and then to reconcile the older and younger brother so that they might celebrate together at the table of fellowship; to sit down with the tax collector and the Pharisee in anticipation of the coming of God's great banquet in the kingdom of God.

If first century Judaism was characterized by debates about what it meant to be the people of God, the question was typically answered with respect to God's law, and disputes about how the law was to be understood and lived essentially divided groups such as the Pharisees, Essenes, and other groups from each other. They all had different takes on the question, what does it mean to be the people of God? How does one live out the Torah in faithful obedience? What can one do on the sabbath? Which is the greatest commandment? When Jesus was asked what the greatest command in the law was, he answered, "'You shall love the Lord your God with all your heart, and with all your soul, and with all your mind.' This is the greatest and first commandment. And a second is like it: 'You shall love your neighbor as yourself.' On these two commandments hang all the law and the prophets" (Matt 22:37–39 NRSV). The heart of what God calls his people to know, to be, and to do lies here, in the Scriptures of Israel as summarized in these commands. Jesus' interpretation of the heart of the law as the love of God and neighbor reflects the Old Testament witnesses to this same point: God's people are to be those who do justice, love mercy, and walk humbly with their God; whose worship of God is neither noisy nor hateful, because from them righteousness rolls down like an everflowing stream.

Jesus' mission as a teacher of God's will is not the whole story of the Gospels, nor of the calling together of God's people. Jesus also gave his life in order to seal and complete what his ministry of proclamation, teaching, and healing had begun: to call and shape a people who would be God's holy people. This was not God's first initiative to gather together a people who would belong to him: Moses sealed God's covenant with the people of Israel with blood; Jesus' blood seals the new covenant with God's people that God makes through him. A king could be expected to care for and protect his people; so the messianic shepherd-king does the utmost to spare his people from death, willingly sacrificing his life for theirs. God disciplined his people for their disobedience by sending them into exile, but restored them again to their inheritance; so Jesus' death is a death for the forgiveness of sin, so that his people may be restored again to their inheritance.

This Messiah, this anointed one, fulfills his mission of gathering God's people through giving his life for them. He does not shirk from faithful fulfillment of his mission, from his messianic vocation, even though it leads to death on the cross. It is in Jesus' own faithful obedience to God, and to the messianic and saving vocation given to him by God, that we see the perfect conjunction of human obedience and God's gracious initiative to gather his people. Through Jesus' life, death, and resurrection, God's people is called, cleansed from all sin, and made holy. In Jesus' life and death, we have the model and the command to love, as well as the context of the gathered community, so that we are empowered to embody that love in this world. The mission of Jesus continues and most fully embodies the one story of that one God to call together a holy people, set apart for God's purposes in the world. To put it another way, Jesus died for the same things that he lived for, to gather a people for God, a people who would love God with all their heart, soul, and mind, and their neighbors as themselves. What holds the Bible together is what we see embodied in Jesus' mission and ministry: the Bible is an account of God's purposes to call together one people, a people who love God and love neighbor.

The Bible further serves to shape God's people into just such a people so that their lives might be a light to the nations. We read the Bible not only for its retelling of this story, but so that it can shape us to be the people that God calls us to be. And we read the Bible this way, because of the way in which Jesus taught us to read it through his teaching, through his life and death, and because in his life and death his work was one work: to gather together the children of God. The Church now takes that vision of God's holy and gathered people to all the world, and embodies it in all the world, calling together Jew and Gentile into one body, bringing together factions long divided, through the redemptive and reconciling work on the cross for all people. And these people live by Jesus' teaching: as Paul writes in Galatians, the followers of Jesus are to "bear one another's burdens, and so will fulfill the law of the Messiah" (Gal 6:2). Among faith, hope, and love, the greatest is love. According to James, the "royal law" is fulfilled when one loves one's neighbor (2:8). And together this gathered people anticipates the new creation, the new heaven and earth, the holy city, where the redeemed from every tongue and nation worship God and the Lamb, lay down their weapons of warfare, and by the rivers there discover the tree of life whose leaves are for the healing of the nations. The mission of Jesus recapitulates the entire Bible and shapes how we read it.

Conversations at the Edges of Things

WHAT THEN? A FEW CLOSING REFLECTIONS

A few closing reflections. First, the steady testimony of Christian faith throughout the centuries is that the Bible tells one story. It does not say one thing only but it tells one story, and often the importance of this distinction has been missed. Of course it is possible *not* to read the Bible as a whole, but to read only the individual testaments, chapters, books, or sentences, so that the question of unity never arises and, indeed, is taken to be an imposition upon the Bible. To focus only on the constituent parts, and to insist that this is all there is, is to believe that, in the end, nothing more than two covers and glue holds the Bible together or, in a more extreme and suspicious reading, that no metanarrative could be more than an ideologically biased and hegemonic account imposed upon incorrigibly diverse materials. But to read the Bible as God's one story for all the world is to read it in continuity with Christian convictions about the unity of God and of God's work in creation and salvation.

Second, as we think about the single story that holds the Bible together we also take seriously how the Bible has actually functioned to shape the life of God's people. That is, the Bible is not only about this one God and this one God's purposes for his people; the Bible serves to shape God's people to be a certain kind of people. There is an important consequence here: people learn to read the Bible by observing the church, and those who do not know the biblical story get a basic introduction to it in part by observing the lives of those who claim to live by it. It is, therefore, crucial that the church embody a winsome and holy witness to God's love and mission to the world. What we are teaches people how to read the Scriptures.

Third, modern study of the Bible is driven by concerns about method. Yet while moderns trust for interpretation to the proper method, ancients looked not so much to method but to content. This is in part why modern scholars struggle with at least some of the New Testament's readings of the Old Testament: the apostles seem to violate modern critical canons for reading Scripture. But for early Christians it was not method that controlled interpretation, but rather the account or story of God's purposes in the world and the climax of that story in Jesus Christ that determined their reading of the Bible.[8] To couch our biblical interpretation more explicitly

---

8. In the preface to the second volume of his Old Testament Theology, called *Israel's Faith*, John Goldingay writes that our postmodern context has led to "our recognition of the importance of narrative as a way of doing theology; it was odd that we had not spotted that the Scriptures spend so much time doing theology this way" (*Israel's Faith*, 13).

within the framework of the *one* story of Christian confession, as early Christian interpreters did, would not force us to become a-critical or anti-critical, but it might well help us to articulate confidently the coherence of the biblical story.

Fourth, to read the Bible as a single story has implications for how we construe the authority of the Bible and how it should be read. To "pull a text out of context" would mean not just to take a text out of its historical context, but out of the context of the larger biblical story. There is only one people of God, but the story of that people has taken some twists and turns, not always expected. To acknowledge the authority of the Bible for us entails taking seriously the place a particular account or passage comes in the Biblical story

As we read the Bible as one story, then we also look for trajectories that run through Scripture, from creation, through Israel and Jesus, on to the church and anticipating the final consummation of God's creative purposes for the world. The Bible has snapshots of God's encounters with men and women, and we learn from these snapshots; but no snapshot captures it all, especially not until the return of Christ for the world's redemption. To recognize the Bible's authority is to take account of both the "freeze frame" snapshots found in the biblical witness, while recognizing that these snapshots are, as it were, pulled out from a moving picture that had a beginning and is still running. Where we are in the story, and how we participate in it, is a matter of discernment.

Finally, even if we assert that the Bible tells a single story for all the world and, by implication, that Christians have a sort of overarching narrative that makes sense of the world around us and of the way we live, we need not fear to acknowledge that this narrative always leaves many questions unanswered. It does so for two reasons. First, the God of this story is sovereign and free, and the final answers to the mysteries and questions of life remain in the hands of this God. Second, the story of the Bible remains unfinished. The Bible anticipates and leans into the future; it is replete with yearnings for the coming of the future realm of blessedness, when swords are beaten into plowshares, when the earth yields its crops abundantly, when God wipes away every tear from our eyes, when human beings dwell together in harmony with each other and with their God, when God's work to call together this holy, worshiping, loving people will be brought to

---

One might add, it is odd that we had not recognized that the church had done theology this way for years as well.

fruition. For that new beginning we trust in the God who made the world and who will redeem it through Jesus Christ. Then the story will not only have its ending, but its new beginning too.

5

Models of Commitment in Paul
A Fine Balance?

STEPHEN TRAVIS

As JOHN GOLDINGAY'S COLLEAGUE in Nottingham for twenty-seven years I learned much from his creative insight into Scripture, including his occasional forays into my own field, the New Testament. I also learned from his frequent ability to be surprising, not least on the soccer field. But perhaps I have learnt most from his honest, gritty, eye-opening writings on Christian living and commitment. In thanks for it all, I offer these thoughts.

Why do many of us get stuck sometimes in our Christian experience? Maybe for some it happens when there are no friends who encourage or challenge us. Others find that nothing has prepared them to cope with a personal tragedy that envelops them. Yet others don't move beyond the mode of discipleship they learned when they first believed, and have had no teaching to show ways of thinking about spiritual growth.

Pondering over such questions has led me to reflect on the rich range of models and images of discipleship to be found in the New Testament, and how we are inclined to privilege a few of these while neglecting the rest. Attention to a wider range of language about Christian living could enrich awareness of the resources available to us. So I attempt here an exploration of the letters of Paul. The spirituality that he embodies and commends might be described as mystical, ecstatic, liberated, strenuous, rooted in awareness of God as Father, Son and Spirit, personal and yet community-focused. I shall group the various aspects under five headings.

ROOTED IN THE GENEROUS ACTIVITY OF GOD, ENERGIZED BY HOPE OF NEW CREATION

Paul would not dream of suggesting how we might live without first inviting us to focus on the foundation of our Christian life and the destiny which we are promised. In a rich range of images Paul stresses that our security as God's people rests on what he has done and continues to do for us and in us. This is logically prior to any human response. We may begin with his vivid portrayals of what God has achieved for us through the life, death and resurrection of Christ.

Some of the words Paul uses are seen by many as heavy technical terms beyond the understanding—or the patience—of ordinary people. Yet in the first century world they were not technical terms designed to explain "how the atonement works" but vibrant images expressing how the achievement of Christ's death and resurrection *changes* us. *Justification* (e.g., Rom 3:24) means that the charges against us are taken away, and we are forgiven and brought into a right relationship with God. *Redemption* means we experience a freedom comparable to that of a liberated slave or of the Israelites delivered from Egypt (Col 1:14). *Reconciliation* is the real experience of being restored to a life-giving, open relationship with our Creator (Rom 5:10).[1] All this is an expression of God's "glorious grace, which he has freely given to us in the One he loves" (Eph 1:6). God's undeserved generosity creates a secure space for us in which Christian living may flourish.

A similar reality is expressed in passages where the apostle assures his readers that they are now *"children of God" adopted* into his family, and therefore *heirs* of all that he has to give his children (Gal 4:4–7; Rom 8:14–17). This is not merely about the "blessings" that God gives, like the toys that parents give to children at Christmas, but more profoundly about the status and security of being the child of a loving parent committed to the interests of his children. And when Paul declares that we are "chosen,"

---

1. I am not denying that the doctrine of the atonement is important or that it is in view when Paul uses these terms, but simply suggesting that these images describe the *experienced impact* of Christ's work at least as much as they define the *means* of it.

"called," "predestined," the message again brings assurance that our faith is no mere accident of circumstances and nothing imaginable can ever "separate us from the love of God that is in Christ Jesus our Lord" (Rom 8:28–38). Such affirmations of the initiative of God the Father are complemented by statements about the self-giving of Jesus: he "gave himself for our sins to set us free from the present evil age" (Gal 1:3); he "loved me and gave himself for me" (Gal 2:20). G. B. Caird, in a sermon on this verse, spoke of "a debt of love, which only love can repay."[2]

However, Paul wants us to be confident not only about our past and our present but about our future, when Christ will be revealed in his glory and God's new creation becomes reality. He expresses both themes together in Rom 5:2: through Christ "we have gained access by faith to this grace in which we now stand. And we exult in our hope of sharing the glory of God." And this hope is not a form of escapism, but the motivation for our Christian living: as people who look for Christ's coming we live as "children of the day," characterized by light rather than by darkness (1 Thess 5:4–11).

"IN CHRIST"

This phrase, or its variant "in the Lord" occurs 130 times in the letters of Paul. "If anyone is in Christ—new creation!" he says (2 Cor 5:17). Noting this frequency, James Dunn comments: "Paul's perception of his whole life as a Christian, its source, its identity, and its responsibilities, could be summed up in these phrases."[3] Sometimes the phrase refers to God's redemptive acts in the past—"In Christ God was reconciling the world to himself" (2 Cor 5:19)—or future—"in Christ all will be made alive" (1 Cor 15:22). But our focus here is on Paul's usage in relation to Christian *experience*. When he writes, for example, "There is no condemnation for those who are in Christ" (Rom 8:1), or addresses a letter "To the saints and faithful brothers and sisters in Christ at Colossae" (Col 1:1), he is conveying the idea of living in communion with, or being somehow surrounded by, the risen Christ. We are so closely united to him that he is like the air we breathe, the atmosphere which surrounds us on every side and is the source of our life, the strength for all our activities. The prayer known as St Patrick's Breastplate echoes this and is a helpful way of reflecting on it:

---

2. Cited in Wright, *Acts*, 130.
3. Dunn, *Theology*, 399.

> Christ be with me, Christ within me,
> Christ behind me, Christ before me,
> Christ beside me, Christ to win me,
> Christ to comfort and restore me.
> Christ beneath me, Christ above me,
> Christ in quiet, Christ in danger,
> Christ in hearts of all that love me,
> Christ in mouth of friend and stranger.[4]

Closely related to 'in Christ' are several other images. Paul speaks of "Christ in me" (Gal 2:20), "Christ in you" (Col 1:27) or being "clothed with Christ," "baptized into Christ" (Gal 3:27). This latter phrase is elaborated in Romans 6: "All of us who have been baptized into Christ Jesus were baptized into his death. Therefore we have been buried with him by baptism into death, so that, just as Christ was raised from the dead by the glory of the Father, so we too might walk in newness of life" (Rom 6:3–4). Baptism is not merely a sign of our commitment to Christ, or a helpful picture of what is involved in being a follower of Jesus. It is for Paul the actual moment in which our lives are joined to his, and we enter into the obedience of which his death is the supreme instance and into the new life which flows from his resurrection.

"Crucified with Christ" (Rom 6:6; Gal 2:20) and "made alive with Christ" (Col 2:13) belong to the same circles of ideas. But images such as these make it clearer that our union with Christ is not so much a static, mystical state as "in Christ" on its own might suggest, but an active and ongoing experience of self-giving which reflects the character of Christ's own self-giving for others. Michael Gorman, who has written much on this theme, comments that though many people think of the cross as the *source* of their salvation, not so many think of the cross in relation to the *form* of their life. "Cruciformity," as he calls it, "is letting the cross be the shape, as well as the source, of life in Christ. It is participating in and embodying the cross," reflecting Christ's "self-giving loyal obedience to God (faith) and self-giving love of neighbor." Paradoxically, it is "life-giving, both to those who live it and to those affected by it."[5] Not only did this perspective sustain Paul in all his experiences of suffering (on which see below), it also shaped his character, his priorities, and his relationships. This is what he had in

---

4. From the hymn "I bind unto myself today," translated by C. F. Alexander.
5. Gorman, *Paul*, 146–47.

mind when he expressed to the wayward Christians in Galatia his longing that "Christ be formed in you" (Gal 4:19).

All this might seem to suggest that Christian life is an abject surrender of the self which obliterates our distinctive personalities and takes away free choice—bad news in today's world where we like to think of ourselves as autonomous. And there are Christians who give the impression that this is the goal. In becoming submissive to Christ they somehow become dull and less human than they were before. However, God's intention was never to make us dull but to make us truly human! God's purpose in creating humanity was for us to be "in his own image" (Gen 1:26), and whatever else that enigmatic phrase means it must include the idea that we are created to reflect the character and concerns of God himself. Now in Christ we are being renewed according to the image of our creator (Col 3:10). And that can hardly be dull, but rather is endlessly demanding and exciting.

So alongside his message that we depend entirely on what God has already done for us and that our response is to be crucified with Christ, Paul makes clear that this involves not the suppression of self but the active engagement of the whole person in response to God's call. Although our life is handed over to God and we "are not our own," we are actively to "glorify God in our body" (1 Cor 6:19–20). We are not free agents in the sense that we can do what we like without restraint. Romans 6 begins by firmly squashing that idea, but the rest of the chapter shows how we are *set free* in a more profound sense to be the people that God can make us. Freed from slavery to sin, we are paradoxically "enslaved to God," commissioned for his service (Rom 6:15–23) and for a life that is (quite literally) infinitely worthwhile (1 Cor 15:58).

DEMANDING ETHICS

Any who would presume upon the grace of God rather than constantly renewing this self-offering in service to God and neighbor should look at Paul's pictures of the *effort* of Christian living. It is like *running a race*, which demands sacrifice and rigorous training, and a constant pressing on until the prize is won (1 Cor 9:24–27; Phil 3:13–14) It involves an *inner battle* to choose the good rather than the evil (Gal 5:13–26; Rom 6:11–23; 7:14–25), though the resources of God's Spirit are always there to be drawn on afresh (Gal 5:22–25). In a world where Christians faced hostility and never knew when they might be roughed up in the street, Paul valued *perseverance* highly (2 Thess 1:4; Col 1:11). In the same context, it was important to *"watch out"* for false teaching (Col 2:8, 16–23) or *"take care"* to avoid any attitude that would undermine their real purpose (1 Cor 8:9; 10:12; Gal 5:15).

One characteristic strategy of exhortation is what scholars like to call Paul's *indicative-imperative pattern*, as in Gal 5:25: "If we live by the Spirit, let us also be guided by the Spirit." Usually this form of expression recalls something that Paul and his readers agree to be the truth and then appeals for a response corresponding to that truth. For example, "Just as the Lord has forgiven you, so you also must forgive" (Col 3:13; see further 3:1–11).

There is no room for complacency or imagining one has reached one's potential. I know that you are showing exemplary signs of Christian character, Paul says to his friends in Thessalonica, "but do so more and more" (1 Thess 4:1, 10). In an ethic based on love rather than on rules, that is what one would expect. One cannot fix a limit for love. But once again Paul stresses that it is through God's enabling that Christians will be "blameless and holy" at Christ's future coming (1 Thess 3:12–13; 5:23). The balance is there in Phil 2:12–13: "work out your salvation . . . for it is God who works in you."

Paul's entire perspective on the wide-ranging demands of Christian living is summed up in Rom 12:1–2: "By the mercies of God . . . present your bodies as a living sacrifice, holy and acceptable to God . . ." It begins with an implied 'indicative-imperative,' since "by the mercies of God" means "because of all that God has done for us as described in chapters 1–11." Then it continues with an appeal to his readers to offer their whole selves to God. And—crucially—this involves the *mind*. "Do not let yourselves be squeezed into the mould determined by this present age, but be transformed by the renewing of your minds, so that you may discern what is the will of God—what is good, acceptable and complete" (v. 2, paraphrased).

The implications of this emphasis on the mind are important. Paul is popularly viewed as a bossy character, always laying down the law, telling people how to behave—or more often how not to behave. On the contrary, the one who writes, "Be transformed by the renewing of your minds" frequently urges his readers to use those minds to work out for themselves and their communities what is right. Notice the verbs in the following examples:

- "Whatever is true, honorable, just, pure, lovely, commendable, excellent, praiseworthy, *think about* such things" (Phil 4: 8; see also 1 Cor 14:20).

- "I speak as to sensible people; *judge* for yourselves what I say" (1 Cor 10:15).

- "Those who are spiritual *discern* all things, and they are themselves subject to no one else's scrutiny" (1 Cor 2:15).

- "*Test* everything; hold fast to what is good" (1 Thess 5:21).

- "I want you to be *wise* in what is good" (Rom 16:19).

And the three chapters which follow Rom 12:2 include examples of what this perspective implies for various areas of life. Paul gives general guidance of what a Christ-shaped life will look like in personal life and relationships (12:9–10) and in the wider society (12:14–21; 13:8–14). In considering the relationship of Christians to the Roman state there are some finely balanced instructions: it is right to be subject to the ruling authorities, but at the same time the authorities are supposed to be "God's servant for your good" (13:1, 4). But Paul does not draw a list of rules from this, except to urge that taxes be paid, not least because any Christian seen to be supporting subversive moves to avoid taxation—a topical issue under Nero—could be landing the whole Roman church in trouble (13:6–7).

In chapter fourteen he addresses differences of opinion which are causing discord in the church: is it acceptable to eat meat, or should one eat only vegetables? Should we observe certain days as holy or are all days the same? And he responds by urging that they respect differences of opinion. "Who are you to pass judgment on servants of another? . . . Let all be fully convinced in their own minds . . . Do not let what you eat cause the ruin of one for whom Christ died" (14:4, 5, 15). Far from "laying down the law," Paul is offering a vision of a community which reflects the generous love of God himself in its thoughtful, generous interaction.

Paul's letters, then, are neither a rule-book nor a cook-book with a detailed recipe for every modern situation. But they can help us become what we are meant to be – people of imaginative love, insight and judgment, able to think responsibly abut God's will in the present.

THE SHADOW OF SUFFERING

Sooner or later, a Christian's commitment is challenged by the experience of suffering, one's own or that of a relative or close friend, or the sheer weight of suffering around the world. We lose our bearings, we wonder where God is in it all. For Paul, suffering came mostly in the form of danger, deprivation and persecution experienced in the course of his missionary work, though he knew too the deep anxiety of seeing a friend close to death (Phil 2:25-27). And it seems that during his two year stay in Ephesus, he experienced severe suffering—maybe persecution and imprisonment (see 1 Cor 15:32)—so that he really felt death was imminent.

This experience deepened his insight as he discovered within his suffering the transformative power of God. "While we live, we are always being given up to death for Jesus' sake, so that the life of Jesus may be visible in our mortal flesh. So death is at work in us, but life in you" (2 Cor 4:11). God did not take away his "thorn in the flesh" (whatever that was), "but he said to me, 'My grace is sufficient for you, for power is made perfect in weakness.' So I will exult all the more gladly in my weaknesses, that the power of Christ may dwell in me . . . When I am weak, then I am strong" (2 Cor 12:9-10).

I once met a Palestinian pastor who spoke vividly of the sufferings of the Palestinian people in the Holy Land, the burdens he carried as their pastor, and the small but significant ways in which God encouraged them from time to time. I studied his face. I had never seen a face in which there was so much pain and so much joy at the same time. For me it was the face of Christ.

SPIRIT AND COMMUNITY

Here of course is the vital element which I have not previously made explicit. Just as Paul loves to say that Christians are "in Christ," he delights to remind us that God's Spirit is in us. In Romans 8, the Spirit is the defining mark of the believer: "Anyone who does not have the Spirit of Christ does not belong to him" (Rom 8:9). The Spirit bubbling up, or creating a calm aura, brings reassurance that God has us in his care (Gal 4:6; Rom 8:15-16). He is the moral energy that shapes our lives and produces a harvest of Christian character—love, joy, peace . . . (Gal 5:22-23), and especially the key qualities of faith, love and hope (1 Thess 1:3; 5:8; 1 Cor 13:13). But note again that such qualities do not simply drop out of the sky without intentional effort on our part. First Thess 1:3 speaks of the "*work* of faith, *labor* of love, and *steadfastness* of hope." The Spirit will be the wind, but we must set the sails and navigate the ocean.

The Spirit is the creator and sustainer of community. Yes, other people can be difficult, and the temptation is either to get annoyed with them in return, or to give up on the project of community by withdrawing into a private spirituality. An open-eyed reading of Paul's letters to the early churches will show that this was their experience too. But for him it is simply inconceivable that Christian life should function without community. To be "in Christ" means necessarily to be linked closely to others who are in Christ. As Paul put it, "We, who are many, are one body in Christ, and individually we are members one of another" (Rom 12:5).

And in sharing out a variety of "gifts of grace" (*charismata*, Rom 12:6–8), or "spiritual gifts" (*pneumatika*, 1 Cor 12:1), or "ways of serving" (*diakoniai*, 1 Cor 12:5) for the building up of the community (Eph 4:7–16), the Spirit equips the church for its service to each other and to the world. God, who as Father, Son and Spirit *is* divine community, has devised a system whereby his people can function only as community! Thus it reflects his own nature.

Another of Paul's paradoxes appears in 1 Corinthians 12. The gifts we have are God's choice for us, not ours (v. 11), yet we are urged to "strive for the greater gifts" (v. 31). As with Paul's other paradoxes, we have to hold together both truths. We must recognize these gifts are entrusted to us for use in God's service, and not complain if we seem to have a gift other than one we might have preferred. But at the same time we are encouraged to long to serve God as fully as we are able and therefore to be actively open to the possibility that God may trust us with other gifts also. It is part of progressing in our Christian journey.

In this range of perspectives there is enough to keep me grappling with the questions raised by the different moods and circumstances of life. And then there is the rest of Scripture, as well, and nineteen centuries of thoughtful reflection upon it.[6] For the time being, we may conclude that our discipleship is founded on God's grace, that it rests on, and is shaped by, Christ's self-giving for the world. It engages the mind to work out how the character and purpose of God is to be embodied in the details of our lives. It is demanding, yet energized by the Holy Spirit and sustained in community. It is inspired by hope of the resurrection. God takes our stuttering commitment and uses us as signposts of the new creation. Not that we have already reached the goal, but we press on to make it our own, because Christ Jesus has made us his own (Phil 3:12).

---

6. See, e.g., Longenecker, *Patterns*.

6

In Praise of Mystery

GRAHAM BUXTON

IN HER BOOK *The Ethical Imagination,* Margaret Somerville, the well-known Australian ethicist now working in Canada, quotes the philosopher Charles Taylor, who suggests that we have lost complexity, spirit, and mystery, and replaced them with mind, will, and technology.[1] Over the past year or two, I have found myself reflecting on the notion of mystery as it applies to the practice of pastoral ministry, causing me to wonder if those who are engaged in this privileged calling have fallen into the trap of replacing mystery with methodology. I think John Goldingay would have some sympathies with such concerns. Citing the insights of the orthodox priest and theologian Andrew Louth, he writes: "Scripture is inherently characterized by depth, complexity, and difficulty—not merely the contingent difficulty of the inevitable occasional obscurity of a text from another culture but the ontological difficulty that reflects mystery."[2] John wants to see the sense of the holy preserved in the Scriptures, and it is this sense of the holy that can too easily be lost in the problem-centered pragmatism that characterizes much pastoral ministry today.

My reflections on pastoral ministry have led me over the years to eschew pragmatism in favor of a theology of participation: we are all called

---

1. Somerville, *Imagination,* 207.
2. Goldingay, *Models for Interpretation,* 155.

to enter into the continuing ministry of Christ in the world, participating in what he is doing in people's lives. One of my central convictions is that participation in the ministry of Christ is a liberating privilege, releasing us from the pressures and burdens of 'doing things for God' in our own strength. In our practice of pastoral ministry, we do well to take stock of our lives and to ask, with T. S. Eliot, "Where is the Life we have lost in living?" Called to proclaim the richness and joy of life in Christ, many of us discover a vast gap between the words we speak and the lives we live. A quiet desperation takes over as we struggle to fulfill our vocation as ministers of the gospel. "Where is the Life we have lost in living?" Perhaps I could paraphrase this question and ask: 'Where is the joy of ministry that we have lost in our action-packed agendas that too frequently characterize our pastoral practice?' Endless invention, endless experiment . . . knowledge of words, and ignorance of the Word. Elsewhere, in *Dancing in the Dark*, I have proposed a theology of participation as an antidote to the pragmatic weariness that seems to pervade so much of pastoral life.

But in recent years I have come to see that this idea of participation is not confined to a discerning awareness of God's presence and actions in the world, in which we are invited to play a part today. It also has a lot to do with what is inherently unknowable. There is a distinction between mystery and ignorance, first identified by William Hocking in his book *The Meaning of God in Human Experience*, published almost one hundred years ago. We often confuse the two terms. Ignorance reflects a condition in which you or I are unaware of something that is inherently knowable, and is essentially negative in character—it is an *absence*. Mystery, however, is positive in expressing something that, although unknowable in an empirical—or revelatory—sense, is fundamentally ineffable. It expresses a *presence* that lies beyond human experience.

The definition of mystery, therefore, that I would like to use here is that which is "sensed to be unknowable, and incomprehensible, and inexplicable, or even inaccessible *in its fullness* to the human mind."[3] It is, in the words of Jaroslav Pelikan, "the quality of the known." Mystery does not *inhibit* faith—it *inhabits* faith, though some would not have it that way. In one of his letters Sir Isaac Newton writes: "'Tis the temper of the hot and superstitious part of mankind in religion ever to be fond of mysteries & for that reason to like best what they understand least." Newton subscribed to the rational worship of One God, and maintained that the doctrine of the

---

3. Schilling, *New Consciousness*, 30.

Trinity had been imposed upon the Church by Athanasius, amongst others: scientific rationalism had no place for such "monstrous legends." Away with such superstitions, declared Newton: our understanding of God must be made "as easy and agreeable as possible" in order to convince people of the Truth, and so combat the rise of atheism. So mystery and other such foolishness must be banished.

It may well be that we are tempted to embrace a simplistic faith in our desire to resist the challenge of atheism, and those of a more fundamentalist hue have gone down that path. We might note too that the contemporary age has a Newtonian feel about it, in spite of the fascination with spirituality in all its forms. The French Jesuit philosopher, Pierre Teilhard de Chardin, famously observed that we are not human beings having a spiritual experience; we are spiritual beings having a human experience. But too often human hubris has eclipsed our spiritual core.

D. H. Lawrence once asserted that "the supreme little ego in man hates an unconquered universe. We shall never rest until we have heaped tin cans on the North Pole and on the South Pole and put up barb-wire fences on the moon. Barb-wire fences are our sign of conquest. We have wreathed the world with them. The back of creation is broken. We have killed the mysteries and devoured the secrets. It all lies now within our skin, within the ego of humanity."[4] Such hubris is an offence to the mystery of faith. There is, as Aldous Huxley once wrote in his essay *The Doors of Perception*, an incompatibility between man's egotism and the divine purity.

Mystery lies at the heart of the Christian faith, not in the sense that Christianity is a 'mystery religion,' with all of the cultic implications associated with such a term. The mystery of the gospel is precisely *the mystery of Christ*, as Paul proclaims in a number of places in his letter to the Colossians (1:27; 2:2; and 4:3), and we are now privy to this 'open secret.' Human beings have been blessed with the faculties of reason and discernment, and especially the gift of the Spirit, in order to grasp—or perhaps I should say, be grasped by—the gospel of salvation for all people. But we recognize too that there are aspects of the Christian faith that elude human comprehension, and we do well to allow that insight to inform our ministry. How, for example, do we interpret the relationship between divine sovereignty and human freedom? How do transcendence and immanence cohere in the triune God of Christian faith? How do judgment and divine grace play out at the *eschaton*, when all things have been summed up in Christ? Confronted

---

4. Lawrence, *Reflections*, 281.

by what Harold Schilling calls "the mystery of nature's ambiguities"[5]—the coexistence of good and evil, of beauty and brutality, whether in the natural world or in human behavior—we understandably question the goodness of God. These are matters that rightly concern Christian pastors seeking to serve the people in their communities. They are the stuff of pastoral ministry. Dogmatic knee-jerk responses to pastoral dilemmas do the gospel no service at all.

The problem with knee-jerk reactions is that they often leave no room for genuine dialogue, since they tend to be birthed out of dogmatism. Tom Smail once wittily observed: "I'd rather be a catalyst than a dogmatist!" The starting point in any dialogue has to do with a willingness to listen to others, and you can't be a catalyst unless you are willing to listen. And close behind listening is a willingness to learn from others. We're often not very good at those things. Perhaps we need to take a leaf out of the philosopher's book, and I'm thinking about Socrates here, although of course he didn't leave any writings behind. He left that to his students.

"I am the wisest man alive," he once said, "for there is one thing I know . . . I know nothing." That's an appeal to humility, isn't it? . . . a willingness to sit at the feet of others and recognize that they may have something to teach us. In the science-religion debate, in which I am currently involved at a number of levels, we do well to note the words of Pope John Paul II: "Science can purify religion from error and superstition; religion can purify science from idolatry and false absolutes. Each can draw the other into a wider world, a world in which both can flourish."

A second quote from Socrates is apposite: "The unexamined life is a life not worth living." Socrates said this at his trial for heresy, charged with encouraging his students to challenge the accepted beliefs of the time and to think for themselves. What I'm suggesting here is that we need to be willing to consider why we think the way we do: we need to examine ourselves, our presuppositions and values. And that's not easy. I think I wrestle theologically far more than I used to. I once liked to have things nice and cut-and-dried. No grey areas, just black and white. But life isn't like that, reality is complex and ambiguous.

I have been encouraged by the response from a number of pastors to my proposition that those who are involved in Christian ministry are tired of simplistic certainties, often associated with formulae for church growth, and that what is needed is permission to live with uncertainty, with

---

5. Schilling, *New Consciousness*, 29.

mystery, ambiguity and paradox. John Haught reminds us that we "run the risk of diminishing the mystery of reality and of ourselves if we plunge precipitously into shallow certitudes."[6] In truth, embracing uncertainty causes us to think more profoundly, whereas certainty may well lead us to discard thinking altogether. And that is a very dangerous thing indeed. Vincent Donovan writes in his book *Christianity Rediscovered*: "The day we are completely satisfied with what we have been doing; the day we have found the perfect, unchangeable system of work, the perfect answer, never in need of being corrected again, on that day we will know we are wrong, that we have made the greatest mistake of all."[7]

I need to insert a qualification here: I am not in principle against certainty. I am reminded of some words of the twentieth-century British philosopher of history Herbert Butterfield, who once famously—if rather perilously—said "hold fast to Christ and for the rest be totally uncommitted." Butterfield, of course, was highlighting the importance of placing our faith in a person rather than a system, so inviting us to recognize the contribution of different confessions in our search for the nature of Christian truth—to be discovered, not in a series of faith-statements, but in a living person, Jesus Christ.

So there is a center to hold fast to, a conviction to affirm, even as we acknowledge a boundary that is necessarily ill-defined. Just as Luther proclaimed his unswerving loyalty to the testimony of God's Word and would not—indeed, could not—recant at the Diet of Worms, so we are summoned to affirm the central reality of the living Word, Jesus Christ, a reality, however, that is at its core a mystery. As I pointed out earlier, the apostle Paul writes about the revelation of the Word who is Christ in the language of mystery: "God has chosen to make known among the Gentiles the glorious riches of this mystery, which is Christ in you, the hope of glory" (Col 1:27). He alludes to this mystery in Rom 11:33 following his proclamation of the universal scope of God's redemptive grace in Christ: "Oh, the depth of the riches of the wisdom and knowledge of God! How unsearchable his judgments, and his paths beyond tracing out!" So we affirm certainty as we proclaim Christ, but we also affirm mystery as we confess with Paul that we all "see through a glass, darkly" (1 Cor 13:12).

What I am troubled about, though, is that methodology converts the mystery of life into the problems of life, problems that can be addressed

---

6. Haught, *Mystery*, 57.
7. Donovan, *Christianity Rediscovered*, 146.

and—it is claimed—ultimately solved by methodology. Now this is grist to the mill of all who are concerned to see the church grow and reverse its sad decline in the Western world. And so we embrace techniques that promise to put people in the pews and cash in the coffers. Well, that is the hope, and a forlorn hope it has proven to be in many cases. The fact is, of course, that the church cannot grow as the result of methodology in and of itself.

Church leaders are often under great pressure within their denominations to develop strategies that promise growth. In the second half of the twentieth century, the Church Growth Movement, with which Donald McGavran and Peter Wagner are particularly associated, unwittingly contributed to this pressure, though, paradoxically, it also offered hope to those who were struggling to get their local church out of ruts and into renewal. The literature, tapes, seminars, and conferences spawned by this movement seemed to promise new life: take the pulse, read the signs, develop five-year plans, distribute questionnaires, design new organizational patterns, set targets: the techniques and methodologies proposed were endless.

Many of those churches that were enamored of this formulaic approach discovered that for all their efforts nothing really changed. Pragmatism offered so much, yet delivered so little. The bookshelves of pastors were full of 'how to' texts, designed to get the local church out of maintenance mode into growth and mission; 'spiritually-loaded' numbers, especially seven and twelve, appeared in the titles (*Seven Steps to . . .* or *Twelve Keys to . . .*) as if to guarantee divine authenticity or inspiration. Authors encouraged pastors to be success-oriented and growth-conscious; and so a pragmatic 'what-works' business-oriented mentality began its subtle invasion of the pastoral ministry of the church.

Of course, methods designed to enhance the health and growth of the church are not wrong or inappropriate per se in the practice of Christian ministry: they have their place in mobilizing the community of faith in its witness in and to the world. What concerns me most is the very real danger of losing sight of the mystery of faith when confronted by the attractions of pragmatic methodologies. The truth is that we live in a world which is far removed from the modernist version of reality, with its rational, clinical, and superficial presentation of life. James Olthuis writes that "the world is too complex, too contradictory, too enigmatic, pock-marked with guilt, flawed with folly and pride, scarred by ignorance and arrogance."[8] Ministry today takes place in a world that is rapidly changing and extraordinarily

---

8. Olthuis, "Dancing," 140ff.

multifaceted. Contributing to these changes, the postmodern agenda highlights ambiguity, mystery, and paradox in its understanding of reality, so presenting us with emphases that need to be acknowledged if we are to participate compassionately in the turmoil of the world around us.

As we all know, the Christian gospel is replete with paradox—indeed we might want to argue that paradox lies at the very heart of the gospel: the first will be last and the last will be first; all who will exalt themselves will be humbled and those who humble themselves will be exalted. More weightily, we wrestle with how love and suffering might cohere in God. Doctrinally, we have already mentioned the incomprehensible nature of the Trinity, with its impenetrable one-and-three structure. Earlier in this chapter I identified a number of what we might call 'the mysteries of faith': the relationship between divine sovereignty and human freedom; the coherence of transcendence and immanence within the Trinity; the logic of judgment and divine grace at the *eschaton*. Consider, too, the Christian doctrine of the incarnation, the wonder of which has been expressed eloquently in Charles Wesley's well-known words, "our God contracted to a span, incomprehensibly made Man," so poignantly conveyed in John Betjeman's well-known poem, "Christmas" with its repeated refrain, "And is it true?" and its evocative closing lines: "That God was man in Palestine/And lives today in Bread and Wine."[9]

The Word made flesh. 'Both/and' rather than 'either/or.' Søren Kierkegaard, the nineteenth-century Danish philosopher, regarded Christianity as essentially paradoxical, not because it embraces the impossible but precisely because it embraces the incomprehensible. Such paradoxes are, for him, offensive to reason and reflect the *virtue of the absurd*. Again, note the emphasis: not the impossible or the contradictory, but the illogical and absurd, the incomprehensible. This is the mystery of faith. In *A Grief Observed*, C. S. Lewis writes: "Heaven will solve our problems, but not, I think, by showing us subtle reconciliations between all our apparently contradictory notions. The notions will all be knocked from under our feet. We shall see that there never was a problem."[10]

In *Aurora Leigh*, Elizabeth Barrett Browning's nineteenth-century verse-novel of contemporary early Victorian life in England, the author speaks of a world "crammed with God" but discernible only to one who has eyes to see it—who, like Moses before the burning bush, is humble enough

---

9. Harrison, *Christmas Poems*, 183.

10. Lewis, *Grief,* 83.

to "take off his shoes" in awe. As for those who lack insight, "The rest sit round it, and pluck blackberries . . ."[11]

Here we discern a way of seeing that offers a way forward as we seek to incorporate the element of mystery into all that we do as faith practitioners. What I am proposing here is a mode of seeing that has to do with the imagination, and implies paying attention to 'what is' in a way that takes us beyond observation and into *participation*. Using the imagination is a discipline, and does not come easily to some people, especially those who are locked into an 'either-or' paradigm. But imagination—which is one of God's great gifts to humanity—enables us to experience realities which cannot be accessed through either reason or logic.

What is needed is a whole-hearted engagement in the manner suggested by the French philosopher Gabriel Marcel, who defines mystery as "something in which I find myself caught up, and whose essence is not before me in its entirety." Marcel's distinction between problem and mystery is also very helpful here: "A problem is something which I meet, which I find complete before me, but which I can therefore lay siege to and reduce. But a mystery is something in which I am myself involved, and it can therefore only be thought of as *a sphere where the distinction between what is in me and what is before me loses its meaning and its initial validity.*"[12]

The theologian John Haught suggests that the prophets' visionary pictures of God's future require us to "use our own imaginations to portray, however inadequately, the freedom, extravagance, and surprisingness of God's eternal vision for the world and humanity."[13] Of course, as Haught points out, we need to ensure that our visions are not simply projections of childish wishfulness, rather than images more truly revelatory of mystery. This means that we need to be truthful and honest about our inner motivations. Over the years I have found that my life and ministry have been transformed as I have experienced the paradigm shift—no, it has been more of a *paradigm drift* than a paradigm shift!—from imitation to participation.

We might also note that in pastoral work, the presence of 'limit-experiences' which occur at the edge of ordinary life—moments of deep sadness, ecstatic joy or bewilderment over what life is all about—may open both pastor and parishioner to new, unexpected glimpses of the mystery of life, offering new understandings of what it means to be free, as well as fresh

---

11. Browning, *Aurora Leigh*, "Seventh Book."
12. Marcel, *Being*, 127.
13. Haught, *Mystery*, 9.

courage to step into God's future with confidence and hope. In one of his sermons, Paul Tillich has this to say: "The Kingdom of God is peace and joy. This is the message of Christianity. But eternal joy is not to be reached by living on the surface. It is rather attained by breaking through the surface, by penetrating the deep things of ourselves, of our world, and of God."[14] No better summing up of the role of imagination could be offered.

---

14. Tillich, *Shaking,* chap.7.

7

Evangelical Mary

Christopher Cocksworth

INTRODUCTION[1]

I FIRST MET JOHN Goldingay when he interviewed me as a prospective student of St. John's College, Nottingham. I remember the interview being interrupted by his colleague Tom Smail bursting into the room to congratulate John on a recent academic achievement. That early encounter, and the relationships into which it initiated me, has led me to write about Mary the mother of Christ, and to try to do so from an Evangelical perspective. Let me explain.

I arrived at St. John's College—in part an Evangelical Anglican seminary, in practice much more than that—in 1984. A couple of years beforehand, Tom had preached a series of Bible studies on Mary. As was always the case with Tom, they were closely argued and very rich biblical expositions, but they began with a story that was much less predictable, especially from someone who, at the time of the experience he recounted, was a Scottish Presbyterian recently returned from a pastorate in Northern Ireland.

---

1. The core of this chapter was delivered to the 2011 Ecumenical Marian Pilgrimage to Walsingham, a published record of which is forthcoming.

Conversations at the Edges of Things

Tom spoke of a personal encounter with Mary. By this time he was Director of the Fountain Trust, a body that served and promoted Charismatic renewal in the churches of Britain. He was living on the outskirts of south London, in a town called East Molesey. The previous night, Tom had been reading Cardinal Suenens' chapter on Mary in his influential book *A New Pentecost?* In the morning, in those brief moments between sleeping and waking, he became aware of a powerful presence close to him and a conversation ensued. "Who's that?" said Tom in the twilight of consciousness. "It's the Virgin Mary," came the reply. "What are *you* doing here?" responded the Reformed theologian. "I'm helping you to praise my son," answered the mother of the Lord. "Oh, that's all right, you can stay," said Tom, who then awoke. Tom never claimed this as an apparition. In fact, he did not *see* anything. It was more of an auditory experience, something heard but not seen. He also recognized that his reading the night before may well have been some sort of psychological trigger, but he nonetheless regarded it as an authentic encounter with Mary which has had an abiding effect on his attitude to her. When I arrived at St John's, Tom's story was still being talked about, and John Goldingay was known to be fond of referring to Mary as Our Lady of East Molesey!

The College at which John and Tom taught in the 1980s, and over which John later presided as Principal, was known to stretch some boundaries of the Evangelical tradition, especially when nudged by the renewing work of the Spirit across all kinds of theological traditions. However, despite the lasting impression left on me by Tom's story, my experience of Evangelicalism in the thirty years since then has been marked more by an absence of attention to Mary than by a serious attempt to find her proper place in Evangelical life.[2] We are like the *Frauenkirche* in Dresden—a magnificent Lutheran church that owes its name to 'Our Lady' but whose memory has no real trace either in the edifice itself or, I suspect, in the faith that is nurtured within it. Why is that so when the Bible that we love speaks much of Mary? The Jesus that we follow would not have called us had it not been for Mary. The gospel that has grasped us first grasped her. The Church to which we belong named her among the faithful few on the day of Pentecost. Luther loved her.

---

2. There have been, however, at least two significant Evangelical publications in the U.S.: Tim Perry's scholarly and insightful *Mary for Evangelicals*; and Scot McKnight's more popular but highly engaging *The Real Mary: Why Evangelical Christians Can Embrace the Mother of Jesus*. I have written at more length about Mary in my *Holding Together: Gospel, Church and Spirit*.

Part of the answer lies in a thoroughly good Evangelical emphasis on the vicarious humanity of Christ in which our human nature is reshaped by *his* learning of obedience through suffering (Heb 5:8–10), *his* saying "yes" to God and "yes" to the cross (Heb 10:5–10), *his* ascension to heaven as the pioneer and perfecter of our faith (Heb 2:10; 12:2). That is why many Marian musings fail the test of gospel and Bible. Among them is the claim of the Anglican-Roman Catholic International Commission that Mary is "the fullest human example of the life of grace."[3] Surely that accolade belongs to her son. Of course, the life of Jesus is *God* living out human life, but that does not make him any less than human—the Word is made true flesh. This is exactly the point that Cyril of Alexandria wanted to secure through the *Theotokos* ascription to Mary in the Christological debates of the fourth century, and it is the principle promoted by Augustine, Aquinas and Newman among many others, that whatever we say truly of Mary will by definition (if we really have said it truly) say even more of Christ. It was this very principle that Mary's word to Tom Smail in East Molesey respected, and which is the basis of Orthodox iconography of Mary—she always points to Christ so that we may praise him and, through him, praise his Father.

My own Marian moment took the form not of an apparition or even an auditory experience but of a realization that, notwithstanding the Evangelical commitment to the centrality of Christ and to the role of his vicarious humanity doing for us that which we cannot do without him, there is one thing that Mary can do for us that even Jesus cannot do. That is to show us—and be the first to show us—what it means *to see Jesus*, to love him, to adore him, to hear him, to place one's faith in the grace of God that comes to us in Jesus, and to give one's life over to this transforming grace, and then to follow Jesus as a member of his messianic family. What is more, Mary can show us what it means to be seen by Jesus—to be seen with such eyes of love that you know you will never be the same again having been seen in that way, and that you will be ready to lay your life down for the one who, looking at you in this way, loves you.

That is the theme I would like to explore in this chapter: what we can learn from Mary about seeing Jesus and being seen by him. There is much more that can be said about Mary than this particular lens allows. Indeed, there is much more to say and see through this lens than I will be able to do in these short pages. In what follows, though, I hope to show that seeing Jesus through Mary's eyes, and being seen by Jesus with the love that he

---

3. ARCIC, *Mary*, 65.

has for Mary, yields results that are entirely consistent with the thoroughly Evangelical advice of Thomas Aquinas that "[w]e must not attribute so much to the Mother as to detract from the honour due to her son, who is 'the Savior of all men,' as the Apostle says."[4]

MARY AND THE CONCEPTION, BIRTH, AND PRESENTATION OF JESUS

Jesus was beyond Mary's sight at the annunciation and subsequent conception. Nevertheless, Mary does a lot of seeing in Luke's account, much of it the sort of mysterious seeing by faith that happens as believers hear God's word. We do not know exactly what Mary saw when Gabriel came to her, but that encounter has been fertile soil for the imagination of artist and poet alike. The gaze between Gabriel and Mary is freeze-framed by the Renaissance artist Franciabigio in his carefully staged scene between angel and virgin. They look intently at each other in a moment that seems to have lasted for eternity with, as John V. Taylor saw, "the dove symbol of the Holy Spirit spinning, as it were, a thread of attention between them."[5] "Greetings, favoured one! The Lord is with you," says Gabriel. "My soul magnifies the Lord, and my spirit rejoices in God my Savior, *for he has looked with favour on the lowliness of his servant*" (Luke 1:46–48), sings Mary later. Being looked on with favour by God and believing God's word of favour (Luke 2:45): this is the heart of Evangelical theology and the dynamic of Evangelical spirituality. This is why Mary is *Evangelical Mary*—because the grace of God in all its gracious goodness and mercy and unbounded love has overwhelmed her and transformed her. There is a rather extraordinary statue of Mary in the Chapter House of Ely Cathedral by David Wynne. From a distance it looks loud and gaudy, better suited to a fairground than a Cathedral. But get up close, stand beneath it, and see Mary's joy, watch her stretch out her whole body, straining forward, arms reaching to the heavens and you get a feel of what it is like to be looked on with favor by the Most High and to be found by God the Savior. Here you can see that Elizabeth was right to say that Mary was blessed by the Lord and that Mary was right to prophesy that we would call her blessed. She is indeed.

According to Matthew and Luke, all sorts of people saw the child Jesus and were seen by him at his birth and in his early years: shepherds, magi,

4. Thomas Aquinas, quoted in O'Connor, *Dogma*, 193.
5. Taylor, *Go-Between God*, 10.

inn keepers, towns-folk of Bethlehem and, of course, Joseph. But there was not anything quite like the gaze between Mary and her son. There never is anything that really rivals that sort of look between mother and child. The mother in whose body this new body has been formed; the mother who has risked her life to give life to this new life; the mother who now continues to sustain this life with the nourishment of milk and love. The child who has grown in this womb; the child who has a deep physical and psychological instinct of dependence upon this woman; the child whose experience of life and love is focused on this woman. There is a sense in which every human father, despite the intensity of emotions he experiences at the birth of a child and through those first formative months and years, knows that, in the words of a children's television series of some time ago, he is "not the mummy." At the very least, biology determines that there is a unique vocation to motherhood and for Mary, with her memory of the angel's words, her experience of her extraordinary conception, her pondering all these things in her heart, especially so.

The look of love between mother and child is the overriding theme of traditional iconography of the virgin and child. They look at each other with such love. We are invited, as it were, to step into the stare, to look at Jesus with eyes of love and adoration, and in Christina Rossetti's perfect words, "to worship the beloved with a kiss."[6] At the same time, we are invited to see that we too are looked at with the eyes of love with which Jesus looks at Mary. Yes, there is a unique character to the love a person has for his or her mother, and it would be a denial of the full reality of the incarnation to doubt that Jesus' love for his mother has something unique about it that belongs to the inviolability of that relationship. Yet, there is something inviolable about Jesus' relationship with *each* person, something that belongs to the unique characteristics of that particular relationship. Psychologists tell us that healthy human development involves a child's reaching a measure of independence from his or her mother, not in any sense of rejection but in the sense of broadening the focused love that a child has for his or her mother so that others are included in the frame of reference and relationships with those who are "not mother" can be made. Perhaps, thanks to the healthy loving of Mary, there was something of this going on in Jesus' early development so that, without losing anything of the particular filial love for his mother, he came to embrace others in his loving gaze, looking at us with

---

6. Christina Rossetti, "Mid-Winter."

eyes of love, with an intensity that is able to focus on our particularity and the unique contours of his relationship with each of us.

There is one more moment of seeing we need to mention before moving from the exhilaration of the crib to Mary's agony at the cross, and that is the seeing of Simeon in the Temple. Depicted so tenderly in the glorious golds of Rembrandt's great masterpiece, Simeon, with eyes that though dimmed with age are enlightened with the Holy Spirit, sees the child Jesus, and in seeing him sees the salvation of the world for which he has been waiting and longing. In a profound and mysterious prophecy Simeon shows that he has seen something of the cost of this salvation to Israel, to Jesus and to Mary. "This child is destined for the falling and the rising of many in Israel, and to be a sign that will be opposed so that the inner thoughts of many will be revealed—and a sword will pierce your own soul too" (Luke 2:34–35). Commentators are divided on the meaning of Simeon's words. Of course they are. That is the nature of prophecies, especially ones that penetrate to the heart of the divine plan. Is it that Mary will be pierced by grief as she—in John's account—stands by the cross of her son? Is it that Mary will share in some way in the opposition that Jesus will provoke and will suffer its effects? Is it that the judgement that Jesus brings (which will divide the nation of Israel) will also in some way pass through Mary's heart as it divides even her own household and causes her to choose between, as it were, Church and family? I see no reason why it cannot be all three—personal grief, religious persecution, existential testing and no doubt much more. It is to this event (the suffering of the Savior, the solidarity of the mother and the seeing that takes place between them) that we now turn.

MARY AND THE DEATH OF JESUS

With great skill John draws us into that most poignant of scenes where Mary, "standing near the cross of Jesus" together with the other women, sees her dying son and, together with the beloved disciple, is seen by him, her dying Savior. He is the son and Savior who, even in the suffering of his last, agonising moments, cares for her and commissions her for the new life that is soon to emerge from these terrible events: "When Jesus saw his mother and the disciple whom he loved standing beside her, he said to his mother, 'Woman, here is your son.' Then he said to the disciple, 'Here is your mother'" (John 19:26–27).

John's scene has captivated writers and painters over the Christian centuries as they too have looked upon this exchange of love between mother and son. Before the thirteenth century, depictions of these moments were relatively restrained. Generally, in Miri Rubin's words, "Mary remained a figure of controlled sorrow."[7] This changed dramatically in the thirteenth century, culminating in the publication of the *Meditations on the Life of Christ*, a book that was condemned for imagining Mary losing control of her emotions as she saw the suffering of her son. The same exploration of Mary's suffering was being pursued on canvas. In Giotto's *Crucifixion*, for example, we see Mary overcome with grief, fainting into the arms of her woman friends.

In a similar but more subtle portrayal of Mary's anguish in Ugolino's *Crucifixion with St Francis*, Mary points to her crucified son with her right hand while she turns her head away from the cross. The mother, unable to bear the unbearable sight of the suffering of her son, directs us nonetheless to behold him dying for us all. In comparison, in a lament dating from around 1230 that was added to the late twelfth-century *Carmina Burana*, Mary's resolve will not allow her to turn her face from her son and yet, even though the device is different, the point (in every sense) is the same: Mary calls each of us to look to the cross of Christ and to know that in his death is our life.

> Alas, alas, what grief is mine today and forever,
> Alas, how I now look upon
> The dearest child that ever
> In this world any woman brought forth.
> Alas, my lovely child's body!
> I will look upon it forever.
> Have pity, women and men.
> Let your eyes look there
> And observe the true torment.[8]

It is worth pausing to wonder whether there is anything in this scene John portrays at the cross that is analogous to "the Holy Spirit spinning, as it were, a thread of attention between them" as observed by John V. Taylor regarding Luke's account of the annunciation. Perhaps John is trying to tell us something in the bowing of Jesus' head and giving up his Spirit so soon

---

7. Rubin, *Mother of God*, 243.

8. Bevington, *Medieval Drama*, 219–20; as corrected from the citation in Rubin, *Mother of God*, 246.

after the seeing of Mary and the beloved disciple at the foot of the cross. Is John giving us a hint of what we see more clearly as the reality of Christian existence unfolds: that the attention of Jesus to Mary and his disciples is now to be mediated by the gift of the Spirit? Is this another overshadowing of Mary by the Holy Spirit, this time with the Church that is gathered around her? Is there a suggestion that the presence of Christ given to Mary at the annunciation by the Spirit is now given to the whole Church by the gift of the divine Spirit so that *we* may bear the Son of God in the world?

We have already acknowledged the mystery of Simeon's prophecy that "a sword would pierce Mary's own heart," but let us look at the suffering of Mary again and explore the relationship between the suffering of the mother and the suffering of her son. There are four points to make.

The first is that Mary's sufferings are unique. She suffers the grief that only the mother of Jesus can experience. Second, Mary's sufferings are real but not saving. They are distinct from the saving action of the cross. Mary is the recipient of their effect rather than a participant in their making. In this sense, she is indicative of the relationship that the whole Church has with the cross.

Third, there is yet another sense in which Mary's suffering is indicative of the Church and its relationship to the cross. Her suffering speaks of the suffering of the Church which bears Christ in the world. Although the suffering of the Church is not an atoning suffering, it is nonetheless a suffering of solidarity. In this sense, Mary is situated where every follower of Christ is situated—always looking to the cross, to the salvation won *and* to the cost of standing with the Savior in his suffering. It is a cost that many women have been ready to pay. There is a remarkable chapel in the grounds of what was once a Nazi headquarters in Cologne. In this place that for a short and terrible time was taken over for the purposes of violence, there is a chapel built in the style of a gas chamber dedicated to the German nun, Edith Stein, who paid the ultimate price for standing near the cross of Christ. She was exterminated for refusing to remain silent in the face of the suffering of God's ancient people. The scene on the decoration behind the Lord's Table shows the women around the cross, Edith Stein among them. It is an almost unbearable sight of the cost of discipleship and the sufferings of Christ's followers.

Fourth—and here I hesitate to tread on this most holy of ground—might Mary's suffering in some mysterious way also be a reflection of the suffering of the Father, who suffers the death of his Son? There is an unusual but powerful painting by the sixteenth century Lutheran artist, Cranach the Younger, which hangs in one of Dresden's magnificent art galleries. It depicts the Father holding the body of the dead, crucified Son. One cannot fail to be reminded of Michelangelo's *Pietà*, that most moving example of Marian art, which stands in St. Peter's Basilica in Rome, depicting the sorrowful mother as she holds the heavy weight of her executed son. Of course, there is an absolute difference of being between the eternal, divine Father and the human mother of Jesus, but might the grief of this poor, lowly woman be an echo of a chord that our human ears can hear of the cost of divine love that is borne in the heart of God?

MARY LOOKING AT US

We have been thinking about Mary looking at Jesus and Jesus looking at Mary. What about Mary looking at us? Might there be an Evangelical case for Mary's gaze on us? Dare we even ask, as the *Salve Regina* puts it, for Mary to "turn those two merciful eyes on us"? This takes us back to where we began, which is the question of Mary's present ministry in the life of the Church and of our relationship to her. Mere mention of the *Salve Regina*—with all the implications of its problematic title, quite apart from its content—is enough to alert deep Evangelical instincts to the danger of Mary obscuring the place of Christ in gospel life. There are certainly real and deep pitfalls to avoid and there is still a need for Evangelical correctives of some contemporary Marian practices. But perhaps some clear, scripturally grounded thought on our present relationship to Mary would reveal the particular place that she has in the communion of saints and that as well as joining the apostles in saying, "come and see the Christ" (John 1:41, 46), she also says, as only a mother can, "do whatever he tells you" (John 2:5).

8

Why Psychology Needs Theology (and John Goldingay)

Nancey Murphy

PREFACE

WHEN ASKED TO CONTRIBUTE an essay to *Conversations at the Edges of Things*, I chose to rework a paper I had just given in Iran (a very edgy place these days). It was my second trip to Tehran, to speak at a conference titled "Psychology, Culture, and Religion." During my earlier trip I discovered that the primary organizer of both conferences, Dr. Shiva Khalili, had written her dissertation on a Muslim approach to psychotherapy. In contrast, the other psychologists I met there were importing nearly all of their resources from the U.S.

I had long been interested in the fact that modern Western science was shaped at its origins by various Christian theological assumptions, so the lively debate concerning the possibility of "Muslim science" intrigues me. The paper I gave in May 2011 was meant as encouragement to the psychologists to mine their own theology for resources; I backed up my argument by pointing to the ways in which the understanding of human nature in our shared holy books contrasts with modern individualism.

I often long for the support of a colleague when I lecture on material outside my field. John Goldingay would have been a perfect companion, since he has written on the contrast between the Hebraic conception of human nature and that of the West.[1] My original title was "Why Psychology Needs Theology," but I've amended it in recognition of how much better the paper would have been with his participation.

INTRODUCTION

In the name of God, the Most Merciful.

The thesis of this paper is that philosophical theories of human nature relate, on the one hand, to psychological theory and practice, and on the other hand, to conceptions of the nature of God. My purpose in presenting this here is in hopes of making a small contribution to the question of the possibility, or even necessity, of developing an approach to psychology that is self-consciously Islamic. This is not only because so much of Western psychology is secular, either ignoring the spiritual aspect of the person or even, as with Sigmund Freud, seeing religion as a sign of illness, but also because the individualism presupposed in Western psychology *may* be a distortion of a proper Islamic view of humankind. I am not qualified to make a judgment on this issue, but my suspicion is based on seeing a conflict with original Christian and Hebraic teachings on human nature.

So I present two contrasting sets of views, each involving a theory of human nature and a correlative conception of God, and I will relate each to a current approach to psychological theory and practice. The first set will be based on modern Western individualism. The second will be an attempt to grasp an alternative "dyadic" theory of human nature. Here I'll begin with a current approach to psychology, attachment theory. Then I'll show how it echoes the theory of human nature that is proposed to be that of first-century Mediterranean culture, and finally, I'll describe how scholars have shown that theory of human nature to illuminate Hebraic and early Christian accounts of divine action. I end with a question that my reflections have raised for me regarding Islam and psychology.

---

1. E.g., Goldingay, "The Communal Nature of Humanity," in *Israel's Faith*, 528–29.

Modern Western Individualism

For modern Westerners, individuals are thought to be "self-contained" in two senses: The first is that they are what they are apart from their relationships. The second is the idea that the real self—the soul or mind or ego—is somehow contained within the body. Individualism is the product of a number of factors, but I'll focus here on philosophy.

Individualism in Philosophy

One important source of modern individualism was the seventeenth-century English philosopher Thomas Hobbes. Hobbes developed a political theory modeled on the atomism in physics of his day. The atoms exist prior to their relations with other atoms, and were thought not to be affected by those relations. By analogy, he imagined that humans could have existed prior to all social relations. Social facts such as moral obligations and property rights came into existence only as a result of the "social contract," which is motivated by the individual drive for self-preservation. Social relations do not affect basic human nature.

While contemporary Westerners are aware of individualism in the sense I have just described, they often unconsciously assume that their true selves are somehow *inside* their bodies. For those who are substance dualists, of course, it is common to think of the mind or soul as *in* the body. However, recent philosophers, beginning with Ludwig Wittgenstein in the mid-twentieth century, have made the further point that we think of ourselves as having an "inside" and that our true selves are somehow inside that inner space.

This is an image that comes from the fifth-century theologian Augustine. In reflecting on the location of the soul, he thought of it as a "space" of its own, and bequeathed to the Western Christian spiritual tradition the idea that prayer involves entering into one's soul in order to encounter God. This image had no effect in philosophy until the modern period, when it influenced René Descartes and nearly all his followers. Descartes described himself as observing the ideas *in* his mind. Philosophy since then has been occupied with the problem of how this inner observer can be confident that the ideas or perceptions inside accurately represent whatever is outside. One extreme form of this worry is solipsism: how can I know that there are other consciousnesses apart from my own?

While this concept of human nature began among philosophers, it became so prevalent in Western culture that it affects even children. Contemporary philosopher Brian Magee describes his own "recognition" of the problem while he was still a child. He was in chapel when he reflected on the fact that upon closing his eyes all the other boys disappeared—that is, his visual image of them did. "Up to that moment," he says,

> I had always taken it for granted that I was in immediate contact with the people and things outside of me . . . but now, suddenly, I realized that their existence was one thing and my awareness of it something radically other . . . Even now after all these years, what I cannot put into words is how indescribably appalling I found that moment of insight . . . as if I were for ever cut off from everything that existed—apart from myself—and as if I were trapped for life inside my own head.[2]

Another contemporary philosopher, Mary Midgley, sums up the modern individualist ideal of human nature:

> Crudely—and we have to be crude here to bring the matter out into the open—this view showed the essential self as consisting in reason. That meant an isolated will, guided by an intelligence, arbitrarily connected to a rather unsatisfactory array of feelings, and lodged, by chance, in an equally unsatisfactory human body. Externally, this being stood alone. Each individual's relation to all others was optional, to be arranged at will by contract. It depended on the calculations of the intellect about self-interest and on views of that interest freely chosen by the will. The dignity of the will rests in its ability to assert reason against passive feeling, which is seen as relatively subhuman, emanating from the body.[3]

Individualism and Theology

I'll only address briefly connections between individualism and Western Christian theology. Nicholas Lash, former professor of divinity at Cambridge, notes that a doctrine of God is always correlative to anthropology. The correlations should be mutual, but in modern Christian theology the relation has only been one way: from Cartesian inwardness to conceptions of God. For example, when the human person is identified with a solitary

---

2. Magee, *Confessions of a Philosopher*, 9–10.
3. Midgley, "Soul's Successors," 56.

mind, God tends to be conceived as a *disembodied* mind.[4] Furthermore, if we can only come to know other humans by inference from their bodily behavior, then knowledge of God becomes highly problematic. Just as Descartes believed that all experience takes place inside the mind, modern theologians tended to reduce religious experience to an inner awareness. Thus, all we know for certain is that we have an idea of God *in* our minds. It was easy, then, already in the nineteenth century, for philosophers such as Ludwig Feuerbach to argue that God is nothing but an idea created by humans.

Another problem for modern Christians is that of divine action. It is now widely agreed that it is impossible to begin with a Cartesian account of the human mind and explain how it could have any effect on a material body. Similarly, theologians are still struggling to give an account of how a mind-like God could have any causal interaction with physical creation. Christians in the United States are quite sharply divided between liberals and conservatives. The liberal strategy for dealing with the problem of divine action is to emphasize the traditional claim that God is immanent in all of creation, but in addition they claim that God acts only in and through natural processes. This has created a problem for understanding revelation. If God never does anything apart from upholding natural and historical processes, in what sense can one particular set of texts be called revelation? The typical answer is to turn to the understanding of religious experience as an inward experience, and to describe biblical texts as verbal expressions of that experience. Such expressions can be more or less adequate, but in the end, they are expressions of *human* religious awareness, not literally words of God. While conservative Christians recognize human contribution to biblical texts—they are reflections of their own times—they nonetheless believe that some sort of special divine action was involved in their production. But this claim has been difficult to explain in the modern West.

Individualism in Psychology

I now turn to the effects of individualism in Western psychology. I'll only describe here one theory that is prominent among Christian therapists and pastoral theologians: Family Systems Theory, largely based on the work of American psychiatrist Murray Bowen. He argued that humans, like many kinds of animals, are predisposed to travel in packs for survival. He has

4. Lash, *Easter in Ordinary*, 95.

contributed significantly to the qualification of Hobbesian individualism; in contrast to Hobbes's view that individuals are unaffected by social relations, he drew attention to the fact that, within families especially, people's emotions are very much affected by others.

However, Bowen's focus was on the negative effects of these emotional ties. I referred earlier to Midgley's account of the Enlightenment ideal of humans as guided by intelligence rather than emotion, and with optional relationships with others. Similarly, Bowen saw the goal of therapy as increasing "differentiation," which is the capacity to become independent from one's family of origin and other close relationships. This allows the person to avoid being influenced by others' emotions and by desire for approval, and thus to make decisions on the basis of intellect alone.[5]

I have not studied family systems theory in any depth, but I heard about it repeatedly from my seminary students, who claimed that it gave them brilliant insights into their own personalities. I never thought to question it until I attended a conference on a competitor in the field called Attachment Theory and an associated approach to family practice called emotionally focused therapy. What I learned there gave me the idea for this paper.

While individualism has provided many benefits to Western culture, in particular by promoting equality, many are dissatisfied with its negative consequences and are searching for a better understanding of human nature. I believe that individualism is harmful to families, that it makes it difficult for societies to imagine a common good other than a summation of goods for individuals, and that it has distorted Christians' views of the nature of the church. I realized that Attachment Theory embodies a theory of human nature at odds with individualism. In addition, some of the language the lecturers used fit surprisingly well with concepts of the person in Hebraic and Christian scriptures. In particular, in both cases the term "dyadic personality" is used. So I turn to an exposition of attachment theory, and the parallels with scriptural views of both human nature and of divine action.

---

5. See, e.g., Bowen, "Differentiation of Self."

Humans as Dyadic Personalities

Attachment Theory

Attachment theory is attributed to the British psychiatrist John Bowlby, whose lifespan corresponded almost exactly with that of Murray Bowen—they both died in 1990. Like Bowen, Bowlby paid attention to features we share with some animals. However, as the name of the theory indicates, he focused on the value of attachment within family groups, in contrast to Bowen's differentiation.[6]

Bowlby began with the fact that babies who have their physical needs met but receive little or no emotional interaction fail to thrive, and sometimes even die. Bowlby's colleague, Mary Ainsworth, described three types of personality in small children. Children of the secure type become upset when a parent leaves them alone, but quickly reconnect when the parent returns. Anxious-avoidant children become extremely upset when the parent leaves and then are ambivalent about re-attaching when the parent returns. Avoidant children are little distressed when the parent leaves and actively avoid the parent upon return. Ainsworth's research shows that secure children had parents in their first year who were consistently emotionally responsive, while in the other types the parents were insensitive, inconsistent, or rejecting.[7]

Attachment theory is now being applied to the study of adult relationships, in particular married couples. Here attachment styles comparable to those of infants have been identified. Partners who both have a secure style of attachment are able to read one another's emotions well and provide calming responses during times of stress. In consequence, they tend to be more flexible, curious, tolerant, and compassionate.

The capacity for empathy is crucial for developing secure relationships. Contemporary neuroscience is beginning to shed light on the brain processes that make it possible for humans to "read others' minds." We have neural systems that are specialized for recognizing faces, for interpreting intentions by observing tone of voice, direction of gaze, hand gestures, and other cues. Christian Keysers and colleagues propose a theory of social cognition based on the concept of shared neural circuits. It has long been known that in humans and some primates, when one watches the behavior of another, the same neural circuitry fires in the observer as in the actor.

---

6. See, e.g., Bowlby, *Attachment*.
7. Ainsworth et al., *Patterns of Attachment*.

For example, if I watch someone reach for an object, this activates the same brain process in me that would be involved if I were reaching for the object myself. Keysers argues that this same principle explains our ability to react to others' sensations and emotions. For example, touching subjects' legs produced activation in the primary and secondary somatosensory cortex. There was similar but lesser activation in the same regions when the subjects viewed other people's legs being touched. Similar sorts of corresponding brain activity have been found in the observation of another person's pain, disgust, and fear.[8]

These abilities to not merely make *inferences* about others' feelings but, to an extent, to actually *feel* their feelings lead attachment theorists to reject much of the modern individualist understanding of the person. Sue Johnson says that we have fallen in love with the idea of self-sufficiency, but the essence of being human is the need to connect with others. We use the eyes of those we love as mirrors to reflect back to us a sense of ourselves. Dan Siegel says that we have to change the cultural message that the self ends at the skin. Similarly, James Coan criticizes the definition of the self as "located between our ears." Instead, we need to recognize that our brains are designed to extend ourselves to incorporate others. He claims that his wife and child exist within himself.[9]

This last remark by Coan about his wife and child existing within him called to mind some theories about biblical anthropology that I had read, but could not fully understand at the time.

Biblical Theories of Human Nature

Bruce Malina is a New Testament scholar who uses cultural anthropology to help contemporary Christians better understand biblical texts. In a chapter titled "The First-Century Personality,"[10] he describes a model that is intended to fit the non-individualistic, dyadic self-awareness that characterized the first-century people of the New Testament. A dyadic personality is one who needs another continually in order to know who he or she is. Dyadic personalities internalize what others say, do, and think about them. They conceive of themselves as always interrelated, as needing others for their very psychological existence. Every individual is perceived

---

8. Keysers and Gassola, "Unifying Neural Theory."

9. These remarks were all made at a conference titled "Conversations on Attachment," at Eastern Mennonite University, March 31–April 2, 2011.

10. Malina, *New Testament World*, 51–70.

as embedded in some other. In fact, there are concentric circles of embeddedness: the family, the kinship group, and larger social bodies. In short, he says, "the primary emphasis in the culture we are considering is on dyadic personality, on the individual as embedded in the group, on behavior as determined by significant others."[11]

There are negative characteristics of this perception of human nature, such as a tendency to form stereotypes of other groups and to be suspicious of strangers. Nonetheless, if the attachment theorists are correct, it provides a truer account of human nature than does modern individualism.

A complementary view of human nature is described by Aubrey Johnson in his monograph on the Israelite conception of God. While Malina describes the individual as embedded within closely related groups, Johnson says that the Hebrew personality was thought to be extended in subtle ways among the community by means of speech and other forms of communication. This extension of personality is so strong within a household that in its entirety it is regarded as a "psychical whole."[12] "Accordingly, in Israelite thought the individual, as a [*nephesh*] or centre of power capable of indefinite extension, is never a mere isolated unit . . ."[13]

Hebraic Conceptions of Divine Action

Aubrey Johnson's purpose in describing the Hebraic understanding of the extended self was in order to explain how God's action was understood. The Hebrew word, *ruach*, translated as "spirit," is an extension of God's own personality. Hence God is *genuinely* present in God's messengers (angels), God's word, and God's prophets when they are moved by God's Spirit. "[T]he prophet, in functioning, was held to be more than Yahweh's 'representative'; for the time being he was an active 'Extension' of Yahweh's Personality and, as such, *was* Yahweh—'in Person.'"[14]

I argued earlier that the modern Western conception of humans as isolated minds led to the strange worry, called solipsism, that knowledge of other minds is problematic. In addition, when this conception of humans led to an understanding of God as a disembodied mind, it created problems for explaining how we could know of God's existence. Even for those who have continued to believe in God, there is the problem of how to explain

11. Ibid., 67.
12. Johnson, *The One and the Many*, 4.
13. Ibid., 7.
14. Ibid., 33.

God's action in the world, and in particular, to make sense of claims regarding scriptural revelation. The connections among these positions are not necessary connections, so it's possible to hold an individualist account of humans and nonetheless believe that God performs special acts in history, including revealing himself through prophets. However, the turns that liberal Christian theology has made in the modern era, I believe, should serve as a caution to other people of the book, particularly to Muslims.

Concluding Question

When I address an American audience on the topic of human nature I usually have an accurate idea of how my views will be received. I have been highly critical in this paper of individualism, but I have no knowledge of whether you are in agreement. I spent time before I came here trying to learn what to expect, and of course I've hunted for information in the Qur'an. But even if I read all the relevant suras, would I be able to interpret them correctly? And to what extent has Islamic culture in general or Iranian culture developed beyond the Qur'an, as in the case of Western Christians' post-biblical conceptions of human nature? In the hope of stimulating discussion, I'll end with a question—a long question. I have a book by an Egyptian scholar, Fathi Osman, called *Concepts of the Quran: A Topical Reading*. He has organized quotations from the Qur'an under nine major headings, and has incorporated his own commentary. So of course I turned to the section on human beings. His first quotation is Sura 2, verses 170–71:

> And when it is said to them, "Follow what God has sent down [to you], they say 'No, but we follow only what we found our forefathers believing in and doing.'" Even if their forefathers did not use their reason at all, and were lacking any sense of direction? The parable of those who stubbornly deny the truth [with regard to those who call them to follow it] is that of one who shouts loudly [addressing] that which hears [and recognizes] nothing save [the sound of] calls and shouts; deaf, dumb and blind are they.

Osman comments on this quotation as follows: "The Quran repeatedly stresses individuality and condemns dependency, blind following and imitation of others."[15] So here, finally, is the question with which I'll end. Does the Qur'an in fact repeatedly stress individuality?

15. Osman, *Concepts of the Quran*, 73.

9

Theology with Passion

GORDON OLIVER

STORY

THE FIRST PASSAGE IN the Bible I ever read was Psalm 116. It was a Monday morning after I had 'given my life to Christ' the previous evening in February 1965. I felt overwhelmed by the love of God in Jesus and frightened that my conversion might prove to be just another part of the mental illness I had been struggling with for more than two years. The curate who had prayed with me the night before gave me the psalm to read. What I found astonishing (and still do) is that it described a whole lot that was very real and very raw in my experience: "The snares of death encompassed me; the pangs of Sheol laid hold on me; I suffered distress and anguish. Then I called on the name of the Lord, 'O Lord, I pray, save my life!'" The relief of discovering that I could look forward to a life with purpose made possible by the love of God instead of one of endless misery is hard to describe. There it was in the psalm: "For you have delivered my soul from death, my eyes from tears, my feet from stumbling. I walk before the Lord in the land of the living." Here also was the start of my calling to ministry, "What shall I return to the Lord for all his bounty to me? . . . I will pay my vows to the Lord in the presence of all his people

. . ." My very first encounter with Scripture was filled with emotion and passion as I took the first joyful steps of my Christian life. Thirty six years later, at the threshold of old age, I remain fascinated and challenged, and at times repelled, by the experiences of my own and other peoples' emotions and passions in our journeys through the Christian life. I continue to find myself engaging my passions with the passions of Scripture. And I find myself amazed at people who want to continue in public ministry when they appear to have hardly any spark of passion or commitment as part of their Christian faith.

I want to write about theology with passion in this book for three reasons. First, because I see John Goldingay's biblical scholarship, teaching, and testimony as characterized by passionate emotional and theological questions and commitments, and by rigorous, even relentless, academic enquiry which he has learned to hold together in creative tension. Second, because I think that too often my church (the Church of England) has lived a kind of theology that displays commitment to hard work and practical acts of mercy, but mostly admires warm and passionate Christian discipleship without wanting to get too personally involved in it. Third, I continue to have a personal love-hate relationship with passion as an emotion in my own Christian faith and ministry. I wish I had been wired to be a calm and emotionally cool person who could find fulfilment in careful analytical theological study, a person to whom gaining 'critical distance' would come naturally. But I have not been built that way. I find myself caught between the passions generated in me by the suffering of other people, structural and personal sin, the searing love and grace of fellowship with God and God's people, and the call to attend carefully to Scripture and tradition, to live the life of prayer and to serve with joy the people committed to my care. I live daily with the question of whether theology as rational enquiry about the things of God and passion as emotional commitment can really be held together for very long at a time.

Although John Goldingay is second to none in hard-headed linguistic and exegetical studies, he is also unashamed to use narrative, including his own personal story, to engage with contemporary interpretation of Scripture. At the popular level this is most clearly demonstrated for me in his book *To the Usual Suspects* in which he interweaves parts of the story of his wife Ann's progressive and protracted illness with his exposition of the attempts at so-called comfort by Job's friends. It is this combination of uncompromising scholarship and truthful engagement with human story and Scripture in the same context that demonstrates what I am groping for in this exploration of theology with passion.

There are good reasons to be wary about passion as emotion. It can imply lack of proper control and a tenuous grasp on reality—people blown this way and that by joy or sorrow, elation or despair. Individuals and crowds can be whipped up to celebration or fury, extraordinary generosity, prejudice, even violence by manipulative people with well-honed rhetorical and media skills. I recall being at a huge Christian convention where the speaker was using the most brilliantly delivered (but baseless and incoherent) arguments to condemn Church of England bishops, gays and members of "other world faiths" while the people all around me applauded and cheered to the echo. With a shudder I reflected that there seemed little dynamic difference between this kind of corporate so-called 'Christian' passion and the whipping up of crowds at extremist political rallies. Passion can be a dangerous thing. When it is bound up with something as identity-defining and potentially reality-blurring as religious commitment, it can be a *very* dangerous thing.

Passion as unregulated emotionalism is certainly dangerous when it expresses no more than the excited, fearful, self-focused ego. Passion as emotional investment can be something much more positive. Soccer and other sports stars, rock musicians, politicians, artists, parents, carers, social workers, theologians, and many more would be unable to function effectively in their roles and professions without high levels of passionate commitment. These are mostly examples of how individuals act passionately; but passion as emotional investment is also essential for the welfare of groups and societies. Obvious examples include social justice campaigners, environmental activists, and industrial union leaders; but others would include groups where faith and ethnicity are tied together, such as Coptic Christians in Egypt and Amish communities in Pennsylvania.

We cannot go much further, however, without proposing a definition of passion that has the capacity to hold together the dynamics of life-sustaining investment and the emotional charge that produces the kind of energy that can make them fruitful or frustrate their flourishing. The word 'passion' means to suffer. For the purpose of this reflection, therefore, I propose that passion should be understood as the energy that makes us prepared to pay the cost of our commitments.

PASSION AS HOSTAGE TAKER

The New Testament generally sees passion and desire as having the power to capture people and lock them away from the grace of God. Both the Greek terms *pathos* (suffering) and *epithumia* (longing, desire) are translated to describe human passions that are always at risk of going out of control. *Epithumia* describes desire as a longing, a pining, that fills a person's mind, preoccupies their thoughts, constantly drags them back to the inescapable scripts of their inner life and can show itself in destructive actions. The best you can hope for when passionate longing threatens to be overwhelming is to control it by getting it into some kind of perspective where it can find godly expression (1 Cor 7:36). This is only possible in some contexts (such as marrying to give sexuality a proper means of expression), so another way out of the addictive cycle of passion, desire and sinful action has to be found. In Romans and Galatians, Paul reflects at length about the incompatibility of life "in the spirit" and life "in the flesh." Life in the flesh is dominated by competing desires that leave the person feeling carved up, confused and crying out in frustration because however hard they try, they can't make a difference to how they are: "I find it to be a law that when I want to do what is good, evil lies close at hand" (Rom 7:21).

Paul can see only one way out of this cycle of frustration, failure and alienation from God and it is a desperate one. It involves crucifixion: "Those who belong to Christ have crucified the flesh with its passions and desires" (Gal 5:24). A good Buddhist might expect such a moment of crisis to be followed by a period of tranquillity and a refreshing freedom arising from the absence of desire. But, according to Paul, that is not on the agenda for people who are "in Christ." They are liberated to "live by the Spirit" (Rom 8:13). This involves knowing who God really is, who we really are, and what we really have to face up to. Far from being at a far distance or near yet unapproachable, God really is the God who is Abba, Father! Far from being condemned to fall back into fear, we have the Spirit's word for it that we really are children of God. Far from escaping the pressures and pains of life, we truly are called to engage with Christ's suffering in the face of the world as it truly is. And there is nothing whatsoever in our engagement with that suffering that can separate us from the love of God in Christ. In other words, when we come to Christ we don't exchange a passionate but essentially pointless existence for a life of detached 'holy' tranquillity. As Paul might have said, "Not at all!" We exchange passion focused on no purpose or meaning beyond the self for passion with fulfilment and purpose.

This passion and this purpose are intimately tied up with the purpose and the passion of Jesus Christ. This is why, in the Christian understanding, passion is radically connected to resurrection. It is passion with God's version of personal and community future.

PASSIONLESS GOD?

Christians in the European Reformation traditions have good reason to be wary of religion seen in terms of passionate commitment to faith centered causes. Some of the worst atrocities in our history were perpetrated by Christians seeking dominance over other Christians. Wielding the Word of God as if it were a weapon, it was as if they had never read it. Generation after generation can be seen, with the hindsight of history, to have created and recreated God's will in the image of their own myopic passions. (The likelihood is that future historians will find plenty of evidence of this in the preaching, writing and religious claims of twenty first century religious adherents too). Given the volatile faith commitments and the tragic results of many of these in the decades leading to the mid seventeenth century, it is not surprising that the writers of the *Westminster Confession* of 1646 should declare so strongly: "there is but one only living and true God, who is infinite in being and perfection, a most pure spirit, invisible, without body, parts, or passions, immutable, immense, eternal, incomprehensible . . ." (Article II).

Drawing on Scripture and the eastern Fathers, the writers of the *Westminster Confession* were determined to establish that God is infinitely more than even the greatest projections of human self-understanding. Humanity is created in the *imago Dei*, but humans are not God. Only God is God. Mostly I have no difficulty with the *Confession*'s resort to the apophatic definition methods of early eastern Christianity, except that this chapter, and the *Confession* as a whole, makes God appear to be impersonal, characterless, and passionless. It seems that one can only relate to this God by obediently accepting his sovereign will declared through the faithful preaching of Scripture and trusting to one's eternal election by the grace of God. It is hard to resist an admittedly anachronistic question: Where is the room here for the realities of searching, yearning, protest, laughter, joy and wondering, and the other passions that are part and parcel of so many people's actual experience of faith, unfaith and half-faith as they trust in Christ at the same time as trying to get a grip of what such trust is supposed to mean? My former colleague at St. John's Nottingham, Michael Insley, once helpfully reminded me that the phrase 'without passions' "could be interpreted as imperturbability, that is to say without the ability to be overthrown by passions directed against one."

The western Protestant traditions of theological writing in systematics, biblical studies, moral philosophy and practical theology that formed the main texts of modern theology curricula presented to seminarians prior to the last quarter of the twentieth century were often strong on analysis and exposition, but woefully short on attention to Christian spirituality, mysticism, worship, testimony and mission. At least this is how I experienced them as I prepared for ordained ministry. Even the secondary sources about the eastern Fathers tended to be forensic, foreign and far away from anything that could conceivably be related to the concerns of ministry. What were Christian disciples and future ministers supposed to make of this passionless God and his teachings? Perhaps the best resort would be somehow to survive the rigors of seminary studies, then leave them behind and find a more down to earth theology of our own that would work in the realities of everyday ministry? For some this temptation was irresistible.

Part of the problem, on reflection, was that much of the writing about the great theologians of the past lacked a key piece of information, perhaps on the assumption that it was so blindingly obvious that only a fool could possibly miss it. This missing piece was concerned with who these people were, and the present passions and commitments that were driving their theological reflection. My first meeting with a fellow lecturer at St John's illustrates this well. George Bebawi was hired to teach patristics and I was hired to teach practical theology at the same time. To get the conversation going I asked him why he wanted to spend his life teaching something that had bored me stiff as a student. His eyes lit up and his nostrils flared as his booming voice rang out, "Are you not interested in mission and evangelism? Do you not wonder how to pray? Do you not wonder how to be clear about the Gospel of Jesus?" His torrent continued as he showed me that most of the Fathers were missionaries, pastors, and teachers of the faith in cross cultural settings: mystics who were trying to find the right kinds of language to communicate the truth they found in Christ. As it dawned on me, rather late in the day I fear, that there simply is no theology without biography, and therefore without the lived passions and commitments that go with it, I became increasingly aware of this lack. Detaching a theologian's life completely from a theologian's teachings risks reducing the impact of their scholarship to little else than a few more interesting observations. It is no accident, I think, that the theologian of the early church who is most read in the twenty first century is Augustine of Hippo who explicitly set his reflections in the context of his experience of Christian discipleship and ministry.

I do not mean, of course, that Christian theology can be no more than thinly disguised biography. The commitment to "loving God with your mind" sufficiently to engage in patient scholarship and painstaking research which follows the discoveries of truth is vital if theology is not to become self-referential, an end in itself, even (in the strict sense of the term) idolatrous. There is a paradox here: like any other branch of research, theological exploration must be committed to a certain level of pointlessness. If it is to have rigor and integrity, research cannot start by knowing for sure where it will end. On the other hand, the theologian has to be clear about her prior commitments and starting assumptions if gaining essential critical awareness is to be any kind of possibility. Put simply, it makes a difference if, when you read Aquinas, you realise that he was a monk who was required to spend time each day in community prayer and contemplation of the Divine as the main context of his scholarship. The traditional definition of theology as "faith seeking understanding" implies that the agenda of theological reflection must include attention to the passions of the people God loves—passion understood as the sufferings of the people, and passion understood as the commitments for which people are ready to pay great costs. The recent popularising of Evagrius of Pontus' definition of a theologian ("one whose prayer is true") serves to reinforce this reconnection of theology as thinking about God with theology as the commitment of love to follow where God leads. Theology and passion can again be held in creative tension precisely because they belong in intimate, if not always comfortable, relationship with each other.

WHAT KIND OF PASSION?

It clearly matters what kind of passion we are talking about. It cannot merely be a matter of taming wild human passions so that they become compliant with the will of God, as if following Christ means that some part of you has to be permanently and reluctantly held in check lest it break out in destructiveness and reverts to type. This could be a recipe for a grim, dogged, resentful discipleship. The freedom offered by God in Christ has to be more than that. It seems to me that two things need to happen. First, the full range of human passions needs to be laid wide open to the love and grace of God—with nothing held back. Second, human passions need to be redeemed and redirected so they take on the character of the passion of God revealed in Christ. We see a full range of human passions laid open before Yahweh in the Psalms with their combination of devotion, commitment, praise, paranoia, bitter anger, flatness, longing for justice, thirsting for righteousness, dejection, despair, and boisterous rejoicing. John Goldingay's quip that "the Psalms are 150 things God doesn't mind having said to him" is a reminder that before the face of God there is no place to hide the realities of our experience because there is no need to hide.

People's passions and commitments are more than communal or personal generalisations. They are contextual. In the psalms, people are not just angry, bitter, alienated, lost. They are angry about something, bitter towards somebody, alienated from somewhere they belong. They have lost something they treasure. This means that Scripture will be read differently by people in different contexts. John's commentary on Psalm 137 underlines this:

> From a Nigerian perspective David Tuesday Adamo comments on the fact that the prominence of prayer for God's punishment of one's enemies . . . troubles Western Christians, but does not trouble African indigenous churches. Rather than psalms of violence and hate, these are psalms of protection and defense. People are aware that enemies will use spiritual means such as curses to harm them, and traditional religion gives people charms and recitations to counteract these. When people came to believe in Christ, these means of protection became forbidden, but they discovered the imprecatory psalms and came to use them in this way.[1]

Appropriating parts of Scripture for use according to our passions and commitments, however righteous these might seem, can be limiting, even abusive unless something else happens. They need to be redeemed and redirected so they take on the character of the passion of God in Christ. Much of the Evangelical writing on which I was raised as a young Christian described what was happening at the cross of Christ in transactional and forensic terms. These focused on Jesus "paying the price" and bearing the wrath of God against the sinfulness of humanity, with God the Father somehow (being a bit more God than Jesus at this point) portrayed at a distance

---

1. Goldingay, *Psalms*, vol. 3, 611.

from the violence and bitterness of the cross. There was huge emphasis on arriving at a correct doctrine of the Atonement. This left me wondering what passion considered as suffering meant to God, and therefore whether there was any place in the consciousness of God for the kind of suffering I was dealing with when I was ministering in a community torn apart by bitterness and violence during a prolonged coal strike. Two things alerted me as a parish priest to the suffering of God in the passion of Jesus Christ. The first was reading German theologian Jürgen Moltmann's *The Crucified God* whilst at the same time recognizing what it must have cost Moltmann to engage with the cross of the suffering God in the aftermath of the Holocaust perpetrated by his own countrymen. The second was an encounter in a friary at Alnmouth in the northeast of England.

The chapel of Alnmouth Friary has a large wooden crucifix with the arms of Jesus stretched out in agonising love and triumphant victory. For a long time I had been wondering how the suffering and commitment of God could really connect with my experience and the tornness of our community. One of the brothers told me a story about the crucifix. It had been made by a young man who lived for a time in the Friary after becoming alienated from his family. As he worked on the figure of Christ, he was having great difficulty getting the carving of Jesus' hands as he wanted them. Around this time he was able to meet with his father and explained to him what he was trying to do. The older man held out his hands towards his son and asked, "Will these do?" It was in contemplating the intimate involvement of God the Father in the suffering of Jesus—that on the cross hung a Person of the Holy Trinity—that I came to realise that here the basest and the most sublime of human passions find their true place, their redemption, their new identity, their true purpose. The passion of God in Christ shows how far God will go to meet the cost of his commitment to humanity.

Until recently, the importance of this has been largely masked from Christians in Europe, living in the fading shadow of Christendom. But for Christians in the favelas of South America, in the post-apartheid days of South Africa, in the Hindu majority areas of south western India, or in early twenty first century Iran, how they do theology has direct effects on how—or even whether—they live. In Britain, as I write, many Christians are sensing themselves to be increasingly marginalised in society simply because they are Christians. Discipleship without commitment and theology without passion will not have the capacity to be faith-and-life-sustaining.

In 2 Corinthians 5, Paul connects the passion of Christ with a transformed vision of what people can be expected to be and do. "For the love of Christ urges us on, because we are convinced that one has died for all; therefore all have died. And he died for all, so that those who live might live no longer for themselves, but for him who died and was raised for them . . . we regard no one from a human point of view . . . if anyone is in Christ there is a new creation . . . so we are ambassadors for Christ" (14–20). Here is human passion redeemed and energised to be directed into fruitful living and effective witness as ambassadors for Christ.

John Goldingay is a theologian whose laughter and grief are part of his teaching, who can lead a postgraduate seminar on the Book of Judges while wearing swimming shorts and a loud tee shirt; or signal his mood to a faculty meeting by wearing different coloured socks. His scholarship is born out of countless hours of patient and impatient study by himself, singing to loud music in a rock group, and above all his loving companionship and suffering through the long years of Ann's illness. He has shown me that it is not only possible, but essential, to study and to live theology with passion. Thank you, John.

10

Growing Old in Gethsemane

TOM SMAIL

JESUS NEVER GREW OLD. When, dear John, we reach seventy our earthly career is already more than twice as long as his and the question arises as to whether and how his help can stretch across the gap that divides his comparative youth from our ageing so as to be a relevant support to us in the final stages of our lives. A man in his early thirties has, in the nature of the case, no personal experience, for example, of the deprivations of retirement: of the feeling that what once gave us status and significance is no longer in demand and we have to fade slowly into the geriatric hinterland. Not for him the gradual loss of energy on the physical level (and perhaps on the mental as well), the worries about whether the money will last, or the bereavements of beloved spouses and friends that can reduce us to a lonely singleness. All this can dominate our declining years, and yet all of this a man of Jesus' age, albeit with his own terrible burdens, threats and sufferings, appears to know nothing at all.

What we have been saying is, of course, a particular instance of a question that has theological and Christological roots. When the eternal Son of God became incarnate in Jesus of Nazareth, such an act involved his becoming a particular male human individual, and this put him in a unique historical location that, by its very particularity, excluded him from other historical locations and gave him a human experience whose very distinctness was inevitably different from the experiences of quite different people in vastly varying cultural contexts. In some ways he was like us in sharing a common humanity; in other ways he was unlike us. And so the question from which we started inevitably arises: whether and how far he can reach across these divides to be, as he has promised, our Saviour and our friend.

The patristic Christological principle, "What he did not take, he could not redeem," poses the question in its acute form. Not only has Jesus not taken on our old age, but he has not been, for example, an American black man on death row for tens of years, endlessly tossed between hope and despair as one appeal after another is rejected. He has not been a pregnant teenager trying to make up her mind about whether to abort her baby. Since the life of Jesus is so far removed from the lives of people like this, we are left asking how he can be expected, even if they turn to him, to come to their aid.

THE WOUNDED HEALER

We can, I think, see some pointers towards a general answer to these questions in the strange comment that Matthew makes on the healing ministry of Jesus. Having recorded that on one evening 'they brought to him many who were possessed by demons, and he cast out the spirits with a word and cured all who were sick', he immediately adds, 'This was to fulfil what had been spoken through the prophet Isaiah, "He took our infirmities and bore our diseases"' (Matt 8:16–17).

Matthew does not explain in detail the relevance of this quotation to the healing ministry of Jesus, but he is clearly implying that it is a sharing of suffering between the sick and their healer that makes it possible for him to help them. What makes his healing ministry so effective is not a word uttered from a divine height of invulnerable omnipotence, but the compassionate empathy of the wounded healer who has himself to bear his own suffering in order to free these needy people from theirs.

At the heart of the gospel is the insight that it is not divine power that conquers evil but only divine love. A love that has known nothing but the bliss of heaven will not be much use to those who are being broken by the evils of earth. A God limited by his own impassibility cannot give to a broken humanity the only love that will be of any help to them. As Edward

Sillito put it, "To our wounds only God's wounds can speak, but not a god has wounds but Thou alone."

Nevertheless it is not literally true that Jesus contracted the diseases of those he healed. He did not himself become a leper, a paralytic, blind, deaf or mentally deranged. Consequently, we are left asking: what was the nature of the suffering that gave him a bond with, and access to, all these variously afflicted people?

The answer is that in the suffering of the cross Jesus experiences evil in all its depth of destructiveness. He can heal in Galilee because he is already the suffering servant of God on his way to Calvary. He is beginning to expose himself to the ultimacy of evil that will enable him to reach and conquer the particular manifestation of evil which is afflicting them. He will on the cross plumb the fathomless depths of suffering in all its forms, extremes of physical pain, humiliating exposure, social disgrace, resourcelessness, helplessness, abandoned loneliness, murderous hatred, and spiritual desolation.

All this he experiences humanly, as we do, so that he carries in concentrated form what we suffer; but beyond that he experiences it as God incarnate in its ultimate attack upon the love that made the world, its threatening and destructive contradiction of everything that he is and stands for. That is what he confronts so shrinkingly in the garden; that is what in obedience to his Father and in love to us he willingly endures on the cross.

Because God in Jesus has suffered like this, he has contact with and access to all who suffer evil in any of its myriad shapes. The condemned criminal from Nazareth standing before Pilate is not far from the tortured prisoner on death row; the man who gives himself totally to win life for the last, the least, the lost, has much to say and much to give to the young mother hesitating in the abortion clinic. The thirty five year old contemplating his death in Gethsemane is highly relevant to the seventy year old having slowly to adjust to all that the run up (or should it be run down?) to his own death will involve.

LIFE'S STAGES SHARED

We could indeed say that the short lifespan of Jesus contains within itself all the elements and stages of the much longer lives that we live. That is obviously true of its early stages when he is shaped, as we are, by the family into which he is born, where, as we see him at twelve in the temple, he is educated into the faith of Israel and grows into the unique relationship with God the Father that is to be the vibrant centre of everything he becomes, does and suffers. Soon, this blossoms into the sense of Messianic vocation and empowerment celebrated in his baptism and worked through with intense concentration and incisive purpose in the short years of his ministry.

But what is obviously true of the early part of his life is equally, if less obviously, true of its last weeks. In the one he makes his own the various stages of our living; in the other he makes his own the whole process of our dying. Concentrated into his final days, he faces the same issues that we face spread out over *our* final days. The timescale is very different; he has hours where we have years, but both he and we have to learn how to die, so that the way he approaches his imminent death is relevant and richly instructive to the way we approach our death, however soon and suddenly it may come or however long it may be postponed. That makes Gethsemane, where he explicitly faces his threatening prospects, a good school in which those who are getting old may keep watch with him and learn much about how to face ours.

We have to be careful about how we go about this learning. In Gethsemane Jesus goes a little apart from the disciples he has asked to support him. In his passion he has things to do in which they can have no part; the way he approaches death is to some extent an example for them to follow, but it is far more than that. He has to do *for* them something in which they can have no active participation. He alone has to drink the bitter cup of God's judgement so that they do not have to drink it; he is the high priest of a perfect sacrifice of obedience that they, as sinners, are incapable of offering, so that what they and we have to learn at Gethsemane is not just about what we should be doing, but rather about what we should be trusting him to do for us, as alone and without us he goes to his cross.

The first thing we have to learn from his death is to receive its benefits, undeserved and unearned, from his gracious hand. "Nothing in my hand I bring, simply to thy cross I cling." If that is the central clue to good Christian living, it is also the clue to good Christian dying. When in advancing years we are no longer as able as we once were to do things for Christ, we have to discover with new reality that our hope of salvation rests, as it always has, not on any of our achievements but first and foremost on what once and for all he has done for us. When we come to Gethsemane we have to see not only what we can share with him as we approach death but also what we need to receive from him. We shall bear both in mind as we join him there.

WAITING IN HELPLESSNESS

When we do so, we find him in an attitude of waiting. There in the garden the initiative has passed from him to his enemies; Judas has gone out from the upper room and Jesus is listening for the sound of marching feet that will tell him that he will be arrested, bound and so completely deprived of his freedom, that from now on what happens to him will be in the hostile hands of others.

After Easter he tells Peter that the same thing is liable, sooner or later, to happen to us all. "Very truly I tell you, when you were younger, you used to fasten your own belt and to go wherever you wished. But when you grow old you will stretch out your hands and someone else will fasten a belt around you and take you where you do not want to go" (Jn 21:18). That is a prediction of a martyr's death but it also describes a loss of initiative that will in different ways affect us all.

A few weeks ago I asked for help to get to a plane along the endless corridors of Gatwick Airport in England and found myself propelled in a wheelchair by someone behind me whom I could not see, who, although I had set the destination, was totally in control of how we reached it. Which things are a parable.

Implicit in Jesus' mysterious exchanges with his Father in Gethsemane is the question about whose hand will be propelling him in the period of powerlessness that he is about to enter. Will it be the hands of his enemies or will it be the hand of his God? And so, as he waits for Judas he waits upon God. On the one hand he shrinks in real horror from what God is leading him into, on the other he finds comfort and confidence in the fact that the one who is leading him is still *Abba*, the one whom he has known and trusted throughout his life and ministry.

No doubt Judas, Caiaphas, and Pilate have a will and purpose that is going to drive coming events, but behind them, subtly and quietly, using them and fulfilling his gracious purposes in spite of them and yet through them, is *Abba*; and the fact that Jesus precisely here in these dire straits uses this term of intimacy and closeness is a sign that ultimately he trusts his Father enough to be able to say to him 'Your will be done', even when that will is for the suffering and death of the cross.

This struggle between shrinking fear of what is to come and a serenity that comes from trusting the one who lets it be so, and indeed wills it to come, runs all the way through the passion narratives of the gospels. On the one hand Jesus is devastated beyond bearing by the way he feels abandoned and alone in his suffering, and yet, on the other, he acknowledges that the one to whom he complains of abandonment is still *My* God; and before all is over he regains his trust, confidence and hope in his Father: "Father, into your hands I commend my spirit."

The clash between increasingly dismayed helplessness and his trust in the Father that characterises the last days of Jesus is echoed, however distantly, in the process of ageing that many of us have to face in our own last days. An old Scottish saying reminds us that "Auld age doesn'a come its lane." That reflects all too accurately the experience of many of us, a little bit in our seventies but much more obviously and threateningly in our eighties and beyond. Loss of energy and mobility, failing hearing and eyesight, worries about money, increasing isolation from still-living friends, and bereavements of those who have been sources of love and stability on which we have relied all our lives, deep anxiety about when and in what form death will overtake us: these are but a few of the companions of our advancing years that cumulatively can bring us to the melancholy conclusion that life is going fast from us and is a lot less worth living than it used to be.

DIMINISHMENT AND ISOLATION

Along with an increasing helplessness, we may experience an increasing isolation. Loneliness is the perennial companion of old age; this is when we remember that from Gethsemane on Thursday evening until he died on Friday afternoon, Jesus was utterly and profoundly unreachable and alone. The shared communion of the bread and the wine in the upper room gives way to a series of abandonments that deprive him almost completely of the support he was looking for from those closest to him.

What happens in Gethsemane itself illustrates the two different kinds of loneliness in which Jesus was involved. It was most obviously a loneliness brought about by the failure of the disciples. Peter, James and John, three times invited to watch and pray with him, three times fall asleep. This is followed by the betrayal of Judas, the flight of the disciples and the denial of Peter—Jesus is left to meet his fate all by himself.

But there is another kind of Gethsemane loneliness that is an essential element in what he has to do on the cross. In order to pray he goes a little apart from the disciples because he has issues to settle that are entirely between himself and his Father and in which nobody else can intrude. It is the loneliness not of their desertion but of his own uniqueness. Only he can drink the cup of the Father's reconciling judgement; he does it *for* others, but he does it alone.

BY GRACE ALONE

Both Christ's deprived loneliness and his redemptive uniqueness powerfully address the needs of older people. To take the second first, the final stage of life brings us a deepened awareness of the ambiguity of all that has gone before it. The nearer to God we come, the more clearly we see that the lives we have lived, the decisions we have taken, the ministries we have offered, the loving relationships we have maintained, have all been shaped by God's providential care and the work of the Holy Spirit deep within us. But from start to finish, they have also to different degrees been corrupted and compromised by our own residual self-centredness, by the false gods before whom we have bowed, and the sinful addictions that have again and again subtly seduced us.

We discover, as Peter did, that we dare not rely on our own ability to follow Jesus, but have to trust much more in the Christ who for love of us has drunk to the dregs that cup of reconciling judgement that his Father entrusted to him. Only in the lonely sacrifice of Calvary can the past be purged and our marred relationship with God restored, *sola gratia*—by grace alone.

As I approach the final reckoning, the realisation of that ambiguity makes me see how all my hopes for now and for ever rest not at all on what I have done for God in a whole lifetime, but on what was done in a unique and decisive way by the Son of God who loved me and gave himself for me. I have long since known that as *the* truth: in recent times I have begun to inhabit it as *my* truth.

BY FAITH ALONE

The deprivations and the resulting aloneness that we share with Jesus point us in the same direction. When his friends have gone and his campaign for the kingdom has collapsed, the only one left to whom he can trust and commit himself and his future is his God, who is still as he has always been, *Abba*—who can be trusted to respond to the uttermost offering of filial obedience in his death with the uttermost demonstration of fatherly care in his resurrection.

In that process of trust and vindication, we can see at least something of where God is taking us in our final years. As many of the things and people in whom we have trusted are one by one taken from us, we too stand in our powerlessness and aloneness before our heavenly Father and are asked very simply the one question on which everything else depends: How much do you trust me?

We know that this question has been heard and answered when the priority of trust is reflected practically in the priority of prayer, when doing things for God takes second place to waiting with expectation for what God in his mercy will do for us, when his promises count for more than our achievements, when our hope is based not on what we are for him but in what he is for us.

We have all been hearing, and some of us have been saying, this sort of thing for a lifetime; but when we come to the time of life when all the subsidiary sources of support we have relied on are progressively taken from us and we are left alone with God and Jesus in Gethsemane, the urgency of the question comes home to us in a quite different way. And as we watch and pray and trust in that lonely place with Jesus, with him we rediscover *Abba*. In some of the most devastating and destablizing moments of our lives, we become aware of a benign presence that quietly surrounds us, of a loving providence that is gentle with our weakness but unfailingly opens unexpected doors before us and against all the probabilities gives us abundant reason to go on hoping in him when all the other reasons for hoping have gone. Again and again in a peace that does indeed pass all understanding, we discover that we are indeed nearer God's heart in *this* garden than anywhere else on earth. As the psalmist puts it, "When I walk through the valley of the shadow of death, your rod and your staff comfort me. You spread a table before me in the presence of my enemies and my cup runs over."

FRUITFUL MATURITY

There is of course another much more positive and benign dimension to the old age of Christians that we have not looked at in this paper. In autumn the leaves do indeed fall, but not before the fruit has ripened on the same trees. The Jesus who comes to Gethsemane comes in all the maturity of the lifetime in which he has loved the Lord with his whole being, and in that same love healed and helped his neighbour. Nothing can take that from him; alone and powerless in the garden and on the cross he has a life to offer full of the virtue and goodness that, when it is freely offered, can be the saving of the world.

So elderly Christians come to God not just with their residual sinfulness that needs forgiving but with the fruits of maturity, holiness, and wisdom that God has grown in them over a lifetime, sometimes more obvious to others than to themselves. When the tree that is laden with such fruit is pruned in all the ways we have been describing, when all that we are and have become is entrusted to God in Gethsemane, he will take it and bless it and make us at the end of our life fruitful in surprising and unsuspected ways, and will grow in us a rich harvest ripe for reaping in the resurrection world to come.

11

Biblical Principles of Calling and Training for Mission

Roger Bowen

It is a commonplace that the Church in Western Europe is in a missionary situation and that it needs to ask itself how far it is succeeding in equipping God's people for the kind of mission such a situation requires. The missionary mandate is presented in the Gospels by two classical texts: Matt 28:18–20 and John 20:19–23. These represent two contrasting approaches to the *Missio Dei*. Both emphases are needed but they are in tension with one another. We may rather loosely call them the "traditional" and the "contemporary" perspective, respectively.

THE TRADITIONAL PERSPECTIVE

Ever since William Carey focused on the Great Commission as the prime motivation for world mission, the churches of the Western world have felt constrained by the obligation to utilize their privilege and their power to evangelize the world "in this generation," or at least as soon afterwards as possible. Even in the midst of weakness and failure, many made the ultimate sacrifice and were encouraged by Christ's promise of his power and presence leading to ultimate success, if not in this world, then in the world to come (Matt 28:18–20).

The Twelve were prepared for their mission by accompanying their Lord on his journeys, seeing his works, hearing his words and following his example. They were then sent out on missionary forays of their own, according to the pattern they had experienced. Their activity, like his, was punctuated with periods of withdrawal and reflection. The profoundest reflection took place after the untimely end of his ministry, followed by his resurrection and their realization of its implications for them.

Paul's preparation for mission was not dissimilar to that of the Twelve and contains elements of abiding value. First, his pre-Christian experiences equipped him to relate realistically to the society in which he would exercise his mission. Second, there was a supernatural commission. Third, he had a period of intensive reflection. Fourth, his calling was recognized by the Church and he was assigned a local mentor. Fifth, he had periods of withdrawal and private fellowship with church leaders. Sixth, he engaged in ministry in fellowship with others. Seventh, he and Barnabas were formally appointed for team ministry by a small group of the congregation at Antioch. Much of this process took place in the context of prayer and fasting and in response to the Holy Spirit.

Like his mentor Barnabas, Paul possessed Christian virtues that were recognized by the local church. He possessed an understanding of the Scriptures (Acts 22:3) that he acknowledged to be subject to correction and that he was able to communicate to others (Acts 9:20ff.; 17:22; 19:9–10). Paul believed the local church possessed all the resources both to evangelize its locality and to have an authentic perception of issues of doctrine and discipline. He himself was accountable to the church at Antioch, the Council of Jerusalem and even 'his' congregations in various parts of the world (Acts 14:27; 15:12).

A CONTEMPORARY PERSPECTIVE

A new approach to world mission has forced itself upon the Western Church in the last forty years, without denying the validity of the earlier approach. It is similarly based on Christ's commission to the Twelve, but this time as recorded in John 20:19–23. It reminds us that walking the way of the cross is of the essence of all discipleship (v. 20; cf Mark 8:34; Gal 2:20) and that sharing the weakness, vulnerability and suffering of Christ is of the essence of all mission (v. 21). It focuses on the weakness rather than the power of the missionary and puts a higher emphasis on collaboration and partnership, with one another and with the Holy Spirit (v. 22). Mission is no longer from 'us' to 'them,' whoever 'we' and 'they' might be. It recognizes that the missionary is as much a recipient of the *Missio Dei* as Peter was at the time of his 'conversion' when confronted by the work of God in the Gentile Cornelius. And today the new leadership in mission is to be found in "the poor, the marginalized, the powerless and the oppressed."[1] This has become a decisive corrective to all paternalistic and one-directional mission. It not only condemns the errors of the past; it also constructs a new, no less biblical, model for the future. This is convincingly shown by Sherron Kay George in a truly significant article published in 2002.[2] What is more, this new model has decisive implications for selection and training. "Missionaries must be reinvented, re-imagined and retooled" (54). And although George is thinking of mission from the Western churches to the rest of the world, her insights apply equally—perhaps more so—to those serving in the mission fields of Western Europe and North America.

George invites us to consider some provocative and imaginative New Testament images. First, like the prodigal son, we Western "missionaries must 'come to ourselves' and penitently admit to the non-Western world, we 'have sinned against heaven and before you' and are 'no longer worthy to be called missionaries' . . . Our sisters and brothers . . . will be as compassionate and forgiving as the Father in the parable and will welcome us to the table . . . The Church . . . must repent of all gospel reductionism resulting from our exaggerated individualism and desire to control . . . and must move against the current of our culture" (55).

Second, Jesus sent the Twelve out like beggars. "We may prepare and take our own bread with us, or we may, in the spirit of Jesus, take no bread for the journey (Mark 6:8) . . . Unless we believe that those to whom we go have some bread themselves, and unless we trust that they will share their bread with us, our journey will be a travesty of the Christian mission" (57). Even Jesus acknowledged that he needed the bread which the crowd could supply (Mark 6:38). "The most appropriate image of the missionary today is one who restores and is restored by the wholeness of the body of Christ (1 Cor 12:12–27)" (58). As long ago as 1912 Roland Allen wrote: "We have done everything for them, but very little with them. We have done everything for them except give place to them."[3]

1. Woodward et al., "Changing Face of the Church," 49.
2. George, "Quest," 51–63. The quotations in this section are drawn from this article.
3. Allen, *Missionary Methods*, 184.

Third, this means giving place to, and embracing, those who are alien, and even hostile to, our culture. This is not merely a corollary of the Gospel but is of its essence (cf. Paul's *mysterion* in Eph 3:5–6) and must be advertised both on earth and in heaven (Eph 2:14–18; 3:10). One of our most valuable contributions is as a stranger on the journey (Luke 24:15ff.) or guest at table (Luke 19:7–8), dependent and respectful. Only so can we reflect what God is like. Those who engage in the mission of Christ in the twenty first century will need to dissociate themselves explicitly from the unilateral ideologies that have grown up within the Western world, still often regarded as "Christendom."

Fourth, no one can be a missionary without being first a follower, a disciple, an observer. It is often supposed that leaders should be proactive; but the New Testament pattern is predominantly reactive, whether through the constant modification of apostolic plans, or the Twelve's experience of being continually corrected, or the passivity of Jesus in the passion narrative (cf. W. H. Vanstone's, *The Stature of Waiting*). Here the image is that of Mary (Luke 10:39) "resisting the temptation of our goal-driven, multi-task, Western culture . . . [and] assuming the role of followers, listeners . . . and learners in the global Church" (62). Is this the "only one thing" that is needful for the missionary? This was a feature of the old training model of supervision by a mentor, and today needs to become a permanent habit of life and ministry. George goes on to quote Claude Labrunie: "'It is not biblically possible . . . that the rich church should have the same autonomy as poor churches . . . The poor churches are the Christ for the rich sister.'"[4]

Much of the above is actually not new at all. The New Testament is full of it. Second Cor 4:7–12 is described by Lesslie Newbigin "as almost a classic definition of mission [that] has been (as far as I know) almost completely ignored in missiological writing . . . It is as [Paul] actually participates in the passion of Jesus that he can be the bearer of the risen life of Jesus."[5] This is echoed in 2 Cor 12:5–10, where his "thorn in the flesh" brings him to the end of his resources, and he finds he is like Christ going the way of the Cross. He is "content with a life of weakness, insult, hardship, persecution and distress, all for Christ's sake; for when I am weak, then I am strong," because it is here that God's power is made manifest. The programmatic text of Luke's Gospel in chapter 4:18 uses the word *apostellō* twice—once of Christ and once of "the broken victims"—both are the supremely effective

---

4. Labrunie, "Poor as Christ for the Church," 95.
5. WCC, *Mission*, 24.

apostles of God's mission. Most clearly of all, the humiliation of Christ in incarnation and death has to be the model for his followers (Phil 2:5). Recognition and acceptance of these images of mission is radically counter-cultural but may well bring release from the competitiveness which creates senses of inadequacy and unworthiness in the most devoted disciples of Christ whom God most wants to use.

A GLANCE AT HISTORY

Two hundred years ago, graduation from the universities of Oxford and Cambridge (known collectively as Oxbridge) was generally regarded as sufficient training for ordination in the Church of England. This was sometimes supplemented by a sort of apprenticeship under an experienced mentor. However, the Church Missionary Society recognised the need to train its recruits (who were not Oxbridge graduates) in its own college, which it established in Islington, London in 1825. It offered basic theological studies and also the theoretical and practical missiology needed for its specialist ministry. The first principal of another institution, St. John's College, Highbury (also in Islington), saw the CMS college as the model for his own, founded in 1863 (the forerunner of St John's College, Nottingham). The two colleges developed strong links, both being within the parish of St. Mary's Islington. The bishops of the Church of England began to set up colleges along the same lines for the non-graduate ordinands whom they desperately needed to swell the depleted ranks of the parochial clergy.

The virtues and the weaknesses of this kind of residential training were clear to many of the bishops from the start and both are still with us today. Imagine this: young women and men, captivated by the person of Jesus and on fire to share the Good News with the world, offer for ministry and begin the training process. They develop in community with like-minded colleagues and learn the "language of Zion." Some develop academic gifts, others follow a more ecclesiastical route, but both are in danger of losing the cutting edge which was integral to their original vocation. They become at home in the academy or in the cloister, but not in the street. Their new language doesn't sound street-wise any more. It attracts fewer people, and the more the church declines, the more inclined they are to find contentment and personal value in joining the clergy club. Recognise this picture? These tendencies were noticed back in the nineteenth century. Some bishops felt that, although many college students did better academically than

Oxbridge men (all ordinands were male at that time), their training was too narrow. "No man is a good theologian who is nothing but a theologian. The education of a theological college is necessarily a class education. This is the last thing to be desired for the clergy of our church," remarked Bishop Bickersteth of Ripon in 1867. The Principal of St. John's Highbury likewise argued that non-graduates have an understanding of the mind and the religious needs of the laity and would serve the church better than many graduates. In the words of the principal of St. Aidan's Birkenhead, "It is in the homes of sickness and distress [in Liverpool], amid scenes of suffering and want…that the practical training which the students obtain . . . is one of the most valuable features of their college course."[6]

All this was echoed by John V. Taylor a century later: "The ideal shape of the church is such as will provide the 'one-another-ness' [of small groups gathered and led by the Spirit] with the least possible withdrawal of Christians from their corporateness with their fellow-men in the world."[7]

IMPLICATIONS FOR TRAINING

Much of the ordination training process, at least in the Church of England, has strayed from the principles outlined above. When the Church currently selects people to train for ministry, the Christian community from which they come, or the candidate's family, may have little or no role to play. The procedure may be captive to our cultural individualism, with the emphasis on the individual candidate and recommendations by individual clergy. Despite this, however, it is possible to counter individualism provided that the experience of training occurs in a residential seminary that cultivates and develops a clear sense of community. Where theological students from non-Anglican backgrounds self-select to attend seminary, the individualistic trajectory becomes even more clear.

Moreover, a seminary community typically consists of like-minded people with roughly similar backgrounds. Many will be graduates who have held a professional position in their former occupations. They feel at home in an environment where academic study, assignments and assessment are the norm. What is more, it is an inevitable feature of the history of theological and mission training colleges that they gradually put more and more emphasis on academic performance. The Church Missionary

6. Quotations in this section are drawn from Dowland, *Anglican*.

7. Taylor, *Go-Between*, 148.

Society college, for example, grew in numbers and in academic reputation, so that by the eighteen seventies the students, decked out in cap and gown in imitation of universities, sat the Preliminary Examinations in Theology for Oxford and Cambridge—and twenty years later gained more first class degrees than any other college. Nevertheless, the highly trained often failed in the practical missionary task, while it was the untrained who became heroes of mission. Poorly educated candidates might outstrip their Oxbridge colleagues in mission leadership. Students of CMS and the new Anglican colleges often held an advantage over graduates in maturity, experience of life, and spirituality.

It is beyond doubt that academic expertise is needed, at least for some, so that all may profit from their wisdom, but it too easily becomes the criterion of success—yet there is no correlation at all between academic success and effective ministry.

When John Goldingay was Principal of St John's College, Nottingham, he actively advocated several ventures that attempted to take candidates for ordination out of their comfort zones and immerse them in more challenging environments. John may not have had hands-on involvement in these, but he gave them his whole-hearted support. And in doing so, he showed vision in leadership.

By way of illustration, the Urban Theology Project (UTP) at St John's required most students, in the middle of their two or three-year program, to spend between six and ten weeks outside college in inner-city Nottingham. The UTP built upon students' prior experience plus two terms of basic theological study by inducing continuing theological reflection in a particular socio-economic context. The aim was not to train people to be urban specialists but to train them for all ministry and mission by immersion in one specific context to which they must learn to relate—just as one learns how to interpret the whole Bible by studying a few specific texts as models.

The UTP involved six elements:

1. A two-day supervised community placement among disadvantaged people located at, for example, an Advice Center, Community Health Center, Drug Dependency Unit, Homelessness Center, Disability Center;

2. Sunday with an inner-city church minister for observation and understanding;

3. One day with people of another faith;
4. Twenty hours of lectures and seminars on detailed study of a biblical text, to discover how, or if, theology could relate to urban deprivation;
5. Twenty hours of lectures and seminars on social theology, to provide frameworks for understanding the urban experiences and writing reflections on them;
6. Sessions on key urban issues, e.g., racism, policing, job creation, inter-faith.

Time was made available for networking urban areas, for support group meetings, for corporate meals and worship, for a thirty six hour day off, and above all for space in welcome contrast to the breathless internal college schedule. Unfamiliar, and sometimes uncomfortable, urban settings drew the students together in experience of community, and they probably learned as much from one another as from their appointed teachers. They certainly learned from their supervisors in secular community organisations, usually non-Christian. They saw how unpredictable and hazardous urban living could be. All this modelled the realities of mission. The UTP aimed to transform and enrich their theological reflection, asking them tough questions they would never have met if they had stayed within the comfort zone of their own culture. There were no ready-made answers. They had to think hard.

In the UTP, students took responsibility for their own learning and timetables. The institutions of the college were not in control. One student decided to go on holiday to Portugal with a group of Hindus, another joined a Qur'an study group; both encountered Good News in new and surprising ways, just as Peter did in the home of a Roman centurion. They listened—and learned.

John not only gave his support to the UTP; with Ann, he worshipped regularly in an urban church in one of the poorest areas of the city of Nottingham, where they offered their own ministry but also received much from that indigenous congregation. Since he has been based in Pasadena, he has done exactly the same.

Another illustration was the example given to students to face challenges outside their comfort zones by cross-cultural placements. In this, St John's College was simply following the example set by the Henry Martyn Trust in Cambridge which has for many years awarded bursaries to enable theological students and others to spend a period of time immersed in cultures different than their own. These might be overseas, but could equally well be with a black-led church in Europe, or on the frontiers of sectarian division in Northern Ireland. Such placements required careful supervision and, on the part of students, a presentation of their experiences and the theological reflections arising from them. The unfamiliarity of the context brought spiritual and intellectual challenges which compelled a level of reflection far more profound than was possible within the residential seminary scene. Such reflection is rarely comfortable but is likely to result in long-term change and an ability to face new social challenges with equanimity. A black Pentecostal student discovered in his African placement the roots of his own cultural world-view which he now recognised for the first time.

"If we only experience Christian communities, we do not know what the Gospel is. It is communication of news to those who do not know it. We only understand it as we are involved in so communicating it . . . I have never felt the reality of the Gospel more fully than when I was regularly involved in a ministry to the condemned prisoners in Madurai Jail. Only where the Gospel is really being received as NEWS can you understand what it is."[8]

The culture of 'Christendom' is a culture of power. But as the concept loses its meaning for wider society, the faithful remnant finds it no longer commands unquestioning respect or an instant hearing. It is not surprising if this remnant turns in on itself and develops an inner life focussed on its own spiritual and intellectual growth. It prides itself on its ecclesiastical, or perhaps biblical, orthodoxy. At its bleakest, it can become a clerical club. For some bishops in times past this was a desirable aim: the Bishop of London in 1859 felt many clergy identified too closely with the non-ministerial world and hoped colleges would help them "break off worldly habits and get free of the entanglements of worldly society."[9] Thus a radical question presses upon the contemporary Church: Is this the way the Church of England (and others) are destined to follow, and is this encouraged by their training patterns? Can such Churches effectively bear witness to the good news for the poor?

The question is not new. It was anticipated and highlighted in City-Wise, an intensive consultation on urban mission training held at St John's

8. Newbigin, *Good Shepherd*, 61.
9. Dowland, *Anglican*, 160.

College in 1990. It featured an international team of urban practitioners from the USA, South Africa, India and Australia, as well as Britain. By the end of the second day, however, a degree of boredom had set in. One session was taken up by abstract, conceptual debate where people seemed more interested in scoring points than learning. Another plenary session aimed to identify key issues but finished with an increasingly indigestible list of some thirty issues on a flipchart, leading to tedious attempts at definition. But suddenly an Indian member of the Evangelical Coalition for Racial Justice, a casual visitor, dropped a bombshell: "Where are the Blacks?" he asked. They were not there. They had been invited, but had declined to join a consultation whose agenda had been set beforehand. They had been asked to play the game, but not to change the rules. They had decided it was not worth it.

The discussion that followed in that same session was neither abstract nor tedious. It was electric, as the participants realised that it was they who had the time and the money and the agenda for such a consultation, yet it was only the Blacks who had an effective ministry in our cities, and they weren't there. There followed recriminations and apologies, all traumatic. But was our consultation about to sink into a morass of bitterness and division?

No, the people for the hour came from South Africa and had seen it all before. Malusi Mpumlwana and Caesar Molebatsi pointed out that it is in such areas of struggle that human activity has to be structured and organized. We have different cultures, different wisdoms. We may have failed to include the most significant urban group, but at least we can learn. In the future we need to plan—and let the Black leaders plan. Do this separately by all means, provided we do it in structured relationship with one another. But blurring distinctions will lead to assimilation which disables people and is counter-productive. It is only by recognising and celebrating the differences in our cultures that we are each enabled to bring Christ's varied gifts to the service of his mission. It is, in Andrew Walls' vivid imagery, "as though Christ himself grows as he penetrates"[10] new cultures who see life differently and understand Christ in new ways. This wisdom drawn from experience governed the rest of the Consultation—and probably saved it!

This is why debating theological concepts with like-minded colleagues, fine-tuning our academic accuracy, and refining our ecclesiastical orthodoxy all have their place, but will never be the cutting edge of mission.

10. Walls, "Old Athens and New Jerusalem," 148.

More risks must be taken than this: risks (such as mixing with Muslims and Hindus) that might at times even pose disturbing questions about our own faith.

Perhaps not every trainee minister has the freedom for such explorations. But at least they should always have their feet firmly planted in the world outside the Church. The last dream for theological training John Goldingay had (I think) before leaving Nottingham was of mixed-mode training. This involved those preparing for ordination remaining in their home region, and beginning to exercise ministry among the very people from whom they have come who (hopefully) played a part in recommending them for training. But the program also required them to alternate this with blocks of time in St. John's College, learning, worshipping and living in that community. At first, it seemed a risky departure from normal patterns of training, but it soon became evident that its structured transience offered a clear experiential advantage: the enclosed world of the seminary could never take these students over because it no longer possessed the power to abstract them wholly from the world they knew and to which they were called. For those involved—teachers and students alike—this was a new way of doing theology in which this 'alternating immersion' both tested the theology learned in the classroom and allowed, in turn, this theology to challenge the Church life they experienced. Mixed mode learning provided a virtuous circle of mutual feedback.

We began this chapter by observing that the churches of the West are struggling to get into mission, rather than maintenance, mode. Indeed, we might go so far as to venture that if they fail to become authentically missional, with all that implies, they will simply fail. Marshall McLuhan has shown us that "the medium is the message." Consequently, as we have seen, until the Churches acknowledge that how people learn is as important as what they learn, the message of the Good News will be lost. And central to this, in turn, is a humble acceptance that we need to learn from the poor in uncongenial settings. As we do so, it will become part of our ministerial formation and a lifelong habit that will revitalize both the Church and its members.

12

The Gift of Community
Social Theology for the Twenty-First Century

Francis Bridger

John Goldingay and I are both children of the same social era. He was born in the middle of World War II; I was born only six years after it ended. We are offspring of mid-twentieth century Britain, with all that implies. We grew up at the height of Western modernity confident in itself and its achievements: the triumph of science, the arrival of the welfare state, sustained economic progress, 'progressive' social reforms, enhanced personal freedoms and an assumed future narrative that promised more of the same.

In the second decade of the twenty first century it all looks very different. For one thing, we are now in the throes of postmodernity (or perhaps even post-postmodernity) where many of the assumptions of modernity have either been undermined or have collapsed altogether. Where now is the glad bright morning of permanent economic growth, social welfare and emancipation? And as for value-free, objective science as the only road to truth, the easy confidence of the nineteen fifties and sixties has given way to the suspicion that science has no final answers at all; or, even worse, has been responsible for some of the most horrific events of the last hundred years.

All this is by way of leading into an essay which seeks to offer some reflections upon a central theme that has emerged time and again in the experience of modernity and postmodernity, and which John comments upon in a number of places in his writings, particularly in the third volume of his Old Testament Theology, *Israel's Life*. This theme can be summed up as the *tension between individualism and community in periods of rapid social change*. Or to put it another way: how can individuals relate to one another in community when the very notion of community is under threat?

HEY DUDE, WE'RE ALL INDIVIDUALS AREN'T WE?

The late twentieth century and the first decade of the twenty-first have seen the full flowering of individualism. However, like so many terms in academic discussion (I do not say this pejoratively), it remains a highly contested concept. Not only is it used to *describe* a state of affairs, it is also employed *evaluatively*. And not infrequently, the second is smuggled into the first. Depending on the philosophical viewpoint of the user, individualism can be seen as desirable ("She's a real character; she's a true individualist"), or as something to be avoided ("He's only concerned with number one"). For our purposes, however, I wish to distinguish between two sorts of individualism.

The first is what we might call *personal/existential*. This sees the individual person as the seat of ultimate value, the final arbiter in all things. People are understood first and foremost as individual beings who make their own choices and decisions, who cannot be dictated to by others, who determine their own lives, who by nature possess certain innate rights and freedoms. They cannot be reduced to mere cogs in a machine. Moreover, on this version individuals must take ethical priority over the collective in all but the most extreme circumstances (such as war). Individual freedoms and rights may be subordinated to those of the community if, and only if, individuals judge it is in their interest to do so, or when their security is threatened by external forces that require collective action. We may, as a matter of fact and necessity, be persons-in-relationship, but the community is nothing greater than the sum of individuals who have chosen to associate together for freely agreed purposes; the collective will is merely the expression of the aggregate of individual wills. Community derives from, and is dependent upon, individual consents for its authority. "The collectivity exists for the sake of the individual, and not the individual for the sake of the collectivity."[1]

A second kind of individualism has been described as *possessive*. At first sight, this label might be interpreted as already containing a moral judgment. But in the specialist sense in which it was originally coined, and has been developed, this is not the case. In essence, it refers to the way in which Western philosophers of individualism, such as John Locke, moved from viewing individualism as a philosophical or metaphysical notion about persons in the abstract to seeing individuals as actual persons possessing rights, one of which was the right to "mix" their labour with nature to produce goods and services which they then possessed as extensions of themselves that nobody else could claim. This right may seem self-evident to us today, but in an era that still contained remnants of feudal or royal control of individuals' lives and circumstances, the theory of possessive individualism provided a powerful intellectual motor for social change. Put simply, on this account individuals possess rights by virtue of being human and thereby have the right to acquire and own property and possessions. Nobody (including the State) has the right to deprive them of these without consent.[2] This goes a long way to explaining the ideological resistance to government taxation evident, for example, in some sections of the Republican Party in the USA.

Despite their problems, both concepts of individualism hold considerable attractions. For one thing, they articulate a coherent basis for individual freedom that anyone who has lived in a totalitarian or authoritarian state will recognise as a godsend. For another, they make clear that individuals are, in Immanuel Kant's words, "Ends in themselves and not means only," thus establishing that individuals cannot be others' playthings. And by establishing an intellectual justification for the notion of universal human rights, they provide a powerful weapon in the fight against cruelty and atrocity.

But there is a dark side also to these two views of individualism: the phenomenon of consumerism. Much has been written about this, but perhaps the most pertinent comment is that of Philip Sampson: "Once established, a culture of consumption is quite undiscriminating and everything

---

1. Bridger, *Counselling*, 103.

2. On this view taxation is a necessary evil, not simply because it reduces individuals' wealth but because it constitutes an infringement of their right to own and use their labor and its fruits as they wish.

becomes a consumer item, including meaning, truth and knowledge."[3] Sociologist Zygmunt Bauman further notes that because Western societies have moved from being producer societies to consumer societies, the measure of worth for individuals has shifted from what they produce to what they consume—and woe betide those who do not have the means to consume. They are caught in a twofold trap: on one hand they are assigned low social worth, especially if unemployed or on welfare; on the other, they find themselves forever reaching for the goods and services they cannot afford but which they are expected to have if they are to be counted as worthwhile members of consumer society.

Consumerism also swallows up the self, so that we end up questing after experiences, each more potent than the last, as the self goes in search of the ultimate hit. And since the driving force behind consumerism is the need to turn everything into a commodity designed to deliver instant gratification, it follows that notions of selfhood must be subject to the same imperial process. The individual is seen not as a reflective, feeling, thinking, relating being (as in the models offered by Enlightenment philosophers) but (in Bauman's words), as a "harvester of sensations." The purpose of the individual self is to receive pleasure (now defined as a right), and both mind and body are viewed as no more than instruments to this end. Given that humans are competitive beings, moreover, "One is condemned to live forever in doubt as to whether one's own sensations 'match the standard', and—more poignantly still—whether they reach the peak that other people are capable of climbing."[4] It is little wonder, then, that consumerist societies live in a constant state of psychological and economic anxiety, for who knows how long this frantic existence can be sustained?

The condition charted by Bauman and others describes a world in which individuals are profoundly alienated from themselves and from one another. "The individual is the default state of life."[5] Personhood is defined as individualistic self-fulfilment, and we are invited (nay, required) to see ourselves first and foremost as acquisitive consumers. Luther's description of sin as *curvatus in se* (turned in upon oneself) seems apt.

Individualism, in any of the senses outlined above, poses sizeable challenges for the practise of community. In critiquing them, theology says loudly and clearly that the idea of individuals as abstract entities, separated

3. Quoted in Lyon, *Postmodernity*, 61.
4. Bauman, *Fragments*, 117.
5. Goldingay, *Life*, 20.

from their life contexts and webs of relationships as if they were mere theoretical constructs, is deeply flawed. Not only does it reduce persons to conceptualisations, it threatens the practise of community necessary for human beings simply to be human. "As a person, I am what I am only in relation to other persons. My human being is a relational being. My personal unity is fulfilled in community."[6] In theological language, to be made in the image of God is to be made for community.

Alongside these philosophical analyses of individualism, the British writer Philip Blond has offered an intriguing and penetrating analysis of contemporary social fragmentation. Although he writes about the specifically British context, his analysis can be extended to other Western societies.

Blond begins by offering a narrative of community as having been undermined from both the political left and right. The twentieth century politics of the left, he argues, were concerned with reducing inequality and poverty, empowering the poor and disenfranchised, and enlarging economic freedoms for the worst off. These were (and continue to be) laudable aims. But in doing so, the left assumed that only the power of the centralised State could act (in John Kenneth Galbraith's famous phrase) as a "countervailing power" over and against overmighty capitalism. Entrenched business and other vested interests could be overcome only through collective action by government. And so the combination of governmental intervention in the economy and the establishment of the welfare state came into being, to be continued by governments of the left and right for three decades. In Britain, the vast social experiment launched by the Labour government of 1945–51 involved the creation of universal state health provision, universal state welfare, and state owned industries such as coal, steel and railways. In the USA, Franklin D. Roosevelt's New Deal program of the 1930s pointed in the same direction (though it never went so far as the British program) and can be seen even now (so the argument runs) in the policies of the Obama administration towards healthcare, business regulation and the environment.

In Britain, contends Blond, the effect of this was to create over time a vast centralised bureaucracy responsible for every area of people's lives. By the nineteen seventies, no significant aspect of human life from birth to death fell outside the purview of government. It even took responsibility for determining the individual wage rates of workers through what was known as "incomes policy." The result was that, as government increasingly

---

6. Ware, *Unity*, 206.

intervened in the lives of individuals and communities, the process of disempowerment of a civil society based on voluntary associations set in. "Local requirements, organisations or practices were gradually ignored and rendered redundant."[7]

By contrast, the politics of the right in the nineteen eighties witnessed a rediscovery of anti-collective individualism. Margaret Thatcher in Britain and Ronald Reagan in the USA espoused a philosophy (though not always the practise) of limited government and the importance of individuals as economic actors. State control of industries was rolled back, the welfare state pruned and the market promoted as the engine of economic recovery. Henceforth, individuals were to be re-empowered through participation in a property-owning democracy. The market and the ballot box would march hand in hand. Democratic individualism, rather than democratic collectivism, was to be the way forward.

Unfortunately, Blond argues, the pendulum swing from left to right produced not a revival of civil society and a resurgence of community, but a further diminishment of it. Whereas thirty five years of an ever-growing centralised government had ""made the populace a supplicant citizenry dependent on the state rather than themselves,"[8] the effect of the Thatcher (and by implication, Reagan) philosophy was to produce a no less disempowered population: "Instead of popular capitalism with open and free markets, what we got instead was a capitalism captured by concentrations of capital and a market dominated by vested interest and dominance of the already wealthy."[9] The witches' brew of "modern consumer capitalism" had come fully into flower.

Blond presents a powerful, and in many ways persuasive, analysis. He offers a narrative that endorses neither the left nor the right, and on closer inspection, affirms insights from both. Above all, he reminds us that even the best-intentioned social and political policies always produce unintended consequences that have far-reaching effects on the nature of civil society and community. But as we reflect on this, we find ourselves facing another question: what kind of theological response can be made beyond simply asserting in a general way that anthropologically, theologically and practically, community lies at the heart of a Christian understanding of the image of God in humanity? It is to this we now turn.

7. Blond, *Tory*, 15.
8. Ibid.
9. Ibid., 18.

COMMUNITY: GIFT AND TASK

Much theological writing about community has centred on the social and political significance of human beings as persons who are formed in, and by, relationships with others. The revival of interest in the Trinity as a model for social life has contributed significantly to this. Indeed, in an essay published in 1992, I argued for the "corporate motifs" of the image of God, covenant people, body of Christ, kingdom of God, incarnation and Trinity as supplying "a radical critique both of individualism and of collectivism."[10] However, in what follows I would like to suggest an additional motif, namely that of *gift*.

Gift is one of those words that Christians recognise as fundamental to their faith. Every dimension of faith is a matter of gift: human life, salvation, redemption, reconciliation with God—all are grace gifts to humanity which cannot be earned through our striving, but only received gratefully by faith. This is the good news of the Christian gospel: everything is gift. The principle is so fundamental that it must be seen as structuring our whole understanding of life. Gift is the governing theological concept that overarches all others.

We can quickly see how this bears upon our discussion of community. For if gift lies at the core of what it means to be human and to be made in the image of God, it follows that since we are created to be communal beings, community itself is a gift. "The human being is made for gift, which expresses and makes present his transcendent dimension."[11]

The concept of gift as applied to community has received one of its fullest expositions in Pope Benedict XVI's 2009 encyclical *Caritas in Veritate* (Charity in Truth), applauded by Roman Catholics and non-Catholics alike as a decisive contribution to discussions of theology and social justice. That it was welcomed by 175 leading evangelicals in the USA is itself an indication of its significance beyond the Roman Catholic Church.[12]

The encyclical repays careful reading. But for our purposes, it is worth noting four points about gift that offer foundational principles from which we might develop a theology of community.

---

10. Bridger, "Biblical Theology and the Politics of the Centre."

11. Benedict XVI, *Caritas*, par. 34. All quotations from *Caritas* in the following section are taken from this location; cf. *Charity*, 66–69.

12. See http://www.cpjustice.org/doingthetruth.

Firstly, gift is built into the nature of human existence. It is woven into the fabric of creation. Gift "is present in our lives in many different forms" though we may fail to discern these because the notion of gift has been overlain by self-centeredness. By definition, this is the antithesis of gift. Consequently, the essential nature of human life as gift will "often go unrecognized because of a purely consumerist and utilitarian view of life." This chimes with what we have noted earlier from the writings of sociologists about consumerism and individualism.

Secondly, the principle of gift is not merely a useful anthropological fact or a form of convenient social cement: it reminds us that God is with us and that human beings are created for something greater than themselves. "The human being is made for gift, which expresses and makes present his transcendent dimension . . . It takes first place in our souls as a sign of God's presence in us, a sign of what he expects from us." This last phrase is crucial for it makes clear that the principle of gift carries with it an obligation towards others—a key move, as we shall see, in the application of the concept to community life.

Thirdly, since gift as a fact of creation originates in the graciousness of God, it reflects his overflowing gratuity towards humanity: "Gift by its nature goes beyond merit, its rule is that of superabundance." Once more, the encyclical deftly points us in the direction of a concept of community that goes beyond individualism and the language of rights.

Fourthly, the logical culmination of this theology is that we are called by God to work for communities that express the *nature* of gift (the encyclical uses the language of vocation at this point to suggest that gift is something God actively wills for us). In other words, community should be seen as embodying God's calling to act and live as those called into being by grace: "The human community that we build by ourselves can never, purely by its own strength, be a fully fraternal community, nor can it overcome every division and become a truly universal community. The unity of the human race, a fraternal communion transcending every barrier, is called into being by the word of God-who-is-Love."

Taken together, these four points supply a powerful theological rationale for developing an ethical basis for community that offers something radically different from the assumptions of individualism we observed above. It is to the implications of this that we must now turn.

MUTUALITY AND RECIPROCITY

Is community possible on the principle of gift? At first sight, the idea might seem absurdly idealistic. But when we think about it, societies operate on the gift principle all the time. In doing so, however, they modify the concept of free gift with two further notions: mutuality and reciprocity. Both of these imply that giving in a social context is multi-directional in that although individuals give gifts sometimes in the expectation of return, even where this is not the case, the recipient may choose to reciprocate either out of a sense of obligation or simply out of gratitude. Either way, a pattern of mutual giving is established (think of Christmas gifts) which comes to underlie all kinds of social relationships. Thus is the principle of gift embedded into the structures of society.

Whether a community is built on the notion of *free* gift or gift *exchange*, the result is a social fabric that is much more tightly woven than the free rein of individualistic consumerism would allow. It is the nexus of gift, mutuality and reciprocity that lies at the heart of an alternative vision of community to that identified by Bauman and others as the paradigm of postmodernity.

How this is worked out in differing cultures and societies will inevitably be a question of pragmatics. There can be no single definitive blueprint. Nonetheless, I would suggest that one implication of all that we have said so far is that the practise of community must necessarily involve a combination of mutual action by individuals on one hand (through acts of personal kindness, voluntary associations and charities), and collective action by government on the other. Both are necessary to fulfil the God-given mandate to create and sustain community. Those on the left who remain sceptical about non-state organisations must (as they have increasingly come to recognize) accept that the vocation to gift that *Caritas in Veritate* speaks about is a calling from God *both* to individuals acting as free persons making free choices *and* to the state as the representative of those individuals considered collectively. Those on the right who doubt the value or propriety of state action must accept that the state, too, is called by God to act on behalf of *all* its members in empowering (economically and politically) the poor and vulnerable. They remain members of the community too.

We began by observing that contemporary Western societies are in danger of becoming empty moral shells through the impact of a consumerist form of individualism. Philip Blond's analysis reminds us that the actions of both left and right have undermined community in ways that we have only now begun to appreciate. In Pope Benedict's encyclical, we see a theological articulation of gift that moves us beyond individualistic self-fulfilment to a realization that there is such a thing as the common good. And thus we are pointed towards a moral basis for the actions of individuals-in-community. Surely now it can be seen that notions both of the all-powerful state and the minimalist state are philosophically and theologically flawed? Neither offers an adequate assessment of the human condition, and neither does justice to the Christian vision of human beings as called to live as members bound together in solidarity. Only through a rediscovery of the profound connections between community, vocation, gift and God will this be so.

13

To the Man in the Pink Shirt

Anne Long

Dear John,

I don't think I've ever written you a letter before. Christmas cards, yes; emails, occasionally; phone calls, mostly from my study to yours at St John's College, Nottingham. Now, thirty or so years later, an invitation has arrived to write about you. But it's turning out to be a letter to you instead of a conventional essay because I want it to feel personal.

    I'm in my late seventies now and my memory isn't as good as it was, but I clearly remember our first meeting. It was in 1972 when I came to Nottingham to be interviewed as a tutor at St John's. I knew it was an all-male staff, and I'd expected a formal group of sober-suited men in clerical collars. How wrong can you be? Principal Michael Green's study was the gathering place for a group of men but there wasn't a dog collar to be seen or a vestige of interview sobriety. Instead, there was a riot of rollicking laughter. "And this is John Goldingay," Michael said as he did the rounds of introductions. "He teaches Old Testament and Hebrew." Dark floppy hair, broad Birmingham accent, shrewd, dark eyes and a pink striped shirt. I can't remember what you said but you let out an explosive laugh, more of a shriek really. Later, I would hear that laugh coming from your study, or in the dining-room or faculty meetings. Your quick-witted humour often lifted the atmosphere.

I've been asked to write about you from a spirituality point of view. This sounds rather mystical and other-worldly, and I wasn't at all sure how to set about it. Fortunately, the term itself which formerly implied a distinction between the spiritual and material levels of our human lives, has now shifted away from this dualistic compartmentalization so as to embrace the whole of our human life in all its aspects, lived in the context of relationship with God. Some of what I want to write about you fits that description well because it's your lived spirituality that has challenged, guided, comforted and helped me in ways you probably never knew. And, of course, Ann was a huge part of that. So, in writing to thank you, I'm also thanking her for the ways you've enriched me. But more of Ann later.

You once described yourself as an "enthusiast" and "imaginative" (as well as other things), and those two words in your approach to the Old Testament have meant a lot to me. In fact (confession time now) I never realised the Old Testament could be so exciting until I heard you preaching in the college chapel and engage in teaching and writing. It was not dry and dusty academic theory and speculation. You're every inch a brilliant scholar but you brought the Old Testament alive and let it speak in very immediate and contemporary ways, something I'd not experienced when I was taught the Old Testament. It was partly the language you used (blunt and down-to-earth) but also the way you brought characters to life, your pithy asides and the shades of meaning you brought out from the Hebrew.

I remember how you spoke (and later wrote) on Psalms 42 and 43, vividly bringing alive their setting amidst the drought and dry river beds of Palestine and the dreadful effects that can have on animals (in this case a deer). Then, as a pastor, you talked about prayer in those times when God feels absent. Prayer means "getting things off your chest," you said, telling God how we feel, being straight with him, as Job was, believing that God is "big enough to take it and loving enough to absorb it." You said how trouble comes to us with God's knowledge not by his oversight.

"Better a God whose mystery we cannot understand (but who has given us grounds for trusting when we cannot understand) than one whose adequacy we cannot rely on, or whose interest we cannot be sure of." So you wrote in your book *Songs from a Strange Land*.[1] That was like a word from God for me during a time of depression. It offered renewing hope and prayer. Thank you, John.

---

1. Goldingay, *Songs in a Strange Land*, 75.

Conversations at the Edges of Things

Then there were the titles of your books. When I alighted upon *Men Behaving Badly* I wondered what on earth this had to do with being David Allan Hubbard Professor of Old Testament at Fuller Theological Seminary. But the chapter headings hooked me: "The Brown-Eyed Handsome Man," "The Man Who Loved (too?) Much," "The Replacement Brown-eyed Handsome Man," "The Man Who Died Cold," etc. You brought to life the characters in 1 and 2 Samuel, gave me many new insights, and posed searching questions about the nature of leadership and how it works out in relation to God. You never avoided or glossed over the hard questions but encouraged us to wrestle with them, just as you yourself did.

A few years ago, a vicar who was also a friend presented me with a very heavy parcel. He knew that you and I had been colleagues at St. John's and he'd read your books. When I unwrapped volume one of your *Old Testament Theology* (940 pages, no less), I was a bit nonplussed. Of course I thanked him, but I was also wondering if I would ever read it now that I was retired and catching up on unread novels. One day I opened it and saw in the Preface that you'd written much of it sitting on your apartment's patio with Ann, listening to CDs (it always puzzled me that you could do all these things simultaneously). Because I'd once stayed with you and Ann in Pasadena, I could picture the patio, your table, and Ann's chair. Those fragments of memory led me on. You said you wanted to see what the stories tell us of who God is and who we are. Your focus on narrative grabbed me, as did the way you progressed from God Began, through his Promising, Delivering, Accommodating, Wrestling, Preserving, and Sending. I warmed to your thinking about God having a "vision" for the world rather than the fixed plan of a "micro-manager." And your approach to creation by way of the metaphor of God "birthing" the world includes shades of meaning I'd never thought of. Then there were your little asides, as at the end of the chapter "God Wrestled" on the Exile, where you gave a very contemporary twist by saying that the Church in Europe is in exile. I'd used words like decline and diminished to describe what's happening to our churches, but exile got me thinking (and praying) in a different way. I think you promised, when you were 49 years old, that you'd write an Old Testament Theology before you died. Well, it's done now and still more spills forth from your pen (ahem, computer). Your editor noted that yours is a theology of the Old Testament that preaches. Tell him it's also influencing my praying and helping me join up head, heart and action. I think it's doing something similar for my neighbour who's into Joshua and Judges in your *Bible for Everyone* series. Thank you, John.

When I first got to know you, to be honest I found you a bit scary. In faculty meetings you spoke quickly, rationally, and decisively. I was often still trying to work out what I wanted to say long after the meeting was over! At times your bluntness and quick-fire observations felt aggressive. I remember writing you a note about this. You then came to my study, sat on a floor cushion, listened to me, and were contrite. With hindsight, I realize we were simply different temperamentally. As an introvert I felt threatened by your speed of thinking and speaking. I wish I'd done the Myers-Briggs personality test sooner than I did and realized we needed a variety of gifts to complement, rather than compete with, one another on the team! I gradually came to realize that, although sometimes volatile, you were a self-deprecating person, completely unpretentious. You called a spade a spade and were unafraid to question and challenge what you thought was shallow, but you were also kind and thoughtful. If I wanted to ask you something and you were deep in a book (which you often were), you were quick to put it aside and give generous attention.

Then there was your love of jazz and rock music. Remember how you formed your band (from which you were later squeezed out by gifted students)? You said that rock fed your relationship with God, especially in some of the tough questions you had to grapple with. You joined Ronnie Scott's jazz club, listened to Radio 1 and read the rock magazine Q. Because I came from a somewhat puritanical background, I couldn't get my head round this, and it was a foreign world to me. Also I was inhibited by the jigging-around charismatic songs we sang in chapel (whilst feeling envious of those who could actually jig around). When I read in *To The Usual Suspects* about your visit to the Nine O'Clock Service at St Thomas Crookes church, Sheffield, and how the music made your foot thump and you felt it brought together two parts of your life, that made sense. I love the punk song you wrote:

> I want music with guts as well as music to bless my soul . . .
> I've no objection to tambourines and I like the sound of a flute,
> But I also like to be driven to stamp up and down with my boot.
> Is it really impossible for rock songs to be the Spirit's fruit?

Now that got me thinking or, rather, wanting to take notice of some of what some of these song writers were saying (like Bruce Springsteen and his "Everybody's Got a Hungry Heart"). I even bought a Beatles record!

Then there was your love of film (another suspect activity in my background) and the way you reflected on questions raised by particular films, such as *Presumed Innocent*. You also said *When Harry Met Sally* was one of your favorites and it made you cry. I never saw it but, like you, I did cry in *The English Patient*, not only when the woman dies alone in the cave but also when the man who loved her carried her dead body to his plane and let out that silent scream. You thought that was a moment of 'male' emotional engagement in the film, but it certainly had me sobbing too.

Thinking of drama, do you remember the dramatized script of *Job* you wrote which Pat Travis and I produced as a dance drama in the college chapel? There were quite a few students and their spouses who took part. On each side of the chapel we had a tall pedestal. God stood on one (which was higher) and Satan on the other (which was lower). In working on it we learnt a lot more about Job, thanks to you. And, too, by what you wrote about him in *The Usual Suspects,* and how he reminded you of Princess Diana and Dodi Fayed who had everything but then lost everything. Connections like that make you catch your breath and realize that the Old Testament and its characters are not another world but the same one in which we live.

Something I valued in the same book was your insights into prayer, not only prayer in general but the ways you prayed. I knew how you prayed in public, at faculty meetings and in chapel: nothing flowery, clichéd, or long-winded but usually quite brief, matter-of-fact and to the point. I sometimes wondered, though I don't know why, how you prayed on your own. In any case you don't usually go around asking colleagues that kind of question. So I felt I knew you better when I read how you talk things over with God. You said you weren't very good at Quiet Days or spiritual retreats, and I'm not sure what you meant by that. But you did have long conversations with God on car journeys, talking things through with him, sometimes challenging him, identifying and naming your feelings to him. Was that out loud or inside yourself? And you were aware of him speaking back to you so that between you, you could clarify things. You didn't pretend with God: like the morning you woke up when Ann wasn't well and you said to God, 'I do not trust you with Ann', and even if it was going to be all right at the End, what might God let happen in the meanwhile? Thanks for examples like that which challenged me to be more direct with God.

I liked it too when, one College Quiet Day, instead of using the silent times between talks for other things, you took up the leader's suggestion to write a letter to God. You began, "I like the idea of writing to you, Father: it fulfils the function of getting it out of my head, but doing it in conversation with you, and you can comment."[2] It was all about the invitation to go to Fuller Theological Seminary, and it was a good way of spreading your thoughts and feelings before God, giving your concerns to him and being strengthened to know that this was the right way forward for you and for Ann.

And there were those intimate times in prayer like when you longed to feel arms around you and to be held, and you cried out to God and suddenly felt as if there really were arms around you and that you were being held by God in a way you'd never previously felt. Thank you for sharing personal things like that in such an unsentimental way.

During our overlapping time at St. John's, the Charismatic renewal was in full swing. You said you felt at first as if you weren't an insider because you hadn't had the experiences some people had. But then, one day, you had a mental picture concerning one of the students and it turned out to be absolutely true, though you hadn't shared it at the time. That gave you more confidence to follow your spiritual hunches. You also wrote the booklet *The Church and the Gifts of the Spirit*. Your approach was so spiritually sane. Do you remember your two-thirds rule? "Only one-third of pictures, prophecies, etc., are worth uttering, but better risk uttering the other two-thirds than miss the one-third."[3] I found that helpful.

Do you remember, too, how, in a college chapel service, you wept for a student who was going through a painful time? Your tears were not just a few silent ones trickling down your cheeks but real heartfelt sobs. That left such a deep impression on me. It was a genuine weeping with those who weep. Your emotional openness was a gift to us, challenging any macho-image of masculinity we may have had and making it look like a cardboard cut-out. Real men need the freedom to cry. Your tears helped me to be less embarrassed about my own—and there were plenty of those in my time at St John's!

I guess a lot of that gift of yours was due to Ann and the way God used her to shape you. Through her increasing illness she was a living example of vulnerability. I first knew her when she was a practising psychiatrist. I'd sometimes come across to your house on the college campus for a cup of tea with her before Steven and Mark came home from school, or to discuss

---

2. Goldingay, *To the Usual Suspects*, 190.
3. Goldingay, *Men Behaving Badly*, 79.

something connected with the pastoral counselling classes I was teaching. She had beautiful eyes which creased up when she laughed, and she could be very funny and twinkly at times. But, as multiple sclerosis took its toll, Ann's presence amongst us became a constant reminder of the vulnerability we so often try to avoid: our uncertainties, our need of others, and our frailty. John, you once said that Ann "brings these demons out into the open in such a way that they cease to be demons."[4] Indeed, they are part of being made in the image of God. Ann was a wounded healer amongst us, offering her own challenge to those preparing for ministry in the Church. Ann helped to shape me, as she did so many others in the college. Perhaps I had, until then, assumed that with someone disabled, I was in the role of giver. Wrong, because I received so much from her just as she was.

I remember the time a friend and I came to California and stayed with you for two days. The evening we arrived you said we were going out for supper. Taking the handles of Ann's wheelchair you skipped along the pavement, singing and making her chair zigzag and dance. Her eyes sparkled and she chuckled with delight as we tried to keep up with you. The next day, before leaving, we gave her some flowers and tied a balloon to her reclining chair. Her whole face lit up as we said goodbye: her smile was like the sun appearing from behind a cloud. That was the last time I saw her. But I've never forgotten that smile, for it was a parting blessing given quite gratuitously. How closely entwined our joy and pain can be.

And that's how it was on Friday July 10, 2009, at the Memorial Service of Thanksgiving for Ann in St Alban's. Steven had made a beautiful PowerPoint presentation of photographs of her life. We sang three beautifully poignant hymns: "Take my life and let it be / Consecrated Lord to Thee," and "May I run the race before me/Strong and brave to face the foe," and "I am the resurrection/I am the life."

You shared with us how, the evening before Ann died, you took her to the George Gershwin open air concert and how, the following day, as you were with her in Urgent Care, she suddenly stopped breathing and you held her, prayed for her, and gave her to God. You brought her ashes back to England and scattered them in the valley where you had spent the first night of your honeymoon. We listeners needed to hear that story so that we could complete our own memories of her. After the service I came up to give you a hug and you picked me up (six feet tall) and cried and laughed, which freed me to do the same.

4. Goldingay, *To The Usual Suspects*, 93.

Do you remember the time (it must have been at least 30 years ago) when a word from God was given to you through Tom Smail: "I will make the north wind your warmth, the snow your purity, the frost your brightness, and the night sky your illumination"? Amazing words. Again, it's the pain and joy being so close together. One of the Bible readings at Ann's Memorial Service was from Ps 73:21 to the end. Recently you sent me some comments on this: "The heart needs to be the locus of trust within us, otherwise we become embittered . . . The pressures of life may mean that we come to the end of our heart's resources; but even this need not be a catastrophe, because when our heart comes to an end, God is still its place of refuge." And you have shown me, John, how that can be fleshed out. I never heard you being bitter about the journey you were on. I never saw you at the end of your resources (at least publicly, whatever you were feeling privately). I saw a man with a big heart and a big mind who trusted God amidst the pressures of life and showed me how God can, indeed, be our place of refuge.

Thank you, John, for showing me what a truly lived spirituality looks like.

> With love from
> Anne

p.s. Do you still have a pink striped shirt? (even if not the original one!)

14

When Choristers Grow Up

Vivienne Faull

As a student at St. John's College, Nottingham in the late nineteen seventies and early eighties, I remember talking to John Goldingay about music. The conversation moved from discussing the varieties of Christian rock groups (I was about to join the Board of the Greenbelt Arts Festival and needed a tutorial) to cathedral choirs. Cathedrals were in the doldrums at the time, with declining attendance and few signs of innovation, and John hardly seemed a cathedral type, so when he told me he had been a cathedral chorister I was very surprised. I am now Dean of an English cathedral (Leicester) with responsibility, among much else, for encouraging surprising people to become choristers. This piece is about those cathedral choristers and their place in the current (I hope much livelier) cathedral context. Not always trusting my memory at the time of writing, I asked John to confirm (or deny) that he had indeed been a cathedral chorister. He responded at once: "*I confirm! I owe much of what I am to that fact!*" This essay teases out the ways in which the life of a cathedral chorister is powerfully formative, as well as the ways in which cathedrals are now including more children in that formative experience to the enrichment of the Church's life.

THE BEGINNING

Imagine this: It is a Thursday afternoon late in the school term and two hundred children aged eight to ten years are returning to their seats in Leicester cathedral after an afternoon break for refreshments. A hundred or so parents have joined them. Most of these children and adults have not been to the cathedral, or any other church, before. Some are from the range of Leicester faith communities. Many have no religious affiliation at all. There is a happy buzz: the children have had their final rehearsal after ten weeks of preparation in their schools. Now they will join the cathedral choristers for the once-a-term Evensong for the Chorister Outreach Program (COP). As the last of the children returns from the toilet, the cathedral choristers, robed in cassocks, surplices and ruffs, process into the cathedral. The watching children fall silent instantly. They observe the choristers intently, and later listen with fascination to them singing the anthem. They leave the church to the sound of our great organ and some of the loudest music they have heard that afternoon. It is a great occasion, enjoyed by all.

Two thousand children from Leicester and the county of Leicestershire have been part of the COP over two years, and the project continues to expand. Nationally, sixty thousand children have taken part in similar projects in other towns, and over three thousand teachers, supported by specialist training, continue to encourage their pupils to sing. This is one of the many ways in which cathedrals are now simultaneously at the center of ecclesiastical life, and are open to wider culture in ways parishes often find difficult.

Cathedrals have a particular place in both the history of England and in English society. They contain the seat, the *cathedra* of the diocesan bishop, and have a particular responsibility to support the bishop as he (still "he" in England) gathers the people of the locality and the diocese for worship, for prayer, for learning or for debate. The Bishop's role is rooted in worship and in mission, as is the cathedral's. As part of its worship ministry team, English cathedrals typically have a choir with a "front row" of up to twenty children and young people. What's more, this is not new: the first mention of child choristers in England is in 597 at the abbey founded by St Augustine in Canterbury. Since then the tradition has been continuous except during the English Revolution. Every English cathedral has boy choristers, and in the nineteen eighties the smaller cathedrals began additionally to recruit girls. Salisbury established a girls' choir on the same basis as the boys' choir in 1987.

Conversations at the Edges of Things

All the choristers are kept busy, *very* busy On average, over twenty services take place each week in a cathedral, with Sunday services attracting the highest numbers. Attendance at these "routine" services has doubled from one to two million in the last ten years. The decline of earlier years has been decisively reversed. Up to a third of these services will be led by the cathedral choir, and the numbers of choristers attending weekday services has doubled in the last decade. Choral Evensong remains typical of routine services, and a service from one of the cathedrals (or a university college chapel) has been broadcast weekly on BBC Radio since the nineteen thirties. In addition to these regular services there are also numerous specially arranged occasions that add around one million attenders each year. Civic and diocesan services, funerals and memorial services, weddings and baptisms dominate these, ranging from around eighty each year in the sixteen smaller cathedrals (such as Birmingham and Leicester) to one hundred and forty in the larger ones. The music sung is much more diverse, but still depends on the daily routine of rehearsals, at the heart of which is the singing of scriptural texts: the Psalms, the *Magnificat* and the *Nunc Dimittis*. Cathedral worship is thus soaked in the Word of God one way or another, a fact all too easily overlooked but nonetheless significant. Moreover, cathedral choirs of all sorts reach high, and aim for professional standards. Up to a quarter of cathedrals' expenditure is committed to this work. In recent years, beginning with Truro, cathedrals have created outreach programs as part of the national Sing Up! Scheme to provide support to local schools, many of which now have no singing provision at all.

Cathedral choirs draw on ancient tradition. The people of Israel were a singing people, the followers of Jesus and the earliest church sang songs of praise, of consolation and of credal affirmation, and the Psalms were their richest resource. This Book of Praises is the most quoted Hebrew text in the New Testament and has given the church words and forms for lament, for thanksgiving and for praise. It is no surprise that from the earliest days of the Church the Psalms were central. The Egyptian desert fathers recited the complete book daily, later monastic communities weekly (as set down by St. Benedict's rule), and the English church (using the Book of Common Prayer) monthly, with Psalm 1 beginning at Morning Prayer on the first day of the month and ending with Psalm 150 at Evening Prayer on the last day.

We know very little about how the Psalms were sung in the First or Second Temple at Jerusalem, or the earliest church musical forms, but what became the most important was the way of singing known as Gregorian

Chant, named after Pope Gregory the Great (c. 540–640). The eight "tones" of Gregorian chant and its form (intonation/recitation/cadence: recitation/cadence) reflected the form of Hebrew poetry, particularly the parallelism of the verses, the second half of each verse repeating or building or contrasting with the first half. Anglican Chant continues this form. Developed in the seventeenth and eighteenth centuries, it continues to observe the division of verses and the system of "pointing" allows the speech rhythms of Coverdale's translation of the Bible to be supported by shifts in reciting notes. It is a subtle art and remains one of the first skills choristers have to grasp. In those places where the Psalter is still sung over the course of a month, it sets the routine of life. Choristers remember the fifteenth Evening because it is the day Psalm 78 is sung, the second longest in the book, making Evensong that night longer than usual, and consequently taxis and meals need to be delayed. Archbishop Cranmer in Reformation times placed it deliberately so: with its perspective on Israel's history, it lies exactly halfway through the monthly cycle of the Psalter.

Of course, choristers sing much more than the Psalms. They will sing Canticles and anthems drawn from six centuries of church music; they will sing in more than a dozen languages; and they will often be the first to sing commissioned works. The busiest choirs are singing (either in services or rehearsal) for twenty hours per week. These are at the "ancient" cathedrals where the daily singing of services has a long history. Most have choir schools with boarding houses. But only half of cathedral choirs have such boarding houses.

Between 1877 and 1927 the Church of England established eighteen new dioceses, each with a cathedral. Choristers were recruited from local schools and weekday sung services were only introduced over time. Choristers were often educated at a distance from the cathedral, at a range of schools, travelling to the cathedral by bus or taxi. In 2010 Leicester Cathedral choristers came from eighteen different schools and the commitment of families and friends was crucial. It has been estimated that at Guildford in 1994, choristers were driven 50,980 miles between home, cathedral and school: the equivalent of twice around the world.[1] It is some commitment!

---

1. Mould, *Chorister*, 215.

Conversations at the Edges of Things

CHORISTERS HAVE TO BE GROWN UP . . .

Why do the choristers do what they do, and others support them? Of course, mostly because they enjoy it (though this was not always so, as the television journalist Jon Snow records of his time at the Pilgrim's School attended by the Winchester choristers). But what is it that they remember most?

For many it begins with dressing up. Cathedrals (and their cousins, the college chapels) know this and play out the process of "clothing" publicly: probationers are given a cassock, but are only clothed when they join the main choir at a point acknowledged liturgically with a "surplicing." This sets choristers very obviously apart. They are aware that what they wear can make them seem odd, that the clothes are anachronistic and sometimes uncomfortable. And this makes choristers fiercely defensive and proud.

James May, the motoring journalist, puts it very directly: "As a choirboy, you were required to prove yourself. And you were required to prove yourself because, as a choirboy, you wore a dress."[2]

A close second in the memories of choristers comes the music. Howard Goodall writing in "The Chorister Thing" remembers that after the "fancy frocks" the most significant part of the chorister experience was the rigorous vocal training, so voices and breathing and concentration all developed.[3] By the time they left the choir, choristers could sight read almost any piece. David Lammy, a member of the British parliament and former government minister, won a music scholarship to the King's School Peterborough and sang in the choir, discovering, he remembers, for the first time what excellence meant. He told the *Guardian* newspaper that the experience was "priceless."[4]

Lammy also spoke (in the eulogy at the funeral of one of his fellow choristers, James Adam)[5] about the experience of being the only black child in the school and developing friendships with others who were in some ways different. James had a severe stammer and sitting in class, and in cathedral alongside one another, the two boys forged a lifelong bond.

Goodall found not just friends, but a great team. Many gifted children find music making is competitive and individualistic as they face hours of

2. May, "Frocks."
3. Goodall, "Chorister Thing."
4. Lammy, "Guardian."
5. Lammy, "Extracts."

solitary practice, enter graded exams and are put on display at competitive concerts. Cathedral choirs, which produce such a special and glorious sound, achieve their distinction by working collaboratively and living communally. "We sang as a group, we played and worked and joked and fought and caught flu as a group. Collectively, we soared. There's no other word for it."

The England cricketer Alastair Cook, a chorister at St Paul's, has reflected on the experience as instilling in him the discipline he needed to excel at sport: "They were the hardest five years you could ever expect an eight to thirteen year-old to go through. It teaches you to be independent. It was bloody hard work, twenty four hours a week singing, eight to nine in the morning at choir practice, then school, then four to six for a service and more practice. The concentration was the best thing about it. You couldn't make a mistake. There were times I wished I wasn't doing it but my batting has probably got a lot of what went into the choir."

And James May wrote: "If you're in a really tight spot and all hope seems to be lost, you want to be sharing the blood-spattered shell hole with a chap who once sang the solo in Samuel Sebastian Wesley's *Blessed be the God and Father*. He's your man."[6]

It has also become evident that singing helps thinking.[7] Howard Goodall, speaking to teachers (reporting on his negotiations for *Sing Up!*), talked about the unexpected benefits singing brings for children, developing their social skills, physical wellbeing and sense of identity.[8] Above all singing enables the brain to develop. Getting the right pitch, producing a good sound, repeating a rhythm correctly, remembering words or the shape of a song accurately utilizes different parts of the brain simultaneously and this has a significant positive impact on a child's development.

Additionally, though few former choristers can find the language for it, the act of singing for many people also involves a spiritual experience. Augustine of Hippo is reported as saying, "He who sings, prays twice." In fact, these are the words of a contemporary who wrote the following: "He who sings well prays twice." What Augustine did write was even more powerful: "Those who sing praise, not only praise, but also praise joyously; those who sing praise, are not only singing, but also loving the one about whom they are singing. Or, more simply, singing belongs to one who loves."

6. May, "Frocks."
7. Welch, *Chorister*.
8. Goodall, "Singing."

Beginning in 2008, the work of the Chorister Outreach Program, although giving children only a tiny glimpse of chorister life, had significant educational impact.[9] Here are some stories from around the UK:

Norwich: "This school needs a miracle," were the opening words of one head teacher. It needed, not a miracle, but merely a harnessing of the children's evident zest for life and creativity. From claiming that they could not sing, the children became increasingly confident, and by the end of the project were clamoring for "more next time please." Class teachers were considerably taken aback, then excited, both by the level of talent on display and how they the teachers could lead and harness the talent in the future. The trickledown effect was also evident as other age groups realized that the years five and six were having so much fun that they wanted to join in.

Leicester: Individual children with behavioral issues were encouraged and reached a new level of attainment.

Chelmsford: A child with special needs is now proud to be a singer and is more positive in other areas of school work.

Ely: A head teacher pointed out four children who had engaged fully in the program, saying that they had Attention Deficit Disorder and required one-on-one attention during normal school hours, being very difficult to manage. They engaged fully in singing sessions with no assistance.

Bradford: Teachers from an inner city school with a great number of nationalities represented among their students commented how singing allowed them to bridge the language barrier and allowed children to learn something from the same starting point.

Peterborough: "For some of our children, learning new things is a struggle; however their ability to learn words in such a short period of time was outstanding."

Worcester: "An elective mute joined in."

Bristol: "At first I thought singing was just for girls, but now I know it's for girls and boys and men and women and anyone."

Carlisle: The choristers particularly impressed the boys in the school. Some of the boys were not very interested in the singing program and didn't completely engage with it. However, when they heard the choristers singing, one boy turned to his teacher and said with awe, "He is good!" This

---

9. Choir Schools. "Chorister."

impacted on the boys' attitude towards the singing program and helped to improve their interest in school in general.

AND WHEN CHORISTERS REALLY DO GROW UP . . .

Again, Howard Goodall reports how singing in a cathedral choir had a life-long positive impact not just on him, but on others who have gone on to careers in music and the arts.

Seasoned performers who have moved out of the comfort zone of classical choral music include Rod Argent of the Zombies (St. Albans Cathedral); Gareth Gates (Bradford Cathedral) whose professional career began with *Pop Idol*; the actor Tim Pigott Smith (Leicester Cathedral), and politicians Michael Mates (Salisbury Cathedral), James Wilkinson (St. George's Chapel Windsor), Robert Key (Salisbury), and Simon Hughes (Llandaff Cathedral). Others have excelled in finance, entrepreneurialism, the food industry, and academia. Occasionally we are given glimpses of other heroic and humble vocations formed by cathedral choirs, as David Lammy MP noted at the funeral of his friend James Adam: "I knew he was truly connected to the music and to his faith, which even in those days was very powerful. His music came from vulnerability, an awkwardness that at its core made the man I know, a man of tremendous empathy, truth and compassion."[10]

James went on to work in financial services and, combining this with his role as a church Deacon, become one of the conveners of the pressure group Make Poverty History. He died in the Russell Square terrorist attack on 7/7/2005.

In short, cathedral choirs can produce remarkable people. The ability to listen, the skill of performance, the striving for excellence, the years of laughter and of tears shared with a close team, the confidence to be oneself, the courage to defend others, a life shot through with the texts of the Psalms and a vocation to breathe life into those texts.

So why was I in any way surprised that John Goldingay had been a cathedral chorister?

---

10. Lammy, "Extracts."

15

Encountering Abraham in Africa
Reflections of an Ethnomusicologist on the Road

Roberta R. King

Journeys are a common occurrence in my life. Just as Abram and Sarai set out on an ambiguous journey and engaged with God along the way, I have also known God's guiding presence wherever he has taken me. In writing about Abraham, Eugene Peterson reflects, "Every time we set out, leaving our self-defined or culture-defined state, leaving behind our partial or immature projects, a wider vista opens up before us, a landscape larger with promise."[1] I began my journeys in Africa in 1978 asking God how a woman and a musician could do mission. While I thought I was going to Africa to take the Christian Gospel there, what I encountered was God working in the midst of African contexts in ways that presented new theological insights and deepened my reverence of Him. Whereas in many other cultures major theologizing takes place through music and performing arts, here I found that conversations at what I imagined to be "the edges" brought divine encounters that have moved me closer to "the center." John Goldingay has reminded Western scholars that "Old Testament theology will be wise to keep closer to the Old Testament's own categories of thought in order to give it more opportunity to speak its

---

1. Peterson, *The Jesus Way*, 44.

own insights rather than assimilating it to Christian categories," and the significance of this counsel is especially relevant in engaging the global church, particularly in the southern hemisphere.[2]

HEARING ISRAEL'S GOSPEL IN 3-D

As an ethnomusicologist, one who studies local and global music traditions in relation to communities' cultural patterns and processes, I have come to learn that there is more to music than meets the ear. Music is not merely an aural phenomenon nor just an object for analysis. Rather, music-making, and in particular the setting of scripture to song in groups, provides means for dynamic processing of everyday life events in light of cultural, spiritual, and socio-religious considerations. During the processes of both composition and performance, music not only touches on the transcendent but also brings together multiple strands of deeply embedded life values, beliefs, and issues into liminal realms where musical synapses and dynamic transformative impacts on a people's cognitive processes occur.[3] More specifically, music-making processes offer Christian communities opportunities to interact thoughtfully with the Scriptures and to initiate critical theological discussions.

The experience behind this essay arose out of a new song workshop that took place February 11–20, 2002, in Ferkessedougou, in the north of Côte d'Ivoire, West Africa, where emerging communities of African believers were hearing and interacting with passages of the Abraham narrative that recently had been translated for the first time into their own languages.[4] Two aspects of what took place stood out: (1) the recognition of cultural similarities and contrasts of Old Testament passages as they impact African believers, and (2) the insights and theological discussions behind newly composed scripture songs. Overhearing samples of the scripture discussions that took place at this workshop affords us the gift of hearing 'Israel's Gospel' in three dimensions, toggling between the original Old Testament context, the local receiving Senufo-Nyarafolo believers with whom

---

2. Goldingay, *Israel's Gospel*, 18.
3. See King, *Pathways in Christian Music Communication*, 165–203.
4. See King, *A Time to Sing: A Manual for the African Church*. This volume explains and lays out an approach to setting Scripture to song in groups and emerged out of multiple workshops conducted over a period of ten years with the Nyarafolo believers in Ferkessedougou, Côte d'Ivoire.

the songs were composed, and the Western perceptions of the workshop facilitators.

... ON THE ROAD TO FERKÉ

As the van pulled out of Abidjan, the commercial capital of Côte d'Ivoire, I was pleased to be returning to work among the Senufo in the North.[5] We had been working on a chronological translation of the Scriptures by doing group composing with the goal of setting scripture to song in the Nyarafolo language, one of 21 Senufo language groups in the region. With a non-literacy rate above 85%, oral media such as song, dance, and drama are essential means for hearing the Scriptures. Working in close collaboration with a local translation team, we continually were discovering that verbal, written, and musical translations of the Scriptures share similar tasks. As Linnea Boese, my colleague and translation team leader, explains: "The Bible translator faces two distinct challenges while searching for the right expression to effectively communicate a concept. One is to clearly describe a completely foreign notion; the other is to effectively reveal a connection between what comes from so long ago and far away to ideas currently held by the receptor people."[6]

With translating the Abraham narrative into song as our goal, I wondered how the music-composing arena would contribute to linking foreign, ancient notions in meaningful ways to the life of Nyarafolo believers and non-believers. Drawing upon periodic work over fifteen years in the region, I had come to appreciate Bediako's argument that "Scripture and culture are like merging circles, gradually coming to have one centre as we increasingly recognize ourselves in Scripture and Scripture becomes more and more recognizable as our story."[7] How would this occur in setting the Abraham story to song?

As we finally arrived in Ferkessedougou after an arduous ten-hour drive, we were immediately confronted with a collection of bleating, all white and seemingly flawless sheep. They were tied up against a brick wall bordering the open courtyard across the town square where our new song workshop would take place. It was the time of Muslim preparation for

---

5. My earlier PhD research was carried out in the 1980s among the Senufo-Cebaara in the Korhogo region of Côte d'Ivoire.

6. Boese, "Canaanite, Israelite and Nyarafolo Worldviews," 1.

7. Bediako, "Scripture as the Interpreter of Culture and Tradition," 4.

the celebration of the Great Feast, or *tabaski,* the tradition that focuses on Abraham and Ishmael (rather than Isaac) in relation to sacrifice. The story of Abraham had arrived in Ferkessedougou long before Bible translators and mission workers[8] first arrived in the mid-twentieth century. I immediately realized that the merging of 'Scripture and culture' was going to occur during the workshop in more ways and dimensions than I had imagined.

. . . WALKING THE JESUS ROAD[9]

CALL: *Yahweh told Abraham to go out (3x)*

RESPONSE: *Yahweh told Abraham to go out*

CALL: *. . . that he go to Canaan country*

RESPONSE: *Yahweh told Abraham to go out*

CALL: *. . . and Abraham obeyed him*

RESPONSE: *Yahweh told Abraham to go out*

. . .

CALL: *"The person who honors you, I myself will honor,*

RESPONSE: *Yahweh told Abraham to go out*

CALL: *the person who curses you I myself will curse"*

RESPONSE: *Yahweh told Abraham to go out.*[10]

8. I am very grateful to my WorldVenture colleagues, Linnea and Glenn Boese, for their long years of collaboration and appreciation of the importance of ethnomusicology in mission. I am also grateful for Linnea's contribution to this paper through provision of her translated notes from the new song workshop and interviews with the local Nyarafolo translation team, KONE Nayergue Moise (referred to throughout this paper as Moise) and SILUE Mienougoh Abdoulaye (also known as Speedy). I am grateful to the whole translation team and Nyarafolo believers who invited me to come and facilitate composing Nyarafolo scripture-based songs, and to walk the Jesus road with them in a way that has led to our mutually enriched lives in Christ.

9. All song selections cited in this article are used by permission; the full texts are available from the author at rking@fuller.edu.

10. Song title: "Ôe Yewe 'jo Birama wi- yiri yo" ("Yahweh Told Abraham to Go Out"),

In this first song, the call to get up and leave, to travel on the road sets a familiar scene for Nyarafolo and other Senufo believers. They are well acquainted with walking long dusty roads to connect with others in this northern region of Côte d'Ivoire. Just as Abraham responded to Yahweh's call to leave and enter into a new territory not exactly knowing where his path would lead, so new Nyarafolo believers follow a parallel path by joining what they call the Jesus Road. Leaving the traditional, animistic practices of the peasant Senufo world takes courage and is an overwhelming challenge. Local cultural practices, such as sorcery, taking more than one wife, dependence on healing and success via sacrifices to spirits, and reliance on traditional diviners and healers surround new believers as they forge new paths and 'walk the Jesus road.' Similar to Hebrew images, the concept of Christians walking the Jesus Road, Path, or Way is used on a daily basis.[11]

Additionally, Senufo believers worship Yahweh in ways similar to the Hebrews who struggled to worship God in the midst of the pagan, polytheistic societies of Canaan. As the new song workshop began, I reflected on how Senufo believers are on a journey similar to that of Abraham in discovering and following *Yahweh*, with an emerging sense of who this new God is. For them, the turning away from local, everyday practices toward *Yahweh* is radical and previously unknown. As an outside facilitator, I was confronted anew with questions. What is it like for new believers to "leave family and relatives" because they have moved into a new religious arena in which they, like Abraham, are following a new, unexplored road? What is it like to not know the biblical stories as part of one's historical heritage, to hear them for the first time? Or only to be aware of a Muslim version of the Abraham story that focuses on Ishmael rather than Isaac? As the Senufo believers began hearing and discussing the Abrahamic narrative, multiple cultural links and contrasts began to emerge. Three of the most immediately striking ones are:

1) *Yahweh draws close and interacts with his people:* The traditional Senufo concept of a high creator god is that of a deity who is far off, distant and uninvolved. *Kulocelie* is the indigenous Nyarafolo term for the revered

by Tene Soro. The text is based on Genesis 12:2–3.

11. According to Moise, many images translated into Nyarafolo from the Psalms, for instance, reveal how the Hebrews saw the world just like Nyarafolos. One example is:

> Make your way straight before me. (Psa 5:8b TNIV)
> Muɔ koligo sìɛn gè mi yiʔɛ mɛ́ gè, gàa muɔ 'jo mi líɛ gè.
> (Nyarafolo: Straighten out the path before me.)

Creator God and is used for translating the word, *Elohim*. When the story references *Kulocelie,* Senufo believers immediately grasp the significance of his sovereignty. The striking contrast, however, is that the divine actions "reveal something they never knew about God before: that he intervenes in human history, and is in relationship to human beings."[12] The opening call of the first song, Genesis 12, immediately sets this out when the singer declares three times, "*Yahweh told Abraham to go out.*" Rather than the Senufo tradition of pleading with lesser, local spirits to control and maintain their world,[13] *Yahweh* as the high Creator God breaks in, comes close, and closes the gap that Senufo peoples have long attempted to overcome through mediating spirits. It is astonishing for them that *Yahweh* speaks directly to Abraham. Something radically new and different is happening; people are compelled to listen to the story.

2) *Yahweh Promises Blessing and Protection* (Gen 12:2–3): The promise of God's blessing, help, and guidance as believers walk the Jesus road remains prominent in Nyarafolo thought as they continue to hear the story. Blessings and curses are a common everyday occurrence in the Senufo world. Yet, once again, this God is radically different. He is not requiring appeasement through intermediary spirits demanding costly sacrifices of chickens and goats. Not only does God promise blessings, but God also takes it further with an amazing pledge to curse those who curse them, a commitment to protecting them. As they learn of Abram's sojourn in Egypt and the plague sent on Pharaoh for taking Abram's wife, for example, they reason that Pharaoh could have killed Abram, but "God was keeping his promise of protection and blessing." In seeing Abram's lack of trusting God while in Egypt, they also reason that Abram still did not believe God's promise to protect him. The lead translator and workshop co-leader, Moise, concludes that Abram "was a man like us, he had faults."[14] They are beginning to relate the story to their contemporary world and to consider what it means for them in their everyday life. Additionally, in the song, "God Sent a Plague on Pharaoh Because of Abraham's Wife," Moise, the singer-songwriter, recites the story of famine and how, "while they are on the road," Abraham instructs Sarah to tell Pharaoh she is Abraham's sister. In the closing verses of the song, Moise imparts stunning advice:

12. Boese, "Canaanite, Israelite and Nyarafolo Worldviews," 9.
13. See ibid.
14. KONE Nayergue Moise, "Interview Notes," from L. Boese.

CALL: People, so Pharaoh called Abraham and talked to him,

RESPONSE: Because of Abraham's wife, people![15]

CALL: ... and said, "Abraham, why did you deceive me? Abraham, why did you deceive me?"

RESPONSE: Because of Abraham's wife, people!

CALL: "Abraham, here's your wife, take her and go!"

RESPONSE: Because of Abraham's wife, people!

CALL: Pharaoh sent Abraham away, people, and sent him out of Egypt.

RESPONSE: Because of Abraham's wife, people!

CALL: People, my companions, come, let's protect our women!

RESPONSE: Because of Abraham's wife, people!

CALL: Women, you protect your men, women you protect your men!

RESPONSE: Because of Abraham's wife, people!

CALL: Men, let's protect our women, people let's protect each other!

RESPONSE: Because of Abraham's wife, people!

Closing Refrain (sung twice):

CALL: God sent a plague on Pharaoh because of Abraham's wife, people!

RESPONSE: God sent a plague on Pharaoh
Because of Abraham's wife, people!

---

15. The Nyarafolo song style employs a call-and-response form, uniquely complex, dynamic, and appropriate for telling long stories. It also facilitates dialogical interaction between the musical participants. Especially suitable and appropriate for oral audiences, the call-and-response evokes immediate attention, involvement, and memorizing of the story.

In this text, it is significant that the singers are not only reciting the textual story, but also starting to integrate scriptural lessons into their own lives. The application and merging of scripture and culture is indeed beginning to take place.

3) *How did the Nyarafolo Culture Get into the Bible?* As the storytelling continues in the workshop, cultural parallels continue to grow and abound. In working on the story of Sarah giving Hagar to her husband in order to have a child,[16] the believers immediately understand the immense shame of not having an heir since their own culture likewise considers this a great burden. The custom of finding a surrogate woman for childbearing is one they know themselves. As one astonished participant exclaims, "The Nyarafolo custom is much like this—scandalous to see in the Bible! The custom is that if a woman gives another woman to her husband, usually the woman becomes the titular wife and the other is chased away. How did a Nyarafolo custom get into the Bible?" They are surprised that the same custom and issues are appearing in a "foreign" book from a "foreign" land. God paying attention to the situation is even more astounding. Moise explains, "Sarah's act in giving Hagar to her husband is viewed as appropriate, a good thing, but Sarah doesn't understand that this is going to be a trap for her, with suffering in it. The impact of the song is in that outcome, that the servant-wife is sent away due to conflict; it is thus a warning that resonates since people have often experienced conflict in polygamous families and in situations such as this."[17] The narrative crescendos with significance and relevance in their lives as they learn of God's interaction with Hagar, "the one God sees."

However, the most profound Biblical lesson was yet to come.

---

16. Song title: "Sarah, she took Hagar and gave her to her husband," by Nyiheneyugo Ouattara.

17. KONE Nayergue Moise, "Interview Notes" from L. Boese.

Conversations at the Edges of Things

Abraham Took His Son and Went to the Mountain[18]

CALL: *He took his son and went to the mountain,*
Abraham took his son and went to the mountain.

RESPONSE: *Abraham took his son and went to the mountain.*

CALL: *This is something new; men and women, listen!*

RESPONSE: *Abraham took his son and went to the mountain.*

CALL: *So they started the walk along. When they had gone a long way Isaac said, "Father Abraham, please let me ask:*
I ask you, here is the fire; I ask you, here is the knife . . ."

RESPONSE: *Abraham took his son and went to the mountain.*

CALL: *Abraham said, "My son Isaac, be quiet, and let's go on.*
God will provide the sheep"

RESPONSE: *Abraham took his son and went to the mountain.*

CALL: *When they arrived—listen, my friends! -*
this is a new thing, listen: Abraham tied up Isaac!

RESPONSE: *Abraham took his son and went to the mountain.*

CALL: *And God said to Abraham, "Don't kill the child!*
Abraham, let your son go! Today I know that you fear me."

RESPONSE: *Abraham took his son and went to the mountain. . . .*

CALL: *So Abraham seized the sheep; he caught the sheep and killed it to worship God.*

RESPONSE: *Abraham took his son and went to the mountain.*

CALL: *My dear ones, come! If God talks to you,*
accept what he says, listen to him!

RESPONSE: *Abraham took his son and went to the mountain.*

---

18. Song composed by Moise.

As the story of God asking Abraham to take Isaac to the mountain begins to unfold, three key terms immediately carry significance in Nyarafolo thought: mountain, sacrifice,[19] and sheep. The key term "mountain" (*nyagurugo*) is viewed in a way very similar to Hebrew thought. "It connotes strength and protection, due to being seen as high and hard (a rock), and is the most important of the various places where sacrifices are made; second is the wetland, and then also certain trees."[20] Made up of small granite outcroppings, a "mountain" is significant in this flat, desert region and is naturally seen as a place where one can have connection with the spiritual world. Upon hearing that a father and son are taking fire and wood to a mountain, the Nyarafolo listener also understands that a sacrifice will take place.[21] Finally, a sheep is seen as the animal used in a truly important sacrifice.[22] Thus, the implicit expectation of what is to come builds tension and generates difficulty in understanding *Yahweh's* demand.

The group spends lengthy discussions questioning how *Yahweh* could demand such an awful thing. Child sacrifice, although rare, is sometimes practiced, but is considered condemnable. At first, there is outright refusal to set this part of the story to song; they cannot bring themselves to witness to a god who demands such an abhorrent act. As Moise, the lead Nyarafolo translator, comments, "one expects that from the 'charlatans' and other fetishers but not from God."[23] This cannot be the same God of the New Testament that they have come to know and revere. Yet, amazingly, before knowing the end of the story, they reason that it is God's Word that they are hearing; they must remain obedient to Him. They agree to continue on. Moise explains how the discussion progressed: "When the substitute sheep is provided, the testing finally makes sense, and it is understood that God is not bound by our ideas in the kinds of testing he may send our way. The

---

19. "Almost every people group in Africa seems to have had some form of traditional sacrificial system . . . The animal . . . had to be carefully chosen. . . . The animal offered had to be of a uniform colour. While the exact colour preferred differed from group to group, black, red and white were the most common colours for sacrificial animals. . . . The animal needed to be perfect in every respect, with no birth defects or injuries" (Ngewa, "Place of Sacrifices," 1502).

20. KONE Nayergue Moise, "Interview Notes" from L. Boese.

21. It is also very common to "take fire" in the form of some burning coals to the field during work or to another village or camp; this is another way in which the story resonates as normal action.

22. Lesser sacrifices are composed of chickens and rice, for example.

23. KONE Nayergue Moise, "Interview Notes" from L. Boese.

tension in the story, the way Abraham does not fully reveal the purpose of the trip to his son, also strikes at the heart; people do not want division between father and son. So the resolution is very comforting."[24] Yet, they ask, "Why would God wait until the very last minute? Then one sees that it was a test of whether Abraham truly feared God, how far his faith would go . . . His act shows that he has chosen God, trusting him."[25] The significance of God's providing the sacrificial sheep does not escape them. It is indeed something new; they conclude that a musical equivalent that adequately connotes the profound implications of the story is required.

In terms of musical analysis, a brief word is appropriate here. Although the Nyarafolo believers had been developing their own songs based on their vernacular language, they continued to use the wood-frame xylophone, *balafon,* employed by Cebaara Christians. Yet, Moise, the composer of the Abraham and Isaac song, realized that the melody and text were not compatible with the *balafon*. Reaching back to traditional Nyarafolo music, the group decided on a particular rhythm played on the traditional drums called "pire" (pronounced 'pray' with a flipped "r").[26] Not yet having such a drum available to them, they borrowed *djembes* to get the accompaniment needed. Stylistically, the whole song resembles those that are sung in the last days of funerals (never the first days), at the most significant part of the funeral rite. Moise characterizes it as nyinimɛ wuʔu—a compassionate one, one intended to bring comfort and consolation.[27] The group participants are really excited during the workshop to compose a song that reached deeper into their particular ethnic music. Through it, deeper significance and weight pervades the performance of the song, speaking powerfully in combined verbal and non-verbal dimensions that *Yahweh* is drawing even closer into their world and has an important message for them. They are

24. Ibid.

25. KONE Nayergue Moise, "Interview Notes" from L. Boese.

26. Five years after the workshop, "Moise rerecorded the song once the Nyarafolo group had a set of *pire*. These drums are a paired set, one larger and louder, the other smaller, which complement each other's rhythms. It was partly the experience of composing that sacrifice of Isaac song that motivated Moise to look into acquiring the drums, about five years ago. They are traditionally used for many celebrations, particularly for agricultural competitions, youth festivals and marriages, but also in the latter parts of the lengthy funerals given to older people who die 'naturally.' Once the group began using them, and taking them around town with them when visiting various courtyards, it began to be said that the Christians were bringing back true Nyarafolo music" (see Boese, "Canaanite, Israelite, and Nyarafolo Worldviews"). The redeeming of culture is also taking place through the telling of the Abrahamic narrative via story-songs.

27. Boese, "Canaanite, Israelite, and Nyarafolo Worldviews."

becoming more authentically true to themselves as they interact with God. Here is yet again an important case of Scripture and culture merging closer together resulting in a deeper understanding of the story's significance for the Nyarafolo people.

Joy and celebration break forth as they understand the expanded Gospel that has come to them through the Abraham narrative. They have come to see more fully "who God is and who we are through the ongoing story of God's relationship with Israel."[28] They are growing in their identity in Christ via Abraham in cultural settings directly linked to their own. Stories from biblical cultures with surprisingly close parallels and contrasts easily relate the Bible message directly to peasant societies;[29] reading the biblical scriptures through Western theological categories first is not required. Scripture has become their own history where "all believers in Christ become children of Abraham (Gal. 3:26–29) and are grafted into the original olive tree (Rom 11:7–20) . . . All of us have been adopted into Christ, with our traditions, and are therefore transformed, with our traditions. The God of Israel is not a tribal God but the God who created all humanity."[30]

. . . ABRAHAM ON THE JESUS ROAD

Following a day of recording the songs and dancing in joyful worship in praise of God's blessings and promises, it is time for me to leave yet again for another journey. As we are departing Ferké, the Muslim *tabaski* sacrifice is finally taking place in the town square. I wonder if the new Abraham songs that point to the Jesus Road have jumped the wall into the town square. Grateful that they will be sung again, I continue on.

Surrounded in Ferké by sacrificial practices that are enslaving and costly, there is a profound impact in recognizing anew the significance of God's provision of a sacrificial lamb on our behalf. Encountering Abraham in Africa has personally led to walking with Jesus on a deeper level. I cannot help but fall down in reverence and adoration before our high priest. I find myself praying for the peoples of Ferkessedougou, that their life journeys might open to new vistas, landscapes larger with promise as they sing the Abraham narrative and choose to faithfully walk the Jesus Road.

---

28. Goldingay, *Israel's Gospel*, 30.
29. See Koehler, *Telling God's Stories with Power*.
30. Bediako, "Scripture as the Interpreter," 3.

16

Filming the Bible
Crossing the Red Sea

PHILIP JENSON

BOTH JOHN GOLDINGAY AND I are fascinated by films, or (since he has now crossed the Atlantic) movies. I don't know any survey that indicates how many like-minded Old Testament scholars there are, but it is very probable that we are not the only ones. For interpreting the Old Testament and appreciating a film have much in common. In the first place, film is a pre-eminently narrative and dramatic medium, and the Old Testament has a profusion of gripping stories. God engages with the world through interacting with a vast cast of characters, from leading men and women to hardly noticed extras. And are those never-ending credits at the end of a film that different from the genealogies of 1 Chronicles 1–9? John has taught us much about how to read biblical narrative in his commentaries and other writings.

Second, interpreting either a film script or a biblical passage requires a disciplined imagination. The text is only the starting point. The casting department, the location finders, the costume designers, the set designers, the make-up artists, the camera operators, the soundtrack composer, and above all the actors and director, all co-operate in bringing a bare script to life. And that is before the special effects people get to work. It is the same for biblical interpreters. The Bible is generally bare and sparse, fraught with a background that we are invited to enter and inhabit and make our own. Readers of scripture are always required to go beyond the text, albeit in a way that is faithful to what is in the text. I have always enjoyed the creative and imaginative dimension to John's writing.

Third, both Bible and film set before us a world different from ours in time and space. The Bible comes to most of us in translation, and the most challenging films to watch are often those from another culture and in another language. Interpreting these foreign worlds often requires a journey of understanding, with multiple re-readings and re-viewings. This is not an impossible task, for however bizarre the landscape, the scenery remains that of the universe God created, and it stars the same kind of people we are: sons of Adam and daughters of Eve, reacting to age-old problems and opportunities. John has done more than most in helping us tackle the interpretive challenges of the scriptures.

THE CROSSING OF THE RED SEA

It is possible to explore any film from a Christian point of view, but I would like to focus on those special cases where the Old Testament has been made into film. More specifically I have been intrigued by three movie interpretations of a particularly memorable passage, the crossing of the Red Sea. The first is from the renowned *The Ten Commandments* (1956), directed by Cecil B. DeMille, with Charles Heston as a rugged Moses (referred to from here as 10C). The second is in the animated DreamWorks production, *The Prince of Egypt* (1998), directed by Brenda Chapman (referred to as *PE*). The third is simply called *Moses* (1996), a two-part adaptation directed by Roger Young and starring Ben Kingsley as Moses.

Rather than treating them individually, I'll compare their approaches to two key issues that the story raises.

History and Fiction

How does a film or a biblical text relate to the world we know? One popular modern answer is that it has to be either history or fiction. Biblical scholars divide sharply on the status of the Exodus. A few consider it a sober documentary, others a fantasy full of special effects invented centuries later. However, those interested in film will be aware of the complexity of evaluating from this point of view movies that begin with the claim that it is 'based on a true story'. A writer or director will often change the when, the how and even the who of the story for dramatic effect. If they do it well, it becomes impossible to tell from the film alone. One historical inaccuracy in *The King's Speech*, for example, is that the Duke of York began to work with Lionel Logue, the voice coach, ten years before the abdication crisis. This reflected artistic rather than historical values. The benefit is an increase in the tension and a plot that highlights the remarkable achievement of the central characters. Pedantic historians might complain, but this is not the only value by which we judge the truth of a film, or indeed much else.

It is often impossible to disentangle how much history has shaped a biblical text, and how much it has been shaped by the author's desire to tell a great story, or to communicate important truths about what God is like. The desire to make sharp distinctions between history and fiction is a relatively modern concern that can hinder us appreciating a text or a film for what it is, as opposed to what a modern reader might be familiar with or prefer.

The miracles of the Bible raise the question sharply. Some scholars consider that the parting of the Sea was based on natural events. Exodus itself tells of a strong east wind driving the sea back all night (Exod 14:21). But it is harder to find a natural explanation for the wall of waters on the right and the left, let alone the pillar of fire and cloud (14:22, 24). Do these reflect different sources? Is the miracle an additional artistic highlighting of some natural event? Or is it a combination of natural event and miracle? What a reader brings to the text is also important. Some scholars dismiss the account as fictional on the grounds that miracles do not happen. Believers are less doubtful because they know that God can work both miraculously and through the natural order of things. We pray for healing as well as go to a doctor.

One specific difficulty for those who are skeptical about the historical and miraculous character of the event is that they are required to replace the biblical account with a quite different one. While this may satisfy a modern historian, it is of little use in reading the only text we have, in which it is hard to avoid the miraculous. Wisely, all three movies take this dimension seriously. What is of interest is how far they do justice to the complexity of the account in Exodus 14. In verse 21, Moses stretches out his hand, a strong east wind drives the sea back, it then becomes dry land and the waters are divided. It is in the next verse that we learn about the water forming walls on the right and left. Verse 21 might be a natural phenomenon, but verse 22 is more clearly out of the ordinary.

The only film version that takes this order seriously is *Moses*, where we wait with Moses and the people for several minutes in the dark. The result is a powerful heightening of our awareness of the helplessness of the people, with their (and our) growing awareness of complete dependence on God, along with doubts whether the God of Israel will do anything. The dividing of the two parts of the film during this long period of waiting is an ingenious use of the practical in aid of the dramatic. The other two accounts telescope the action, with a rapid gathering of dark storm clouds leading to the dividing of the sea and spectacular walls of water.

This is just one example of how directors (or storytellers) have to make decisions on the choice of events to portray and their timing. In Exodus there is a complex sequence of events: Pharaoh draws near, the Israelites complain, the cloud comes between, there is the night of waiting, the Israelites cross, the Egyptians pursue, the Lord throws them into panic and clogs their chariot wheels so that they determine to flee back. Finally Moses stretches out his hand and the waters return on the entire army of Pharaoh with not one remaining. In *Moses* we only have someone reporting that they are half a day behind, and there is no cloud or fire preventing the Egyptians pursuing. In *PE* everything happens at the same time. In all three portrayals the Egyptians begin pursuing before the Israelites have completed the crossing, increasing the dramatic tension and highlighting once again the need for God to act. In *PE* the chariots are overturned by rocks rather than clogged by mud, and the Egyptians keep going. In 10C and *Moses* the waters overwhelm them as they continue to speed ahead unhindered. As for not one remaining, the same two versions decide that it is more dramatic for Moses' chief opponent to witness the destruction of his army.

How far do the versions respect the practicalities of the journey through the wilderness? However miraculous the events, a people on the move require a great deal of stuff. In *Moses* they are equipped mainly with staffs, and they cross the Red Sea at a run. In *PE* the Israelites suddenly have access to hundreds of torches, and they too cross much of the end of the path at a run. It looks spectacular, but highlights the artistic rather than the realistic character of the event. Only in the 10C is there a concerted effort to convey the practicalities of the journey, with heavily laden men and women, flocks, carts and much else moving along at a steady pace—only the last few at the rear have to hurry as the chariots appear from behind.

There is no absolute distinction between history and fiction in telling a good story. All three versions have taken license with the text. *PE* is the most simplistic in imagining the practical implications for the people, but gives the most spectacular portrayal of the crossing. 10C has impressive special effects, but these go along with a realistic portrayal of a people on the move. *Moses* is weakest as regards the special effects while also lacking the practical touches of detail of 10C. Of course, a number of these differences depend on the format (animation or not), audience (children or adult) and budget (*Moses* is the poor relation).

Text and Interpretation

Deciding whether the Exodus account is history or fiction is just one aspect of interpretation. It is important because history is often seen as the source of truth, and truth is of interest and relevance. But there are many ways in which a work or a text can be true and relevant without being simple history. A more interesting criterion is how far it combines action and reflection. Relentless action films become boring because we have not been allowed to appreciate the significance of the action, and there is no time to allow the characters to become more than one-dimensional and uninteresting. On the other hand, a verbose dialogue and characters that do nothing are equally boring. A satisfying story integrates plot and character. A good story needs a problem or tension that has to be resolved, but it is complex and interesting people who do the resolving in their own fascinating way.

Now the Bible is consistently more interested in reflecting on the significance of events (historical or fictional) rather than the details of the action. The battle between David and Goliath is, for example, over in one verse. Far more important are the speeches that clarify the personal and theological implications of what will happen. It is striking that there are two portrayals in Exodus of the Crossing of the Red Sea. The prose chapter fourteen has a good deal of action, while the poetic chapter fifteen is mostly reflection. Moses and the Israelites sing an eighteen-verse song, followed by another verse of song from Miriam accompanying a dance of the women.

Relative to the account in Exodus, all three films emphasize action rather than reflection. *PE* has the least reflection, both before and afterwards. There is one divine statement that Moses remembers just before he strikes the Red Sea with his staff, and the only word said afterwards is a curious "thank-you" by Moses to his wife, Zipporah. In 10C Moses responds with a combination of Exodus 15:10, the first phrase of verse eleven, and the final phrase of Psalm 90:2, to which the people respond. The most extensive response is *Moses*, where a selection of phrases from Exodus 15 is used (parts of verses 1, 2, 11, 13, 18). I would have loved to hear the reasons why the scriptwriters included and excluded what they did. And when Charles Heston intones "Thou didst blow with thy winds" (rather than the singular original "wind"), was that his innovation, or the scriptwriter's, or Cecil B. de Mille himself?

PE's minimalism illustrates a general tendency to make the story a universal human one rather than a specifically Israelite one. The focus of all three versions is also very much Moses rather than the Lord or the people. It is he who speaks in both 10C and *Moses*, rather than Moses and the Israelites together. *Moses* is particularly interesting in the way that Moses says to himself the verses in the first person singular ("The Lord is my strength and my might; this is my God and I will praise him") but then, in a louder voice, invites the people to join with him in the second and third person praise ("In your steadfast love you led the people whom you redeemed. You guided them with your strength. The Lord will reign for ever and ever.") From a Jewish point of view there is no need to make the distinction, for many of the "I" psalms were traditionally read as statements of the people (for example Ps 23). Moses represents the people as well as leading them.

Another significant move is the loss of references to other gods in the films. In 10C we only have Moses reciting "Who is like unto thee, O Lord?" rather than "Who is like unto thee, O Lord, among the gods?" *Moses* has "Who is like the Lord? Who among the mighty?" Modern readers are often embarrassed by what look like primitive remnants of an earlier polytheistic phase of Israelite religion, and it is likely that the scriptwriters wished to avoid the problem. More recent discussion has suggested that this embarrassment is unnecessary. What matters above all is that the God of Israel, the Lord, is different in kind from all other gods, not merely different in degree. This is what the incomparability statements express with great power and vividness. Whichever gods people believe in (and we are welcome to think of them as true fictions), even the mightiest and holiest of them merely contribute to the incomparable character of the God of Israel. How far do these movies conform to modern ideas, rather than respecting the distinctive theology of the original?

While *PE* has the least explicit theology, the freedom of animation enables an awe-inspiring presentation of the power and glory of the parting and the crossing. I was particularly moved by the appearance of whales at one point during the journey. Exodus 15 is a hymn in praise of the warrior God (v. 3: "The LORD is a man of war"), but in the ancient world this was required for creation itself. The storm god created by triumphing over the chaotic forces of the sea, represented by the sea monsters (Ps 74:12–15). Only by defeating such forces could God set up the boundaries that allowed the dry land to be formed and human civilisation to flourish. In Isa 51:9-10 we have a similar juxtaposition of the motifs of creation and Exodus. *PE* is unique also in integrating the powerful motif of light and dark, another reminder of creation for those with eyes to see (Gen 1:3). Only the good creator God has the will and the power to bring about the birth of a people who will live to his praise. The defeat of Pharaoh and his chariots is at the same time the defeat of the forces of chaos and anti-life. Ironically God uses the ultimate expression of chaos and death, the waters of the deeps, to fulfil his will. While I am fairly sure the makers of the film were unaware of these motifs, their intention need not limit how an interpreter can go beyond the text.

The portrayal of Moses also differentiates the versions. In 10C Charles Heston's Moses becomes notoriously distant and god-like. Not for him the uncertainties, the doubts and the surprise of the character in *PE* and *Moses*. Both are possible because the biblical portrayal of characters is mostly external, indicating very little about their thoughts and feelings. Preachers and film directors have to do a lot of work in filling in these gaps, and it is no wonder that the eventual product reflects in good measure a modern conception of the man of faith. It is worth asking how faithful the result is to the original text. I am not particularly convinced by any of the portrayals. That of the 10C lacks compassion and a sense of on-going dependence on God; that of *PE* is too clueless, while that of *Moses* is too withdrawn and introverted, perhaps (dare I say it) too British. All of them are too young. But it is doubtful that taking advice from an Old Testament scholar is a priority for anyone thinking of updating the story for the twenty-first century.

The Moses of *Moses* also led me to reflect on how different introspective doubt is from complaining to the Lord, which is one intriguing note in the Exodus narrative that none of the three mention ("Why do you cry out to me?" Exod 14:15). The complaints of the Israelites against Moses hardly feature in *PE*, where people are united in their fear and wonder, and everything happens too fast anyway. *Moses*, too, has little of this, except for a question about whether he intends the Israelites to swim to the Promised Land. It is in 10C that complaint becomes a major motif, located above all in the quarrelsome Dathan. He it is who asks the awkward questions, followed by assertions of doom ("Deliverer? Yes, deliver you to death.") Nor is it just Dathan. Others join with him in blaming Moses and even wanting to stone him. This is a more realistic portrait of a people whom the text repeatedly describes as regularly grumbling and rebelling against both Moses and the Lord.

CONCLUSION

All interpreters recast their sources. We have seen how three films have done this for one biblical passage, but the same is in all likelihood true of the biblical account itself which was transmitted and shaped over many generations. On the other hand, all the films preserve the main features of the event. I believe that it is still possible to say of the Exodus account that it is "based on a true story," even though I could not reconstruct a detailed account of what happened.

The films illustrate a more general feature in the history of interpretation, namely the imaginative and creative filling out of the sparse biblical record. How this is carried out reflects a great number of factors: How far we understand the sources, the audience, the intended message, and our understanding of God? The call for Christian readers, preachers, and filmmakers is to do this in a way that goes beyond the text but remains faithful to the underlying portrayal of the characters in the Bible—not least the God who will one day be the ultimate critic of all our work.

17

Pausing for Thought

SARAH GOLDINGAY

WHAT FOLLOWS IS A collection of two-minute talks I was commissioned to create and perform for BBC radio. As an academic, writing for the radio is an odd experience. The genre demands a different way of thinking about those we are communicating with. In this situation the small, specialist academic readership I am used to writing for expanded to become a wide-ranging audience, listening in their homes and cars, at their desks or on the move. The format gives no time for in-depth, nuanced arguments. Instead, it demands bold statements, simple (though not simplified) ideas and crisp narratives that resolve elegantly at their end. In many ways, creating each of these short scripts was more demanding in range and scope than an extended chapter for a scholarly publication. It was, in all sorts of ways, a challenge.

This writing challenge was compounded because the stakes were high. BBC Radio 2 is a national station with millions of daily listeners. And it is a significant part of the fabric of everyday life for many people. Its public funding demands that content follows a collection of nationally agreed policies and guidelines, rather than sponsorship-driven concerns. These set out to represent the complex, multifaceted communities that constitute the UK, and stipulate that some of the BBC's programming should reflect the nation's multicultural and multifaith makeup. In this setting 'religion' is far from straightforward for it includes a diverse range of religious and spiritual beliefs and practices. My talks needed to somehow speak to, and speak about, this wide-ranging complexity in a way that would feel personal to each individual listener.

The contribution I was writing, *Pause for Thought*, is an important vehicle for the BBC's religious and spiritual output. It is embedded in Radio 2's weekday early morning show and provides a daily, two-minute section dedicated to reflections on questions of life and faith, and their interpretation in relationship to topical news stories and themes. What follows are the six scripts I created for broadcast in January and February 2012 in response to the given themes of *Inspirational Language, Second Chances, Love, Holiness, Leadership,* and *Womanhood.*

All of these themes might make us think of John Goldingay: John the scholar and pastor who creates and shares inspirational language; John as someone who embraces his second chances, something we've all shared in (with a sense of wonder) when he and Ann became adventurers and moved to a new continent, and more recently, in his joy of meeting and marrying his new wife Kathleen; John the leader in the academy and his community; John a passionate advocate for the equal rights of women; John, whose journeys and struggles with questions of holiness have inspired many. But for me, the John I've been thinking about most in writing this is the wonderful father-in-law who fills life, in all its complexity, with profound love.

INSPIRATIONAL LANGUAGE

2011 marked the 400th anniversary of the King James Bible. And 2012 marks another landmark for a significant Christian text: the Church of England's *Book of Common Prayer* is 350 years old. It is now translated into numerous languages across the world, but was first created by Thomas Cranmer who was Archbishop of Canterbury and an influential leader in the English Reformation. When writing the book, Cranmer didn't create it from scratch. He collated and adapted existing texts, before contributing his own words. As a consequence, the Book of Common Prayer, as we now know it, contains writing and wisdoms from other sources which are even older than its 350 years. But it is not simply a relic. It is a vibrant text that continues to be used today as the basis of many acts of public and private worship.

The book has had a turbulent history: it is one that has seen it move in and out of favour against shifting religious and political backgrounds. Yet its inspiring language means it has survived these challenges. In particular, it continues to give us familiar words at times of great change. It contains the rites of passage that form the landmarks of our lives: birth, death and marriage. Even if you've never been to church, or even attended a wedding ceremony, the words "to have and to hold from this day forwards, for better for worse, for richer for poorer, in sickness and in health" will be familiar to you. They run through our everyday lives. We even see them in films and in soap operas. And, when we lose someone we love, the words "earth to earth, ashes to ashes, dust to dust" remind us how the cycles and patterns of life continue. They help us mark our loss, and find ways to move on.

These familiar words have been with us for generations. They are embedded in the very fabric of our lives and our language. But the *Book of Common Prayer* is more than these landmark rites and rituals. It supports everyday reflection and meditation. Its rhythms match the weekly pattern, the daily schedule, the momentary breath, and transient heart beat of the reader. At 350 years old, it continues to be a useful work of inspirational beauty. We can be thankful for it.

SECOND CHANCES

We're all fortunate to get second chances in our lives. They're a time when we can be more aware of the process we're undertaking, whatever it might be. We can, we hope, learn from our previous mistakes. A second chance gives us the opportunity to use our knowledge to change our future. This sounds simple: it's a straightforward process. But what if your second chance doesn't work that way? What if you find yourself at a landmark change in your life, living through something that you've already been through before, but where you simply don't know how the past and present fit together? What if you don't have the experience to draw upon to make the most of this opportunity second time around? This spring, I'm working with a remarkable group of young people in foster care—and the team that support them—who are themselves in a similar place with a second chance.

2012 is a significant point in these young people's lives. They're leaving their foster families to live on their own for the first time. For these young people this is a second chance: it's an opportunity to create a new life, a new community and, perhaps, a new family for themselves. But because these young people had little say in their first experience of leaving home, finding a new way to live, and creating a community to be part of, is far from straightforward. When they're taken into foster care, they're separated from families and friendship groups and taken to live with a new family, in a new location. Their experience of finding and creating a new community this first time around was a challenging and turbulent process. And so, as they move on this year, to live independently, their second time around is more like a first time—a time to create a new way of doing something, one that is unique to them and an expression of who they are.

Their experience is a good reminder that sometimes our second chances don't simply have to be about repetition, but can also be about finding a new way of doing something that is a unique expression of who we are and where we are today. Second chances don't simply need to be a replaying of the past, but they can instead provide the transition into an authentic reinvention of ourselves in the present, for the future.

LOVE

Love takes many forms: a platonic love for our friends, a familial love for our family, our affection for a thing of beauty, a passion for our football team, or our altruism when we give to another. Around Valentine's Day our focus tends to be on the hearts and flowers of romantic love. Scientists have been able to take the complexity of love and map its chemistry. But in so doing they have also recognised that love is not about shifts in hormones and chemistry alone. It's also about what we do: it's about how, by repeating loving actions, we sustain and deepen our human bonds.

Last summer I was fortunate enough to return to the pilgrimage site of Lourdes, in France, to spend time carrying out research with colleagues: one a medical doctor, the other a neuropsychologist. They both have a rich and complex understanding of love that acknowledges its mapping in terms of chemicals and hormones, attraction and human bonding; but they also recognise that it is expressed in many different ways in our day to day experience. When we were with the pilgrims, and the volunteers who act as their carers, we all also saw an abundance of altruistic love expressed through human actions.

In Lourdes, there is both time and space for people to be their "better self," a self that is less selfish, more generous, less suspicious, more kind, less stressed, more altruistic. This is a joyful state that allows people to express aspects of an authentic self that is often suppressed by the complex conventions of everyday life. St. Thomas Aquinas defined love as "to will the good of another." Perhaps, beyond the hearts and flowers that signify the romantic love of St Valentine's Day, we can also take this time as a reminder to be loving and generous in spirit and, as Aquinas suggested, to will the good of another.

HOLINESS

Holiness is a complicated idea. The philosopher and theorist W. B. Gallie came up with a helpful way to explain how we use and understand words when describing complex things. He proposed the idea of the "essentially contested term" as way of grappling with those words that we all pretty much understand in the same way in general, but that become less certain when we begin to think about them in detail. In this way, we might think about holiness as an essentially contested term. Broadly, it seems to be straightforward: a state of absolute purity, a state of perfection. But if we begin to think about holiness on a case by case basis, and how it works in the world, it becomes less clear cut.

Perhaps it is not simply a fixed, single state of being. Instead, it might be helpful to think about holiness as something more fluid; a process, or even a journey. We might, for example, recognise holiness in another: where their life and works are the inspiration for our daily lives. Or perhaps their experience can be a guide and comfort for those on a spiritual quest. Or their example can be an encouragement to be a better person, so that their lives and actions become a pointer towards being the best people we can be. In all its complexity then, perhaps, holiness is simple; it is that which inspires us to live better and more fulfilling lives—to be our whole selves.

LEADERSHIP

I'm fortunate because my work is varied: I teach and research. My teaching includes all sorts of topics and takes all sorts of forms, which includes training people in acting skills for theatre. I also teach some of these acting skills to people who are training for the Church, both lay readers and ordinands who are going to be ministers. In these workshops, our conversations often centre on the topic of leadership. To be the leader of a church is a complex role, one that includes both speaking in public settings and presiding over services and ceremonies as varied as funerals and school assemblies. It ranges between developing a long-term, meaningful plan for the life of a fluid community, and the day-to-day running of a busy public building with often strained finances. But perhaps the most complex act of leadership that a minister repeatedly carries out is to lead an act of worship.

In our performance skills workshops, when we talk about the complexity of leading a service, we often disagree about the style of delivery—about the benefits and pitfalls of leading from the front, or pushing from the back. But we seem to find agreement on one point of leadership that we all value: the capacity of someone to "hold open a space for others." This idea of holding open a space was introduced to us by Chris Southgate at the South West Ministerial Training College. It encapsulates the ways that organisations sometimes simply need their leaders neither to lead from the front, nor push from behind, but rather to create an environment for consolidation and reflection. To hold open a space, away from daily pressures, that provides a safe environment for people to think, discuss, and share in takes great leadership. It requires the capacity to recognise that relentless change and uncertainty can be frightening and exhausting for those you lead. A great leader will, regardless of the pressures coming down from the "powers that be," find a way of pausing this pressure, and hold open a space in which their community can catch breath and take stock: somewhere to regroup, recharge, and begin the journey again refreshed.

WOMANHOOD

We are living in tough economic times. And we know that some sectors of our society will be hit harder than others. One of those groups is women. A report released in November 2011 by the Fawcett Society, in collaboration with a number of other charities, showed that financial cuts are pushing women out of the workforce. This, in turn, reduces their income and has a knock-on effect on other parts of society such as an increase in child poverty. These economic challenges are also having other worrying impacts; they are limiting women's access to justice and protection from violence. And because many women are also the principal carer for another, a partner, parent or child, these changes also have a wider impact on us all. None of us exists in isolation: we are all part of a fluid organism—society.

Society is not landlocked. Increasingly we are members of an international community that exchanges knowledge, goods, culture, and ideas.

As that crossover grows, it becomes evident that the difficult relationship between womanhood, money and being a carer is not simply a British question. It is an international one. This was made clear in a recent exhibition at Dartington Hall in rural Devon called *Tin Girls*. In the exhibition, documentary photographer Alice Carfrae shared images she'd taken in northeastern Nepal. It is a region that is particularly affected by human trafficking, in particular the trafficking of women. In Sindhupalchok it is said you can tell which household has sold a daughter, or lost a mother, by looking at the rooftops of the village. The ones with corrugated tin roofs as opposed to the traditional timber and slate indicate that a sacrifice has been made, a selfless act to try to better the family's situation. The unaffectionate nickname given to these women, who give their lives, is "Tin Girls." It's hard to comprehend a situation where a new roof is a fair exchange for a person, but the roof is both a real and metaphorical expression of that which protects the family from the worst storms of life, keeping it safe and whole. And, perhaps, for many this description is apt, reflecting the sacrifice they choose to, or are forced to, make as women.

The responsibilities of womanhood often involve both caring and personal sacrifice. It is important to remember, however, that, particularly in challenging times, these burdens are not women's alone, but responsibilities that we all need to share.

18

A Paradigm for the Interpretation of Sacred Space

KATHLEEN SCOTT GOLDINGAY

INTRODUCTION

How are we to understand "sacred space"?[1] What paradigms can we turn to for its interpretation? At the beginning of his two-volume work on how the church should think about the interpretation of Scripture, John Goldingay reflects on the importance of discerning and using a variety of models, especially those which emerge from scripture itself:

> It is an important feature of the use of models in theology that a multiplicity of models is commonly required to do justice to its subjects. "An endless number of metaphors and models . . . is no 'death by a thousand qualifications.' . . . Rather, it is life by a thousand enrichments." Varied models offer independent, though not necessarily rival, accounts of their subject. It is less appropriate to seek to interweave them or argue for one rather than another, more appropriate to consider questions such as what aspects of

---

1. "Space" and "place" have important distinctions and complexities about their definitions which will not be addressed here. Both terms will be used interchangeably as well as "environment" and "location."

the object they represent well, what aspects of the model need to be ignored because nothing corresponds to them in the object, what characteristics of the object can only be brought out by other models, and how the varied models act as mutual qualifiers that mark points at which any one model ceases to apply . . . It may not be wise to look for one model for scripture that takes precedence over the others or holds all the models together.[2]

The same may be said of developing a viable approach to the interpretation of sacred space, an equally confounding area for theological hermeneutics. The aim of this essay is to suggest a multivariate *generative paradigm* that examines various potential sources of a space's initiation and/or persistence as a sacred place. The paradigm consists of five key interpretive aspects that may be addressed to any sacred space as generative sources: elements from the *physical character* of the space; a shared story or *narrative* that defines the space; one's own appropriation of the space due to *individual experience*; the role of *community ritual* in forming or sustaining sacred space; and finally the elusive aspect of a sacred space as the locus of *numinous participation*.

Once this generative paradigm is in place, it can become the basis for a tapestry that includes other aspects and exposes a rich but grounded matrix of meaning. For example, once the nature of a generating source is established (i.e. narrative in scripture and physical elements of a river), we have a common basis for discussing how specific sacred spaces (i.e. the Jordan) are related to Christianity (Is the Jordan a physical place or a metaphorical ideal, does going to the river shape the ideal in us, or does only the story do that, or both?).

Models grounded in the generative paradigm and drawing upon a collection of interpretive aspects can address some shortcomings in current approaches. For one thing, this approach would give voice to all the unique features of a particular sacred location and not just to those that are highlighted by a particular theory or found in sacred spaces of a similar type. The use of a multivalent approach also guards against the limitations of an "either-or" duality. For example, rather than viewing all places according to Eliade's dichotomy of "sacred" or "profane,"[3] an interpreter could make room for other categories, such as place as a blessing, a designation that is

---

2. Goldingay, *Models for Scripture*, 16 (citing Ramsay, *Models and Mystery*, 60).
3. Eliade, *Sacred and Profane*.

neither intrinsically holy nor profane.[4] Finally, an approach beginning from these five aspects of sacred space offers a simplified and consistent structure that clarifies sources of meaning without eliminating the complexity and mystery of the actual locations.

The five key dimensions were chosen without a prejudice towards an anthropocentric view. Scripture tells us that creation was brought forth before humans, and God saw that it was good; before Adam and Eve were put into the garden, God planted it (Gen 1:1–25; 2:8). It is appropriate therefore to allow concrete creation and supernatural participation a voice differentiated from (latecomer) humanity's stake. Moreover, by giving narrative its own dimension, we also acknowledge that stories carry on far beyond individual human lives and even vanished communities of storytellers. Stories and histories can be dormant in the landscape and in architecture for thousands of years, only to be picked up by a generation in the future who, with the Spirit's guidance, reinterpret the story and coax the sacred location to speak (as we are now doing at Qumran).

If we do not give priority to simple, intrinsic criteria in our analysis of sacred space, we are likely to be unaware of the effect of the presuppositions we bring to the task. Much work on sacred space has been dominated by culturally embedded agendas: political power (Chidester and Linenthal),[5] religious apologetic moves (Spicer and Hamilton),[6] religious power (Kilde),[7] sociological and technical developments (Kilde),[8] prejudice towards the aesthetic (van der Leeuw),[9] theological formation

---

4. Being free to receive creation as a blessing protects us from two possible traps: (1) pantheism, including the dissection of creation in the search for revelation, and (2) a dualism that portrays our physical existence and its challenges as diametrically opposed to spirit or, worse, views all matter as embodied evil. Cf. Northrop Frye's articulation of the challenge to "steer some sort of middle course between the Gnostic contempt for nature and the pagan adoration of it" (*The Great Code*, 112–13, cited in Fretheim, *God and World*, xi).

5. Chidester and Linenthal, eds., *American Sacred Space*, 1–5 (cf. the example in their discussion of Hawaiian sites in the introduction).

6. Spicer and Hamilton, eds., *Defining the Holy* (many examples of territorial battles between Catholic, Protestant, and secular interests).

7. Kilde, *Sacred Power, Sacred Space* (relationship of church architecture to authority and spiritual empowerment).

8. Kilde, *When Church Became Theater*.

9. Leeuw, *The Holy in Art*, ix, xiii (how beauty and holiness approach each other; how God speaks via beauty).

(Hammond),[10] spiritual path theory (Barrie),[11] implications of geographical analysis (Park),[12] even economic motives.[13] Lack of consensus about the nature of the created world as either "hindrance to" or "revelation of" the sacred further contributes to the cacophony and obscures our ability to receive creation's blessing and to communicate with God.[14] The modeling structure proposed here can unveil cultural agendas that, while they may be credible in their own right, could mask a comprehensive understanding of what place has to say when they are used as dominant criteria for analysis. So, rather than casting about by intuition, or seeking a single-perspective theory, or developing a non-existent utopia on paper, consistently anchoring analysis with the five dimensions explored below can free us to eat at the full table Wisdom has set.

PHYSICAL ATTRIBUTES

Environments speak of the sacred act of creation through physical attributes even when not informed by human presence. High places inspire clouds to gather and compel them to shower the earth with rain (Job 38:26); the paths of the seas guide migrating whales (Ps 8:8b). Creation awaits, ready to imprint interpreters. That interpreters may not perceive or make use of all that is spoken by places does not alter their created wisdom, the underlying principles that make them significant. Both nature and architecture[15] can articulate meaning solely through physical form. Architecture also interacts

---

10. Hammond, *Liturgy and Architecture* (how architecture impacts and communicates theology).

11. Barrie, *Spiritual Path, Sacred Place* (how religious architectural elements reflect religious and spiritual development ideals).

12. Park, *Sacred Worlds* (religion from a geographer's perspective).

13. A visitor to Sedona, Arizona, can't miss advertised opportunities to spend, linked to the area's sacred reputation.

14. For example, Belden Lane provides a substantial survey of the lack of consensus in Christian thought by listing its attempts to explore embodied means of experiencing divine presence: creation as God's glorious theater trappings, world as Body of Christ, nature as the "second book," dignity of matter via the Incarnation, divine milieu and creative matter for the Cosmic Christ, reactions to Gnostic heresies of an evil Demiurge giving form to the material world, *a*sensuality as a vice, sins of making the concrete abstract, the distinct nature of creatures in relationship with God, glory in the tiny ordinary dimensions of nature, God engaged in all God has made. Lane, *Landscapes of the Sacred*, 244–47.

15. "Architecture" includes all human built structures.

with and depends on created order (material properties, weather, geology) and social order (tools, labor, engineering). Following are three examples of how the sacred can emanate from physical attributes.

First, the sacred can be recognized through physical nurture. The Nile became sacred because of the blessing (and sometimes curse) it was to those living along its banks. Its sacred designation acknowledged its crucial nurturing role in life.

Second, physical features can orient and structure who we are and where we are; they enable human beings to "gain an existential foothold" in the world.[16] Crossing a threshold can tell us who we are; Gentiles were forbidden from entering the temple in Jerusalem on pain of death, as the inner court was accessible only to Jews[17] and the inner sanctum only to the high priest. When you entered, you knew Yahweh was your God and you were Israel.

"High places" have always been connected with the divine. Stature alone can make them unapproachable, uninhabitable, and diminishing; shrouded peaks manifest greater-ness, mystery, awe (a possible dwelling place for something beyond humanity). Their very towering presence (or that of a steeple) also reassures us of our location in the landscape ("to the east of").

Third and less overt, physical features can symbolize and transcend; they can exert a theological claim (Jesus' baptism in the Jordan) or illustrate abstract ideas and emotions (dark forests can evoke/represent fear). Physical features are not confined to earth and architecture. Ringing of church bells denotes auditory territory. Burning incense can be used to set the divine apart from the smells of the world, drive away evil spirits, and represent sacrificial offerings.

Sometimes built meaning can transcend time: the entrance to an ancient city is made obvious by an elaborate gate even though the ancient gatekeeper has vanished. Early churches in England were placed near yew trees, sacred to pagans as symbols of death and resurrection, co-opted to represent Christ.

But sometimes original meanings are obscured and places blindly adopted, encouraging idolatry based on superstition. It is important to be clear that even though Scripture provides many instances of specific or even minute details of physical attributes, nowhere in Scripture are physical

---

16. Norberg-Schulz, *Existence, Space, and Architecture*, 12.
17. Achtemeier, Green, and Thompson, *Introducing the New Testament*, 384.

features designated as "touchstones" that guarantee us a connection, communication, or presence of the divine.

NARRATIVE

Story creates place and place can tell story. Unlike the kind of sacred space that is most significantly recognized from its physical attributes, some locations are sacred without being distinguishable from the rest of a city or a landscape. The temple mount in Jerusalem is usually a surprise when seen for the first time; it is not physically the "high place" promised (see Psalm 48). This humble mound is changed into something sacred by the stories that endear it to multitudes. Sometimes there is more than one narrative about the same place, layering the sacred claims. Jerusalem can be the contemporary place in Israel, a people, a church, a place in the past or in heaven, or even refer to a new creation in the future. It is significant to the Jewish, Christian, and Muslim stories for different reasons, some of which overlap.

The same point that John Goldingay asserts about Scripture is also true for sacred places: "The task of understanding the meaning of the story cannot be reduced to the task of establishing the historical facts that underlie it."[18] For sacred places, such a factual focus may or may not result in the loss of significance altogether. Are the Stations of the Cross verifiable and accurately located in Jerusalem? No one can prove their historicity in a way that satisfies the modern scientific mind. The number and locations of the Stations of the Cross in Jerusalem have changed many times over centuries. But no one can deny that regardless of configuration and location the stations tell a powerful story that affects millions of people as they walk or contemplate the Via Dolorosa, "the sorrowful road."

Physically experiencing an environment seems to manifest the truth of a story, to provide witness of it in a unique and profound way. When asking people about their encounters with sacred space, the most common and passionate replies go like this: "Being there (Gettysburg, the beach at Normandy, Jerusalem) made history come alive for me, blood cried out from the ground, I knew those people were real people like me and you, and I could not forget I was part of their story."

Some sacred spaces cannot be located on earth but necessarily exist in scriptural imagination (Mt. Sinai, Garden of Eden). The Israelites could not

---

18. Goldingay, *Models for Interpretation*, 16.

sing the psalms with any credibility if the memory of the exodus didn't create another "place" to live in, an alternate reality or another world than the broken one before their eyes. But the Psalms' events do not merely belong to the past or to one place, they offer something for any worshiper's present time and place.[19]

INDIVIDUAL EXPERIENCE

Our personal histories, which are an overlap of story and experience, can create personal myths and realities that are attached to locations. Eliade speaks of the "private universe"[20] made up of one's birthplace, love scenes, a first encounter with a foreign city, and religious experiences. "What Rudolf Otto described as the *mysterium tremendum*, the profoundly disturbing encounter of the holy as 'other,' is inevitably associated with the particularity of place."[21]

If one person's encounter gains significant resonance with other individuals, enough momentum can be created to designate a place as sacred. It is highly unusual for individual experiences to be duplicated. The experience of apparitions by fourteen-year-old Bernadette Soubirous at Lourdes, France, is a well-known example. But it is not unusual for individual experience to provide a basis for initial site designation, which then takes on a life of its own. We see this in the phenomenon of pilgrimage to the site at Lourdes. "Pilgrimage is one of the clearest manifestations of the significance of sacred space to believers."[22]

Religious experience is embodied. Belden Lane notes that a vivid encounter of the holy is often anchored in the memory of place. Paul's conversion is located on the Damascus road. Constantine describes a vision in the sky over Milvian Bridge. Augustine's life is changed in a garden of the Villa Cassiciacum outside of Milan. John Wesley's heart is "strangely warmed" at a prayer meeting on Aldersgate Street in eighteenth-century London.[23]

---

19. John Goldingay points out numerous times how psalms contain descriptions of horrific situations that the singers are in, but the singers express how they "know" that Yahweh delivers because they "live" in the truth of the exodus, no matter how long ago or far away it was.

20. Eliade, *Sacred and Profane*, 24.

21. Lane, *Landscapes of the Sacred*, 6.

22. Park, *Sacred Worlds*, 249.

23. Lane, *Landscapes of the Sacred*, 244.

These are places where we feel acted upon instead of our initiating the action (Eliade's *hierophany*).[24]

What about the incarnation? Jesus' earthly life had to be associated with enough concrete specifics (Jewish, male, Bethlehem) for us to comprehend it. The results of his ministry (healings, miracles, exorcisms) and vocation (teaching community, social revolution) are part of many named locations, few of which we can positively locate today. Perhaps this is because those places might become revered in a manner not intended by the incarnation—places are not God—so sacred spaces associated with Christ mostly come to us from scriptural story, not from Jesus' footpaths.

COMMUNITY RITUAL

Community worship craves, creates and is validated by environments: "When Chartres was being built, Robert of Torigni reported glowingly that 1,145 men and women, noble and common people, together dedicated all their physical resources and spiritual strength to the task of transporting in hand-drawn carts material for the building of the towers. Such accounts suggest that raising an edifice was an act of worship . . ."[25]

Commitment of significant resources can indicate what is sacred to a community, and long after peoples are gone their sacred spaces cry out. Nothing certain can be known of either the use or the meaning of the megalithic structures constructed on the island of Malta as early as 3500 BCE, but archaeologists interpret them as temples, concluding that the accurate celestial alignments, the massive twenty-ton stones, and accompanying artifacts are both communal and ritual in character.

The vital role of such places in community belief is acknowledged in Deuteronomy 12 by God's strict order to Israel about nations they were about to dispossess: demolish completely all the places where nations served their gods. The command is to completely break down their altars, smash their pillars, burn their sacred poles, hew down idols and even blot out their name.

In satisfying the community need to gather for ritual or to mark events, ritual spaces seem to become consecrated as sacred and remain so, whether theologically appropriate or not. Community shrines can appear spontaneously on roadsides, on public pathways, and more permanently

24. ". . . something sacred shows itself to us." Eliade, *Sacred and Profane*, 11.
25. Tuan, *Space and Place*, 106.

in public squares to commemorate the death of a beloved member. Many British churches were established on former pagan sacred sites. Gerardus van der Leeuw points out that "no matter how Calvinistically we may think, [we] have not been able to free ourselves completely from the idea of a house of God . . . The primitive form of thought of God's dwelling in a house built for him has been given up, but . . . the essential content of that idea is once more receiving new life."[26]

Just as Jesus warned the disciples not to make booths for him and Moses and Elijah on the mountain of the transfiguration,[27] valuing place over practice must be guarded against. Even though "stones cry out," many religious practices which signify sacredness—and which God might render holy—would leave little or no physical trace in the archaeological record.[28] In the case of the Torah, Tent, and Tabernacle (2 Sam 7:6), the holy or sacred "place" moves with the community. Thus sacred place, like the location of the Body of Christ, can be elusive, may not be found when sought, and may not leave a trace because it only exists with a people.

NUMINOUS[29] PARTICIPATION

For the faithful, participation of the supernatural (Holy Spirit, angels, other spirits) can neither be denied nor manipulated in the creation of sacred space. This category is heavily dependent on the other four: God's participation we must read about in narrative, we hear about from individual witness, we seek in community, and we sense in creation as God's handiwork. We can consider these examples:

> Jacob went on his way and the angels of God met him; and when Jacob saw them he said, "This is God's camp!"[30]

> Isaiah had been accustomed to passing through the temple in Jerusalem all of his life, when unexpectedly in the year King Uzziah died, he "saw the Lord there, sitting upon a throne, high and lifted up." The very foundations of the thresholds shook and the house

---

26. Leeuw, *The Holy in Art*, 202.
27. Matt 17:1–9; Mark 9:2–10; Luke 9:28–36.
28. Spicer and Hamilton, eds., *Defining the Holy*, 3–4.
29. Rudolf Otto's term for realization of an indirectly-sensed, overpowering being outside the self with whom a dependent relationship is formed (*Idea of the Holy*, 8–11).
30. Gen 32:1–2.

> was filled with smoke (Isa 6:1–4). The overly familiar sanctuary had suddenly become for him a new place of dread and wonder.[31]
>
> A peasant, Juan Diego, experienced a vision on December 9, 1531, which became the basis of what is now one of the most visited Catholic pilgrimage destinations in the world at the Basilica of Our Lady of Guadalupe in Mexico City.
>
> Simpson offers a catalogue of British sites which "have religious significance, because they are places where traditional narratives assert that a supernatural event once occurred which endorsed Christian values, and which left a lasting mark on the landscape."[32]

Yahweh clearly chooses his own dwelling place. Christians must also be mindful that in the Bible, there are no "spirits" specifically attached to places and no instructions about how to draw spirits into a particular place. It is embodied humans who seem to need a place where we can take our communications to God and bend our knee. Scripture is clear that Christ, not a particular place, is our only mediator.

But the fact we cannot command God's presence does not mean there is no holy ground or sacred space. Belden Lane points out: "Even though we stand on the inaccessible ground of the holy, we may never yet have been brought into any relationship to it."[33] The sometimes obscured nature of sacred environments may not result only from God's desire to protect the holy place, but to protect us; God loves us and knows we may not be ready for the searing refinement a holy environment might require.[34] The sacred is only revealed on God's terms; John Goldingay contends that God shares some things with us, but about some things God says: "I'm keeping that—that is something holy."[35]

CONCLUSION

This proposal explores a generative paradigm for interpreting sacred space by suggesting five sources: its physical nature, the narratives about it, individual experiences, community rituals that take place there, and

---

31. Lane, *Landscapes of the Sacred*, 30.
32. Park, *Sacred Worlds*, 252, citing Simpson, "God's Visible Judgements," 53.
33. Lane, *Landscapes of the Sacred*, 29.
34. As Aaron's sons discovered in Lev 10:1–2.
35. 2011 conversation.

participation of the numinous. Other perspectives, theories, or multi-disciplinary topics could be considered in relationship to these five primary sources in order to form a rich matrix of interpretation; for instance, the role of memory or apologetics or immigration or ethics could be considered for any particular sacred location. Or a survey of a group of spaces by type (grottos for example) might yield surprising results. The design of this interpretive paradigm is purposely flexible and open and has the potential to embrace multiple layers of meaning. Even though interpreters may be restrained by their own blindness and cultural nuances, a model with broad horizons can coax sacred spaces to impart unexpected blessings. After all, sacred space does not depend on the wild flower or the mortal; we depend on sacred space.

> Mortals: their days are like grass;
> like a wild flower—that is how they bloom.
> When the wind passes by and they are gone;
> their place does not recognize them anymore.[36]

---

36. Psalm 103:15–16, adapted from John Goldingay's translation, *Psalms*, vol. 3, 173.

Bibliography

Achtemeier, Paul J., Joel B. Green, and Marianne Meye Thompson. *Introducing the New Testament: Its Literature and Theology.* Grand Rapids: Eerdmans, 2001.

Ainsworth, Mary D. Salter, et al. *Patterns of Attachment: A Psychological Study of the Strange Situation.* Hillsdale, NJ: Erlbaum, 1978.

Allen, Roland. *Missionary Methods: St. Paul's or Ours?* Chicago: Moody, 1956 [orig. pub. 1912].

Alter, Robert. *The Art of Biblical Narrative.* New York: Basic Books, 1981.

Anglican Roman Catholic International Commission. *Mary, Grace and Hope in Christ.* London: Morehouse, 2005.

Barrie, Thomas. *Spiritual Path, Sacred Place: Myth, Ritual, and Meaning in Architecture.* Boston: Shambhala, 1996.

Barton, John. *Ethics and the Old Testament.* Harrisburg, PA: Trinity, 1998.

———. "Reading for Life: The Use of the Bible in Ethics and the Work of Martha C. Nussbaum." In *The Bible in Ethics: The Second Sheffield Colloquium,* edited by John W. Rogerson et al., 66–76. JSOTSup 207. Sheffield: Sheffield Academic, 1995.

Bauman, Zygmunt. *Life in Fragments: Essays in Postmodern Morality.* Malden MA: Blackwell, 1997.

Bediako, Kwame. "Scripture as the Interpreter of Culture and Tradition." In *Africa Bible Commentary: A One-Volume Commentary Written by 70 African Scholars,* edited by Tokunboh Adeyemo, 3–4. Nairobi: WordAlive, 2006.

Benedict XVI, His Holiness. "Caritas in Veritate" (2009). No pages. Online: www.vatican.va/holy_father/benedict_xvi/encyclicals/documents/hf_ben-xvi_enc_20090629_caritas-in-veritate_en.html.

———. *Charity in Truth [Caritas in Veritate].* San Francisco: Ignatius Press, 2009.

Berlin, Adele. *Poetics and the Interpretation of Biblical Narrative.* Bible and Literature Series 9. Sheffield: Almond, 1983.

Bertman, Stephen. "Symmetrical Design in the Book of Ruth." *Journal of Biblical Literature* 84 (1965) 165–68.

Bevington, David, editor and translator. *Medieval Drama.* Boston Houghton Mifflin, 1975.

Birch, Bruce C. *Let Justice Roll Down: The Old Testament, Ethics, and the Christian Life.* Louisville: Westminster John Knox, 1991.

Blenkinsopp, Joseph. "The Social Context of the 'Outside Woman' in Proverbs 1–9." *Biblica* 72 (1991) 457–73.

Blond, Philip. *Red Tory.* London: Faber & Faber, 2010.

Boese, Linnea E. "Canaanite, Israelite and Nyarafolo Worldviews: A Meeting of the Minds in the Pentateuch." 1–26. Unpublished essay, 2005. Cited by permission.

Bibliography

Booth, Wayne. *The Company We Keep: An Ethics of Fiction*. Berkeley: University of California Press, 1988.

Bowen, Murray. "Toward the Differentiation of Self in One's Family of Origin." In *Family Therapy in Clinical Practice*, 529–47. New York: Aronson, 1978.

Bowlby, John. *Attachment and Loss*. Vol. 1, *Attachment*. 2nd ed. New York: Basic Books, 1969.

Bridger, Francis. "Biblical Theology and the Politics of the Centre." In *Politics and the Parties*, edited by Jonathan Chaplin, 96–118. Leicester, UK: InterVarsity, 1992.

Bridger, Francis, and David Atkinson. *Counselling in Context: Developing a Theological Framework*. Pasadena, CA: Fuller Seminary Press, 2007.

Browning, Elizabeth. *Aurora Leigh*. London: Chapman & Hall, 1857.

Brueggemann, Walter. *Theology of the Old Testament: Testimony, Dispute, Advocacy*. Minneapolis: Fortress, 1997.

Buchanan, Colin. *Encountering Charismatic Worship*. Nottingham, UK: Grove, 1977.

Bush, Frederic W. *Ruth/Esther*. Word Biblical Commentary 9. Dallas: Word, 1996.

Buxton, Graham. *Dancing in the Dark: The Privilege of Participating in the Ministry of Christ*. Carlisle, UK: Paternoster, 2001.

Calvin, John. *The First Epistle of Paul to the Corinthians*. Translated by John W. Fraser. London: Oliver & Boyd, 1960.

Camp, Claudia V. *Wisdom and the Feminine in the Book of Proverbs*. Bible and Literature Series 11. Sheffield: Almond, 1985.

Campbell, Edward F. *Ruth*. Anchor Bible 7. Garden City, NY: Doubleday, 1975.

Chidester, David, and Edward T. Linenthal, editors. *American Sacred Space*. Bloomington: Indiana University Press, 1995.

Childs, Brevard S. *Biblical Theology of the Old and New Testaments*. Minneapolis: Fortress, 1992.

Choir Schools. "The Chorister Outreach Programme." No pages. Online: www.choirschools.org.uk/documents/COP%20Impact.pdf

Church of England Doctrine Commission. *We Believe in the Holy Spirit*. London: CIO, 1991.

Church of England. *The Charismatic Movement in the Church of England*. London: CIO, 1981.

Cocksworth, Christopher. *Holding Together: Gospel, Church and Spirit*. London: Canterbury, 2008.

Donovan, Vincent. *Christianity Rediscovered: An Epistle from the Masai*. London: SCM, 1985.

Dowland, David A. *Nineteenth Century Anglican Theological Training: The Redbrick Challenge*. Oxford: Oxford University Press, 1997.

Dunn, James D. G. *1 Corinthians*. Edinburgh: T. & T. Clark, 2003.

———. *The Theology of Paul the Apostle*. Edinburgh: T. & T. Clark, 1998.

Eissfeldt, Otto. *The Old Testament: An Introduction*. Translated by P. R. Ackroyd. New York: Harper & Row, 1965.

Eliade, Mircea. *The Sacred and the Profane: The Nature of Religion*. Translated by Willard R. Trask. New York: Harcourt, Brace, 1959.

Exum, J. Cheryl, and J. William Whedbee. "Isaac, Samson, and Saul: Reflections on the Comic and Tragic Visions." *Tragedy and Comedy in the Bible*. Semeia 32 (1984) 5–40.

Fox, Michael V. *Proverbs 1–9*. Anchor Bible 18A. New York: Doubleday, 2000.

Frei, Hans. *The Eclipse of Biblical Narrative: A Study in Eighteenth and Nineteenth Century Hermeneutics*. New Haven: Yale University Press, 1974.
Frye, Northrop. *The Great Code: The Bible and Literature*. New York: Harcourt Brace Jovanovich, 1982.
Fretheim, Terence E. *God and World in the Old Testament: A Relational Theology of Creation*. Nashville: Abingdon, 2005.
George, Sherron Kay. "The Quest for Images of Missionaries." *Missiology* 30 (2002) 51–63.
Goheen, Michael W. "The Urgency of Reading the Bible as One Story." *Theology Today* 64 (2008) 469–83.
Goldingay, John. *Approaches to Old Testament Interpretation*. Rev. ed. Downers Grove, IL: InterVarsity, 1990.
———. *Men Behaving Badly*. Carlisle, UK: Paternoster, 2000.
———. *Models for Interpretation of Scripture*. Toronto: Clements, 2004.
———. *Models for Scripture*. Grand Rapids: Eerdmans, 1994.
———. *Old Testament Theology 1: Israel's Gospel*. Downers Grove, IL: InterVarsity Academic, 2003.
———. *Old Testament Theology 2: Israel's Faith*. Downers Grove, IL: InterVarsity Academic, 2006.
———. *Old Testament Theology 3: Israel's Life*. Downer's Grove, IL: InterVarsity, 2009.
———. "Old Testament Theology and the Canon." *Tyndale Bulletin* 59 (2008): 1–26.
———. *Psalms, Volume 3: Psalms 90–150*. Grand Rapids: Baker Academic, 2008.
———. *Songs in a Strange Land: Psalms 42–51*. The Bible Speaks Today. Downer's Grove, IL: InterVarsity, 1978.
———. *To the Usual Suspects: One Word Questions*. Carlisle, UK: Paternoster, 1998.
Goodall, Howard. "The Chorister Thing." No pages. Online: www.howardgoodall.co.uk/cds/biog/Articles%20Page.htm
———. "Singing." No pages. Online: www.howardgoodall.co.uk/singing/MLL%2008%20speech.htm
Gorman, Michael. *Reading Paul*. Cascade Companions. Eugene OR: Cascade Books, 2008.
Gorospe, Athena. "Comedy and Humor in the Samson Narrative." ThM thesis, Asia Graduate School of Theology, Manila, 1995.
Gorospe, Athena. *Narrative and Identity: An Ethical Reading of Exodus 4*. Biblical Interpretation Series 86. Leiden: Brill, 2007.
Grimm-Thayer. *A Greek-English Lexicon of the New Testament*. 4th ed. Edinburgh: T. & T. Clark, 1898.
Gunn, David M., and Danna Nolan Fewell. *Narrative in the Hebrew Bible*. Oxford: Oxford University Press, 1993.
Haines, Simon. "Deepening the Self: The Language of Ethics and the Language of Literature." In *Renegotiating Ethics in Literature, Philosophy, and Theory*, edited by Jane Adamson et al., 21–38. Cambridge: Cambridge University Press, 1998.
Hammond, Peter. *Liturgy and Architecture*. Foreword by F. W. Dillistone. New York: Columbia University Press, 1961.
Harrison, Michael. *The Oxford Book of Christian Poems*. Oxford: Oxford University Press, 1983.
Haught, John. *Mystery and Promise: A Theology of Revelation*. Collegeville MN: Liturgical, 1993.
Hettema, Theo. *Reading for Good: Narrative Theology and Ethics in the Joseph Story from the Perspective of Ricoeur's Hermeneutics*. Kampen: Kok Pharos, 1996.

Bibliography

Hubbard, Robert L., Jr. *The Book of Ruth*. NICOT. Grand Rapids: Eerdmans, 1988.

Janzen, Waldemar. *Old Testament Ethics: A Paradigmatic Approach*. Louisville: Westminster John Knox, 1994.

Johnson, Aubrey R. *The One and the Many in the Israelite Conception of God*. 2nd ed. Cardiff: University of Wales Press, 1961.

Johnson, Marshall D. *The Purpose of the Biblical Genealogies*. Cambridge: Cambridge University Press, 1969.

Keysers, Christian, and Valeria Gassola. "Towards a Unifying Neural Theory of Social Cognition." In *Understanding Emotions*, edited by Silke Anders et al., 379–401. Progress in Brain Research 156. Amsterdam: Elsevier, 2006.

Kilde, Jeanne Halgren. *Sacred Power, Sacred Space: An Introduction to Christian Architecture and Worship*. Oxford: Oxford University Press, 2008.

―――. *When Church Became Theater: The Transformation of Evangelical Architecture and Worship in Nineteenth-Century America*. Oxford: Oxford University Press, 2002.

King, Roberta R. *Pathways in Christian Music Communication: The Case of the Senufo of Côte d'Ivoire*. American Society of Missiology Monograph Series 3. Eugene, OR: Pickwick Publications, 2009.

―――. *A Time to Sing: A Manual for the African Church*. Nairobi: Evangel, 1999.

Koehler, Paul F. *Telling God's Stories with Power: Biblical Storytelling in Oral Cultures*. Pasadena, CA: William Carey Library, 2010.

KONE Nayergue Moise. Interview notes by Linnea Boese. Personal communication, October 19, 2012. Cited by permission.

Koosed, Jennifer L. *Gleaning Ruth: A Biblical Heroine and Her Afterlives*. Columbia, SC: University of South Carolina, 2011.

Labrunie, Claude E. "The Poor as Christ for the Church." *Church and Society* 84 (1993) 94–96.

Ladd, George Eldon. "The Search for Perspective." *Interpretation* 25 (1971) 41–62.

Lammy, David. "Extracts from the Eulogy." No pages. Online: www.kings.peterborough.sch.uk/_files/opa/131005.doc.

―――. "Guardian." No pages. Online: www.guardian.co.uk/culture/2010/nov/12/coalition-labour-arts-elitism.

Lane, Belden. *Landscapes of the Sacred: Geography and Narrative in American Spirituality*. Expanded edition. Baltimore: Johns Hopkins University Press, 2002.

Lash, Nicholas. *Easter in Ordinary: Reflections on Human Experience and the Knowledge of God*. Charlottesville: University of Virginia Press, 1988.

Lasine, Stuart. "Guest and Host in Judges 19: Lot's Hospitality in an Inverted World." *Journal for the Study of the Old Testament* 29 (1984) 37–59.

Lawrence, D. H. *Reflections on the Death of a Porcupine and Other Essays*. Cambridge: Cambridge University Press, 1988.

Leeuw, Gerardus van der. *Sacred and Profane Beauty: The Holy in Art*. Translated by David E. Green. New York: Holt, Rinehart & Winston, 1963.

Levenson, Jon D. *The Hebrew Bible, the Old Testament, and Historical Criticism: Jews and Christians in Biblical Studies*. Louisville: Westminster John Knox, 1993.

Lewis, C. S. *A Grief Observed*. San Francisco: Harper & Row, 1961.

Longenecker, Richard N. *Patterns of Discipleship in the New Testament*. Grand Rapids: Eerdmans, 1996.

Lyon, David. *Postmodernity*. Buckingham, UK: Open University Press, 1994.

Lyotard, Jean-François. *The Postmodern Condition: A Report on Knowledge.* Translated by Geoff Bennington and Brian Massumi. Minneapolis: University of Minnesota, 1984.
McKnight, Scot. *The Real Mary: Why Evangelicals Can Embrace the Mother of Jesus.* London: SPCK, 2007.
Magee, Bryan. *Confessions of a Philosopher: A Personal Journey through Western Philosophy from Plato to Popper.* New York: Random House, 1997.
Malina, Bruce J. *The New Testament World: Insights from Cultural Anthropology.* 3rd ed. Louisville: Westminster John Knox, 2001.
Marcel, Gabriel. *Being and Having.* Translated by Katharine Farrer. London: Collins, 1965.
May, James. "Frocks Make a Boy a Man." No pages. Online: www.telegraph.co.uk/motoring/columnists/2749504/James-May-Frocks-make-a-boy-a-man.html.
Menn, Esther Marie. *Judah and Tamar (Genesis 38) in Ancient Jewish Exegesis: Studies in Literary Form and Heremeneutics.* SJSJ 51. Leiden: Brill, 1997.
Midgley, Mary. "The Soul's Successors: Philosophy and the 'Body.'" In *Religion and the Body*, edited by Sarah Coakley, 53–68. Cambridge: Cambridge University Press, 1997.
Miles, Jack. *God: A Biography.* New York: Knopf, 1995.
Mould, Alan. *The English Chorister.* London: Continuum, 2007.
Newbigin, Lesslie. *The Good Shepherd.* London: Mowbray, 1977.
Ngewa, Samuel. "The Place of Traditional Sacrifices." In *Africa Bible Commentary: A One-Volume Commentary Written by Seventy African Scholars*, edited by Tokunboh Adeyemo, 1502–3. Nairobi: WordAlive, 2006.
Niditch, Susan. "The 'Sodomite' Theme in Judges 19-20: Family, Community, and Social Disintegration." *Catholic Biblical Quarterly* 44 (1982) 365–78.
Norberg-Schulz, Christian. *Existence, Space, and Architecture.* New York: Praeger, 1971.
Nussbaum, Martha. *The Fragility of Goodness: Luck and Ethics in Greek Tragedy and Philosophy.* Cambridge: Cambridge University Press, 1986.
———. *Love's Knowledge: Essays on Philosophy and Literature.* New York: Oxford University Press, 1990.
O'Connor, Edward, editor. *The Dogma of the Immaculate Conception: History and Significance.* Notre Dame: University of Notre Dame Press, 1958.
Olthius, James H. "Dancing Together in the Wild Spaces of Love: Postmodernism, Psychotherapy and the Spirit of God." *Journal of Psychology and Christianity* 18 (1999) 140–52.
Osman, Fathi. *Concepts of the Quran: A Topical Reading.* Los Angeles: MVI Publications, 1997.
Otto, Rudolf. *The Idea of the Holy: An Inquiry into the Non-Rational Factor in the Idea of the Divine and Its Religion to the Rational.* 2nd ed. Translated by John W. Harvey. New York: Oxford University Press, 1958.
Park, Chris C. *Sacred Worlds: An Introduction to Geography and Religion.* London: Routledge, 1994.
Parker, David. "Introduction: The Turn to Ethics in the 1990's." In *Renegotiating Ethics in Literature, Philosophy, and Theory*, edited by Jane Adamson et al., 1–17. Cambridge: Cambridge University Press, 1998.
Patrick, Dale. *The Rendering of God in the Old Testament.* Philadelphia: Fortress, 1981.
Penchansky, David. "Staying the Night: Intertextuality in Genesis and Judges." In *Reading Between Texts: Intertextuality and the Hebrew Bible*, edited by Danna Nolan Fewell, 77–88. Louisville: Westminster John Knox, 1992.

Bibliography

———. *What Rough Beast?: Images of God in the Hebrew Bible*. Louisville: Westminster John Knox, 1999.

Perry, Tim. *Mary for Evangelicals*. Downers Grove, IL: InterVarsity Academic, 2006.

Peterson, Eugene H. *The Jesus Way: A Conversation on the Ways that Jesus Is the Way*. Grand Rapids: Eerdmans, 2007.

Rad, Gerhard von. *Genesis: A Commentary*. Translated by John Marks. 3rd rev. ed. Old Testament Library. London: SCM, 1972.

Ramsey, Ian T. *Models and Mystery*. London: Oxford University Press, 1964.

Ricoeur, Paul. "Life in Quest of Narrative." In *On Paul Ricoeur: Narrative and Interpretation*. Translated and edited by David Wood, 20–33. London: Routledge, 1991.

———. "Narrative Identity." In *On Paul Ricoeur: Narrative and Interpretation*, translated and edited by David Wood, 188–99. London: Routledge, 1991.

———. *Oneself as Another*. Translated by Kathleen Blamey. Chicago: University of Chicago Press, 1992.

———. *Time and Narrative*. 3 vols. Translated by Kathleen McLaughlin and David Pellauer. Chicago: University of Chicago Press, 1984–1988.

Ricoeur, Paul, David Pellauer, and John McCarthy. "Conversation." In *The Whole and Divided Self*, edited by David E. Aune and John McCarthy, 221–43. New York: Crossroad, 1997.

Rossetti, Christina. "In the Bleak Midwinter." In *Complete Anglican Hymns Old and New*. Buxhall, UK: Mayhew, 2000.

Rubin, Miri. *Mother of God: A History of the Virgin Mary*. London: Penguin, 2009.

Sakenfeld, Katharine Doob. *Ruth* [Interpretation]. Louisville: Westminster John Knox, 1999.

Schilling, Harold. *The New Consciousness in Science and Religion*. London: SCM, 1973.

Simpson, Jacqueline. "God's Visible Judgements: The Christian Dimension of Landscape Legends." *Landscape History* 8 (1986) 53–58.

Smith-Christopher, Daniel L. "Between Ezra and Isaiah: Exclusion, Transformation, and Inclusion of the 'Foreigner' in Post-Exilic Biblical Theology." In *Ethnicity and the Bible*, edited by Mark G. Brett, 117–42. Leiden: Brill, 1996.

Somerville, Margaret. *The Ethical Imagination: Journey of the Human Spirit*. Toronto: House of Anansi, 2006.

Spicer, Andrew, and Sarah Hamilton, editors. *Defining the Holy: Sacred Space in Medieval and Early Modern Europe*. Aldershot, UK: Ashgate, 2005.

Sternberg, Meir. *The Poetics of Biblical Narrative: Ideological Literature and the Drama of Reading*. Bloomington: Indiana University Press, 1985.

Sugirtharajah, R. S. *Asian Biblical Hermeneutics and Postcolonialism: Contesting the Interpretations*. Maryknoll, NY: Orbis, 1998.

Sweeney, Robert. "Ricoeur on Ethics and Narrative." In *Paul Ricoeur and Narrative: Context and Contestation*, edited by Morny Joy, 197–205. Calgary: University of Calgary Press, 1997.

Tan, Nancy Nam Hoon. *The "Foreignness" of the Foreign Woman in Proverbs 1–9: A Study of the Origin and Development of a Biblical Motif*. BZAW 381. Berlin: de Gruyter, 2008.

Taylor, John V. *The Go Between God: The Holy Spirit and the Christian Mission*. London: SCM, 1972.

Tertullian. *The Five Books against Marcion*. In *The Ante-Nicene Fathers*, vol. 3. Edited by Alexander Roberts and James Donaldson, 1885–1887. Reprinted, Peabody, MA: Hendrickson, 1994.

Thiselton, Anthony. *The First Epistle to the Corinthians*. Grand Rapids: Eerdmans, 2000.

———. "The 'Interpretation' of Tongues: A New Suggestion in the Light of Greek Usage in Philo and Josephus." *JTS* 30 (1979).

Tillich, Paul. "The Depth of Existence." In *The Shaking of the Foundations*. New York: Scribner, 1948.

Tuan, Yi-Fu. *Space and Place: The Perspective of Experience*. Minneapolis: University of Minnesota Press, 1977.

Walls, Andrew F. "Old Athens and New Jerusalem: Some Signposts for Christian Scholarship in the Early History of Mission Studies." *International Bulletin of Missionary Research* 21:4 (1997) 146–53.

Ware, Kallistos. "The Unity of the Human Person according to the Greek Fathers." In *Persons and Personality*, edited by Arthur Peacocke and Grant Gillet, 206. Oxford: Blackwell, 1987.

Washington, Harold C. "The Strange Woman ('*shh zrh/nkryh*) of Proverbs 1–9 and Post-Exilic Judaean Society." In *Second Temple Studies*, vol. 2: *Temple and Community in the Persian Period*, edited by T. C. Eskenazi and K. H. Richards, 217–42. JSOTS 175. Sheffield: Sheffield Academic, 1994.

Welch, G. F. et al. *The Chorister Outreach Programme: A Research Evaluation* 2008-2009. London: Institute of Education, 2009.

Wolfenson, L. B. "Implications of the Place of the Book of Ruth in Editions, Manuscripts, and Canon of the Old Testament." *Hebrew Union College Annual* 1 (1924) 151–78.

Woodward, Kenneth L., et al. "The Changing Face of the Church." *Newsweek* 137:16 (April 16, 2001) 46–52.

World Council of Churches. *Mission in Christ's Way*. Geneva: WCC Publications, 1976.

Wright, Tom. *Acts for Everyone Part* 2. London: SPCK, 2008.

Yee, Gale A. "The Other Woman in Proverbs: My Man's Not Home—He Took His Moneybag with Him." In *Poor Banished Children of Eve: Woman as Evil in the Hebrew Bible*, 135–58. Minneapolis: Fortress, 2003.

Yoder, Christine Roy. *Wisdom as a Woman of Substance: A Socioeconomic Reading of Proverbs 1–9 and 31:10–31*. BZAW 304. Berlin: de Gruyter, 2001.

www.ingramcontent.com/pod-product-compliance
Lightning Source LLC
Chambersburg PA
CBHW062041220426
43662CB00010B/1592